RESPONDING TO THE THIRST OF GOD

40 Days to the Heart of Love

An Exploration of Life
*as **Nuptial** and **Trinitarian***

Joshua Elzner

For more information on the author, or for more resources for prayer and reflection, you may visit the websites: atthewellspring.com

The Scriptural passages are taken from:
Revised Standard Version of the Bible—Second Catholic Edition (Ignatius Edition), copyright © 2006 National Council of the Churches of Christ in the United States of America. Used by permission. All rights reserved.

Quotes from John of the Cross, unless within another quote, are from: *The Collected Works of St. John of the Cross*, trans. Kieran Kavanaugh, O.C.D., and Otilio Rodriguez, O.C.D. (Washington, D.C.: ICS Publications, 1991)

Copyright © 2024, 2022 Joshua Elzner
All rights reserved.
ISBN: 9798836453947

The reason of our existence is to quench the thirst of God. I don't say even "Jesus" or "on the cross," but "of God." Try to deepen your understanding of these two words, "Thirst of God." – Mother Teresa

+ + +

*He would take her
tenderly in his arms
and there give her his love;
and when they were thus one,
he would lift her to the Father
where God's very joy
would be her joy.
For as the Father and the Son
and he who proceeds from them
live in one another,
so it would be with the bride;
for, taken wholly into God,
she will live the life of God.*

– St. John of the Cross, "Romances on the Incarnation"

CONTENTS

Introduction: At the Throbbing Heart – A Personal Testimony ... 1

WEEK I: RESPONDING TO THE INVITATION OF THE BRIDEGROOM

Day 1: The Passionate Thirst of God ... 17
Day 2: The Heart of All Reality: Trinitarian Love ... 20
Day 3: The Bridegroom's Tender Invitation ... 23
Day 4: The Thirst of Jesus ... 26
Day 5: Nuptial Spirituality: Responding to Jesus' Thirst ... 29
Day 6: A Second Conversion ... 33
Day 7: Walking into the Arms of Love ... 38

WEEK II: TRANSFIGURING LOVE

Day 8: Liberated by Beauty, Goodness, and Truth ... 43
Day 9: Appropriating the Gift of Redemption ... 47
Day 10: Mystical Love as the Heart of All Life ... 51
Day 11: The Heart of Virtue ... 56
Day 12: Faith, Hope, and Love as the Life of God in Us ... 59
Day 13: The Cardinal Virtues as Incarnate Love ... 63
Day 14: The God Who Acts ... 67

WEEK III: THE ARROW OF LOVE

Day 15: The Arrow of Love: One Alone, Yet All Things ... 73
Day 16: Baptizing the Jailer ... 76
Day 17: My Unique Path of Healing ... 80
Day 18: Resting in the Divine Gaze ... 86
Day 19: Transfiguring Contemplation ... 89
Day 20: Faith, Hope, and Love: The Lived Tangibility of Love ... 94
Day 21: Sharing in the Life of God: The Convergence of All in Him ... 98

WEEK IV: THE NIGHT: BATHED IN HIS HEALING LIGHT

Day 22: A Look At Spiritual Darkness ... 105
Day 23: The Resonance of the Night ... 108
Day 24: The Redeeming Night of Love: Darkness Transformed into Light ... 112
Day 25: The Darkness Crying Out for Light ... 115
Day 26: The Radiance of the Divine Outpouring ... 119
Day 27: Learning to Pray Anew ... 123
Day 28: The Night of Compassion ... 126

WEEK V: RADIANT NUPTIAL

CONSUMMATION

Day 29: Born Anew into Prayer:	133
He Always Fulfills Expectant Faith	
Day 30: The Panorama of Prayer:	137
Heart Speaks to Heart (1)	
Day 31: The Panorama of Prayer:	142
Heart Speaks to Heart (2)	
Day 32: The Spiritual Marriage:	115
Naked Solitude Fulfilled in Intimacy	
Day 33: The Spiritual Marriage:	119
The "Yes" of Total Surrender	
Day 34: The Spiritual Marriage:	123
Totally Permeated by Love	
Day 35: Carried in Perfect Love,	126
From the Beginning to the End	

WEEK VI: COMING FULL CIRCLE

Day 36: A Single Act of Pure Love	161
Day 37: Against His Breast:	168
The Most Profound Communion	
Day 38: At the Foot of the Tree I Awakened You	173
Day 39: Through the Heart of the Paschal Mystery	177
to the Heart of the Trinity	
Day 40: The Divine, Breathlike Spiration	181
Epilogue	185
Prayers of Surrender	188
End Notes	193

Note:

This book has been arranged as a journey of 40 days—40 days of prayer and reflection—and yet it can be taken slower if desired, or at any pace that you find fitting. The density of the reflections, however, are intended to take time to sink into the interior, to be processed, and to be made one's own. And indeed they can even be returned to in different times and circumstances, yielding in this way a deeper understanding and contact with the mystery.

At the end of the book, five "Prayers of Surrender" have been provided, which can be prayed at the conclusion of the 40 days, or along the way, as desired. (They are "climactic" in their significance, and thus may be premature at the beginning, depending on where the reader is coming from.)

Last of all, I simply wish you a joyful, healing, and lifegiving journey deeper into the loving embrace of our awesome God—Father, Son, and Holy Spirit—and radiant peace, born of his love, in every moment and circumstance of your life.

INTRODUCTION
AT THE THROBBING HEART –
A PERSONAL TESTIMONY

From the first moment of our conception in our mother's womb, the God of the universe has been in intimate dialogue with each one of us. Our very birth from the bosom of his creative desire is an act of primal dialogue, in which he has freely spoken us into existence, that we, in turn, may speak to him. Even more foundationally than our conception through the love of our father and our mother (and thus even if such a conception did not occur through love), we have been conceived from the heart of the eternal intimacy and love shared by the Father and his beloved Son, this love that they share in the breath of a single Spirit.

At the origin of our being, therefore, and as the foundation of our existence, is love, calling us into love for the sake of love. We all bear a thirst for God deep within us, a yearning to make contact with the divine "Thou," the most perfect dialogue partner who sees us and knows us fully, and in knowing us fully, loves us totally. We ache to make contact with the One who has brought us into existence, to trace the lines of our own unique history back to their most foundational beginnings in the creative love of God, and thus to understand both him and our authentic selves. Even in a secular and atheistic culture, in which religious values have been all but discarded from public, political, economic, and social life, this thirst is not, and cannot, be entirely quenched. As Saint John Paul II said at the dawn of the third millennium, pointing to the longing present in our secular society, and to the only true and definitive answer:

> Is it not one of the "signs of the times" that in today's world, despite widespread secularization, there is *a widespread demand for spirituality,* a demand which expresses itself in large part as *a renewed need for prayer?* Other religions, which are now widely present in ancient Christian lands, offer their own responses to this need, and sometimes they do so in appealing ways. But we who have received the grace of believing in Christ, the revealer of the Father and the Savior of the world, have a duty to show to what depths the relationship with Christ can lead.
>
> The great mystical tradition of the Church of both East and West has much to say in this regard. It shows how prayer can progress, as a genuine dialogue of love, to the point of rendering the person wholly possessed by the divine Beloved, vibrating at the Spirit's touch, resting filially within the Father's heart. This is the lived experience of Christ's promise: "He who loves me will be loved by my Father, and I will love him and manifest myself to him" (Jn 14:21). It is a journey totally sustained by grace, which nonetheless demands an intense spiritual commitment and is no stranger to painful purifications (the "dark night"). But it leads, in various possible ways, to the ineffable joy experienced by the mystics as "nuptial union." (John Paul II, *Novo Millennio Ineunte,* n. 33)

The thirst for God is not accidental to humanity, a manifestation of a particular transient need or a response to the suffering present in the world. Rather, it is that which is deepest and most central to our humanity, that which, indeed, alone illumines all else: our longing for union with the God who created us for himself. As Saint Augustine so famously wrote: "You have made us for yourself, O Lord, and our heart is restless until it rests in you" (*Confessions* 1.1).

But this longing for God, this thirst for the eternal Creator of the universe, is secondary to an even more fundamental reality: the thirst of God for each one of us. Indeed, he thirsts for us that we may thirst for him, and that, two thirsts meeting, they may give drink to one another. His desire for us gives us the humble confidence to desire him—for how else could we presume to reach out to the ineffable and invisible Mystery that is greater than all things, infinitesimally small as we are? But he comes to meet us first; he comes to engage us in dialogue, seeking us out and entering into communion with us through his Word and his Spirit, his Voice and Breath, his Logos and Love. As the Catechism of the Catholic Church says:

> "If you knew the gift of God!" (Jn 4:10). The wonder of prayer is revealed beside the well where we come seeking water: there, Christ comes to meet every human being. It is he who first seeks us and asks us for a drink. Jesus thirsts; his asking arises from the depths of God's desire for us. Whether we realize it or not, prayer is the encounter of God's thirst with ours. God thirsts that we may thirst for him. "You would have asked him, and he would have given you living water" (ibid.). Paradoxically our prayer of petition is a response to the plea of the living God: "They have forsaken me, the fountain of living waters, and hewn out cisterns for themselves, broken cisterns that can hold no water!" (Jer 2:13). Prayer is the response of faith to the free promise of salvation and also a response of love to the thirst of the only Son of God. (par. 2560-2561)

In my own life, this great gift of dialogue with God was bestowed upon me early, from the beginning, and without any merit or even choice on my part. I was welcomed into the life of faith, into the very life of the Trinity, by the community that preceded me and accompanied me. And it is to this community—to the living Church—that I owe everything that I have or will ever have; or perhaps more accurately, it is to God at work in and through the Church, which he has fashioned to be his own presence throughout history, his Bride and Body, as well as the family of all who are made one in the very likeness of the unity of the divine Persons of Father, Son, and Holy Spirit.

In a word, I was baptized, in October 1990, a month after my birth. And growing up from my earliest years, I had always known God and loved him, as is often the case for those who are baptized as infants (since God lives in them already in the fullness of his mystery, and they feel and know his presence before they can even name it!). Even without much catechetical teaching or even—at least at that time!—a deeply pious family, I had grown up in the orbit of God's love and the security of his presence. I was loved, and that is the most important and fundamental introduction to the God of Love, as Saint Augustine says: "He who sees love sees the Trinity." And from this gift of faith and love I had received, I prayed to him, I relied on him, I loved him. This is a beautiful confirmation that faith is above all a *gift* of God before it is a capacity or choice of the human heart, even though we must accept it and cooperate with it! The seed of the divine life planted within me when I was only a month old was already sprouting and growing and bearing fruit, however subtle, and would continue to do so more and more.

Let me give two examples of this early, childlike relationship with God. I give them to show that the truths of the faith are not far away, inaccessible to all except the learned; nor are they abstract concepts to be grasped by the strength of human reason. As important as reason is, it ultimately falls short before the "reasons of the heart," as Blaise Pascal says, before the wisdom of children who spontaneously relate to God, not as an object of intellectual assent, but as a person to be known and loved.

The first example is one of a small image of Christ that I kept in my room, probably given to me by my parents or some relative or acquaintance when I was young. The artistic value of it was not very high, being one of the recent reproductions of a gentle, and rather feminine, Jesus holding his hand to his Sacred Heart and looking out of the picture at the viewer. But the artistic value didn't really matter, for it was grace that spoke through the image. And, further, it is so much more important that Jesus is felt in his tenderness than anything else, for the true face of God, as we are coming to know more and more by the work of the Spirit in the Church, is Mercy and Love. And I felt this, as intuitively as someone my age ordinarily would, and expressed such love without much thought. Let's just that say eventually that little picture of Jesus was stained from my repeated kissing (and right on the face of Jesus!). This must have been in elementary school and into junior high, perhaps even later.

The second example is one, not only of my relation to Christ, but to the entire Trinity. I would frequently stop what I was doing to make the sign of the Cross: "In the name of the Father, and of the Son, and of the Holy Spirit." I'm sure this gesture raised a number of curious eyes among my friends, and I remember at least once a friend explicitly asking me about it. I did it so often that my mother even asked me about it, worried that it was a sign, not of prayer, but of obsessive compulsive disorder. But even though I have a rather obsessively inclined personality, and this may have indeed had a part to play in it, the truth is that I would not have turned to the sign of the cross so frequently, for any reason, if I had not found in it solace, comfort, and a profound meaning that even then attracted and drew my heart. In other words, I was already praying my little "doxology" to the Trinity from my childlike heart, reaching out to the One —to the Three-in-One—who felt so real, and so close, in the feeling that is beyond feeling.

Despite these inchoate movements of faith, however, I had not yet awakened to an awareness of the totality of God's loving claim upon my life—his desire to be totally mine and for me to be totally his—the radical choice for God that lies at the heart of authentic faith. I had not yet said a firm "no" to sin and to everything in the world that opposes God, and a corresponding "yes" to God and his absolute reign over my life and my heart. I was still in the process of being subtly nurtured by God, like a young child, or subtly wooed by him—until the scales would fall from my eyes and I would come to see his approach and respond to his call is it is in all its grandeur and depth. Let us therefore move forward a little, to the time of this "awakening," to my first full and explicit conversion, in which faith, hope, and love were stirred into flame within me. This was sometime in the first two years of high school, when things really began to change for me. The life of faith had begun to change from the first day that the beauty of the Gospel began to truly "click" for me: the depth of beauty that awaited me in God, and how much he loved me and sought for me. There wasn't exactly a precise moment for this realization, as is usually the case, but God was gradually approaching me more and more explicitly as my own heart matured from childhood to adolescence (as I have tried to show), and thus became ready to welcome and respond to him in a more mature and conscious way.

And thank God for a deacon in our parish, Jim Clements (may he rest eternally in God), who took me under his wing in my early high school career and granted me to glimpse his own deep love for God and for his word in the Bible. I recall one conversation in particular, in which he was present for our (ordinarily very lacking) Wednesday catechism class. Only myself and my friend were present, and Deacon Jim sat down with us and began to speak, without preparation and from the heart, of Jesus Christ. I still remember vividly the moment when he said, "Christ was so beautiful, with olive skin and hazel eyes," while his own eyes filled with tears, as if he was speaking of someone he had actually seen and known in the flesh, and still knew. What moved me so much, then as now, was his deep and tender love for Christ in all the concreteness of his humanity, in his real flesh-and-blood in history. It was something, perhaps, like the simple and spontaneous love that moves a child to kiss an image of Jesus' face every day, though born of a deeper wellspring of contemplation, study, suffering, and prayer.

After this graced introduction to the mystery of the faith into which I had been baptized, I was fascinated...fascinated by the majesty of God's revelation in history, as expressed for us in the words of Scripture. I devoured it, studied it, contemplated it, and began, more and more, to dialogue with the God whose face and love was becoming apparent to me. Everything I had received from God in the incredible gift of faith was set free to grow and blossom (though perhaps it was more like an explosion) whenever I was introduced to the grandeur of God's word, and, through this, to the beauty of the Church's teaching, sacraments, and life.

I had begun to read a great deal, stirred by amazement and curiosity at these truths that I had not known, or known very little, before. It was in this time that I read the Catechism of the Catholic Church, a fabulous book that leads the contemplating heart deep into the core of God's self-revelation in the Old Testament and in Jesus Christ, and into the radiant, expansive beauty of the Gospel present and at work in history until the end of time. I read not so much for intellectual knowledge as for a glimpse of the face of the One whom I had come to know and for an understanding of his designs and his plan for this world in which we live. I read, in other words, simply out of thirst for the truth: God's truth, the way that he saw reality in all of its depth and breadth, as it really was by his design. (Is this not really what reading is all about anyway, and not about abstract intellectual concepts held as one's supposed "possession"?)

It was in the context of this period of intense reading that I encountered the writing and life of Saint John of the Cross. I was sixteen, perhaps seventeen, quite a young age for introduction to such a profound and, admittedly, difficult to understand mystic and Doctor of the Church.* But his words, along with those of other saints such as Teresa of Avila, Thérèse of Lisieux, and Teresa of Calcutta, touched me (or were to touch me) very deeply, to the core of my being, and to accompany me for many years. I grappled with John's *Dark Night of the Soul* during my junior year in high school, as well as Teresa of Avila's *Interior Castle* and Augustine's *Confessions* around the same time.

And this was all in public school, a rather narrow and secular environment focused on the usual "American" values of self-esteem, success, and individuality. This is not to mention all the apathy, cynicism, and sins of adolescence which are sadly so present in our contemporary society, and which, during this period of the first decade of the new millennium, were beginning to take particularly strong root among the young. In the midst of this culture, wounded in many ways but still bearing seeds of beauty and goodness (the culture of rural Texas still bears certain beautiful Christian values, for example), I was discovering a world of values deeper and wider than I could have ever expected. And these values called for me to repent of my own adolescent sin, my own immaturity and self-enclosure, and to open wide my life to God who approached me. This period was like living in a different world, walking in the orbit of a different universe, even though I still remained in the same place as usual, walking to the same classes, sitting through the same lectures, playing and marching in the same band. But everything was beginning to change.

I spoke of my introduction to the mystical doctors of the Church, Teresa of Avila and John of the Cross, and of my desire to come to understand and live the reality of which they spoke. This effort was to continue

---

*This inflow of mystical influence, from John and the other saints, in the earliest steps of the spiritual life had a unique kind of effect on me. It was like being "thrown in the deep end," and yet I wished for it to be no other way. Of course, it took a good number of years for me to be able to situate the specific focus of these mystics into a more holistic and affirming spirituality (as will become clear in this book), in which human desires and the wholeness of creation is given its proper due without fear, repression, or undue rigidity. Two obvious benefits of this "deep end" introduction, however, were: 1) I was saved from a lot of "fluff" in focusing on the wrong things in desiring holiness and union with God, for I came to know, from the beginning, that union with God consists in "poverty and nakedness of spirit" through a vibrant faith, hope, and love; and 2) even from the beginning, the word of Scripture and the Church's tradition, and every insight into this truth, was not something intellectual or abstract, but a ray of light from the face of the Beloved who sought to reveal himself, and to ravish the human heart, from behind the veil. "If only, on your silvered-over faces, you would suddenly form the eyes I have desired, which I bear sketched deep within my heart!" (*Spiritual Canticle*, 12)

on and off with great intensity for eight years, and to flow on as an undercurrent for much longer. I spoke of my junior year, in which—I remember quite vividly—I read the *Dark Night* of John, and felt, tugging upon me, the mysterious divine darkness that is the bearer of incredible light. Then, for Christmas of my senior year in high school, December 2008, I received Thomas Dubay's summary of the teaching of the above mentioned Carmelite Doctors: *Fire Within: St. Teresa of Avila, St. John of the Cross, and the Gospel—On Prayer*. We were visiting my extended family when I received it, a twelve hour drive from my home, and I recall reading almost the entirety of the book within the period of the return drive. One moment in particular stands out. We were only an hour from home, stopping at a gas station in Amarillo, Texas, and I read these words, concluding the chapter in which Dubay expounds the breathtakingly exalted destiny of nuptial transformation in God that is possible already in this life:

> Our being filled with God is, of course, the reason for everything else in the economy of salvation. Since this chapter is a compact formulation of the indwelling summit, we must be content simply to say that the transforming union [or spiritual marriage] is likewise the purpose of all else in the Church. The Eucharist itself, the Sacrament of all sacraments, is, according to the word of the Lord, aimed at producing eternal life here on earth. Jesus declares that whoever eats His flesh and drinks His blood *has* eternal life. It is a life that is to be abundant, to the full. The fullness is the transformation; there is no other. In this Mystical Body of Christ we are to find our fulfillment, not something less. Thus all structures in the Church—institutions, priesthood, curias, chancery offices, books and candles and all else—are aimed at producing this abundance of life, this utter immersion in the triune splendor, this transforming union.[1]

This was a moment of profound intuition for me, a kind of interior convergence in the heart, which was to set the stage for the unfolding path I would walk in God's love for the rest of my life. Despite all that was imperfect in Dubay's treatment, and even in the writing of the saints (for they, too, are not perfect in their expression, and manifest unhealthy tendencies, and we do them no favors by glossing over these things or trying to believe them whenever our hearts know they are not right)—despite all of this, I was moved to the core by the great message that lies at the heart of the Gospel. I was moved by the awesome truth that *God created me to be joined to him in an eternal intimacy so deep that it surpasses even the love of bridegroom and bride, an intimacy that is a true co-indwelling of persons in one another through mutual self-giving. This is an intimacy that is a living participation, already begun in this life, and to be consummated in heaven, of the life that is shared forever by the Father, Son, and Holy Spirit.*

As I would learn more and more vividly over the coming years, I was tapping into the pulsing heartbeat of God's self-revelation in history, into the heart of the Trinity's redeeming love present in the Incarnation, Passion, and Resurrection of Jesus Christ, and into the heart of the Catholic Church as the perpetuation of Christ's Body, of the Trinity's intimacy within this world, throughout time and space until the end of time. Indeed, I was touching—or rather being touched by—that mystery that lies at the inmost heart of each human life. As the beginning of the Catechism of the Catholic Church expresses it:

> The desire for God is written in the human heart, because man is created by God and for God; and God never ceases to draw man to himself. Only in God will he find the truth and happiness he never stops searching for:

> The dignity of man rests above all on the fact that he is called to communion with God. This invitation to converse with God is addressed to man as soon as he comes into being. For if man exists it is because God has created him through love, and through love continues to hold him in existence. He cannot live fully according to truth unless he freely acknowledges that love and entrusts himself to his creator. (*Gaudium et Spes,* 19.1) (par. 27)

Or again, in the very first paragraph, the Church lays out for us, from God's perspective, the breathtakingly beautiful plan that he has for us and for all humanity:

> God, infinitely perfect and blessed in himself, in a plan of sheer goodness freely created man to make him share in his own blessed life. For this reason, at every time and in every place, God draws close to man. He calls man to seek him, to know him, to love him with all his strength. He calls together all men, scattered and divided by sin, into the unity of his family, the Church. To accomplish this, when the fullness of time had come, God sent his Son as Redeemer and Savior. In his Son and through him, he invites men to become, in the Holy Spirit, his adopted children and thus heirs of his blessed life.

Through all of these things—through drinking in the word of God and beginning to learn, with little feeble steps, to dialogue with him in prayer—I was beginning to understand the deeply *existential* meaning of Catholicism, something which, indeed, I had already been touched by from the very beginning of my awakening to a deeper and more conscious faith my freshman or sophomore year in high school. In a specific sense, I was impressed by the truth that *all* that God does within this world is oriented towards playing itself out, not only on the stage of world history, nor even only in the context of the whole Body of the Church, but also in the intimate sanctuary of each individual heart and life. As John Paul II (also a spiritual son of John of the Cross) wrote in his first encyclical after election to the papacy:

> Man cannot live without love. He remains a being that is incomprehensible for himself, his life is senseless, if love is not revealed to him, if he does not encounter love, if he does not experience it and make it his own, if he does not participate intimately in it. ... The man who wishes to understand himself thoroughly—and not just in accordance with immediate, partial, often superficial, and even illusory standards and measures of his being—he must with his unrest, uncertainty and even his weakness and

sinfulness, with his life and death, draw near to Christ. He must, so to speak, enter into him with all his own self, he must "appropriate" and assimilate the whole of the reality of the Incarnation and Redemption in order to find himself. If this profound process takes place within him, he then bears fruit not only of adoration of God but also of deep wonder at himself. How precious must man be in the eyes of the Creator, if he "gained so great a Redeemer", and if God "gave his only Son" in order that man "should not perish but have eternal life." (*Redemptor Hominis*, 11)

To encounter love, to make it one's own, to participate intimately in it...and all through appropriation into the mystery of Jesus Christ, into his passage, through death and resurrection, into the inmost life of the Trinity. Christ came into the world, the incarnate Son of the Father, to be with us in all that is ours as human beings, to participate intimately in our humanity and to our experience of life on this earth. And he did so, not only to accompany us in the darkness of this life, but also to take it up, to suffer through it with the undying light of perfect love, and thus to transfigure the wounded creation that it may be whole again, may radiate with the divine light. And precisely in this way, through the atoning love present in the redeeming sacrifice of Christ, the world is made capable—above all human hearts, in whom alone the world is fully "personalized," are made capable—of participating in the eternal light of the love of the Father, Son, and Holy Spirit.

You could say then that, from the beginning of my life of faith, I had a crash course in mysticism, in the nuptial theology that lies at the heart of the Church's teaching and life, and gives meaning to everything else within her. To be united to God in this life and for all eternity! This is the great vocation and destiny laid before us in this world, in which all other vocations and tasks find their meaning and purpose, and can unfold freely in the lightheartedness and simplicity that are proper to things that are secondary. Of course, over the next decade and a half I was to learn many lessons, to pass through many misunderstandings, and to experience God's activity in numerous ways, all of which were to deepen, clarify, and correct my understanding of the great gift of insight and instruction that was given to me during those early years.

No, it was not only a gift of insight and instruction. It was not something abstract. The encounter with truth, when real, is never abstract. But in particular, I cannot really grasp the depth of my vocation to intimacy with God except by *feeling* God—except by finding myself seen, loved, and chosen by him, and tasting, in a reciprocal gaze upon him set free by his own gaze upon me, the sweetness of his infinite goodness and beauty. He comes. He comes to reveal himself to us in the tenderness of his love. He comes to woo our hearts gently with the revelation of his beauty. He comes to give us the love that we desire, and also to elicit from our hearts the love that he desires in return. Yes, and his love is total; his gift is total. And precisely this total gift awakening total gift is the drama of the Christian life, birthing both intimacy and abundant fruitfulness. As Saint Francis of Assisi said so beautifully: "Hold back nothing of yourself for yourself, so that he who gave himself totally to you may receive you totally."

+ + +

There are many things that I could say about the maturation of my heart and prayer over the years following what I have said above. But let me focus on one thing in particular, which will hopefully open out as a kind of avenue towards the whole. I said that God spoke profoundly into my heart through the words and lives of the Carmelite reformers, Teresa of Avila and John of the Cross. This is true, but it is also true that my life was never merely an imitation of or a focus on their lives alone. They assisted and aided me, mediated and parented me, as I walked forward in relationship with God who spoke directly into my heart, and guided me on my way, as he does each one of his children.

It is also important to recognize that in their spirituality there is still a certain feeling of excess rigidity, even harshness, due to the culture of their time and place, and to the currents present in human and ecclesial thought that affected them. It is also simply important to be able to "translate" what they were trying to say from its particular, culturally conditioned expressions, into the universally valid truth of the Christian life and the expansiveness of the Church's tradition. But back to the danger of unhealthy rigidity. While John and Teresa ultimately escape the main temptations inherent in this through their encounter with the God who is Love, it was not long after this time period that a terrible heresy broke loose, the heresy that hurts the heart of God the most: Jansenism. This heresy portrays God as a harsh Lawgiver and rigid Judge who demands complete reparation from each individual, through suffering and sacrifice, for every slightest infraction of his law, in order to balance anew the scales of justice. It is a heresy that instills fear, and crushes the little ones, obscuring the face of Mercy that lies at the heart of the Gospel and putting in its stead rather the face of anger and judgment. This heresy hurts the heart of God why? Because God, as pure and undimmed Love, desires nothing more than to be desired! Thus, to instill fear in us is the very opposite of his intentions! As he said to Teresa of Calcutta: "They do not know me, so they do not want me..."

However, despite the trends to rigidity in their culture, I encountered in John and Teresa the first radiant *revelation of the face of the God of Love*: the God who seeks out his creature, the human person—me—with ardent love and passionate longing, to unite me to himself as a bride with her Bridegroom. For this is the God whom they experienced, loved, and proclaimed with their very lives and their words. In comparison, certain rigid or unhealthy trends in their culture and in the manifestations of religious life proper to their time pale to nothingness. The blazing fire of the love of God whom they encountered and knew, and with whom they experienced the most vivid nuptial intimacy, consumes all else in a conflagration of radiant light and beauty. Yes, the God whom they portrayed, and above all experienced, was far removed from the harsh and angry judge, the distant lawgiver, portrayed by Jansenism. He was a passionate Lover, and nothing else.

But in the period following the lives of Teresa and John, Jansenism all but swamped the spirituality of the Church, and particularly the lives of the Carmelites who carried on the teaching and life given through Teresa and John. It is only necessary to read about the life inside a convent in France in the 1800's, in Thérèse of Lisieux's convent, for example, to see how far from a God of pure love their experience had become. Convents had become bastions of Jansenism, places of heroic sacrifice to appease the justice of an angry God. But they, in turn, simply manifested a trend, an illness, that infected all the Christian faithful to lesser and greater degree, and with which they grappled in the effort to discover and know the true face of God. But through all of this, God was turning everything to good: allowing all of the lies that we believe about God, all of our false projections, fears, and evasions to come into the open, so that his true light may shine upon them.

Through all of this, in other words, a purification occurred, and the revelation of the face of God as Love grew in transparency and mature expression. And I myself walked, in my own life and growth, the path that history itself walked, the path that unfolded in a straight line from Teresa of Avila and John of the Cross to Thérèse of Lisieux and, finally, to Teresa of Calcutta.[2] History, after all, is never merely in the "past." It is etched in the intimate spaces of our own souls. My own path, therefore, and the path of history over these centuries, was a gradual unveiling of *the depths of the infinite thirst in the heart of God to love and to be loved*. It was a gradual unveiling of the nature of Gods' very being as *self-diffusive love seeking nothing but intimacy, nothing but drawing us to participate eternally in his own life of communion and joy*.

My own tendency to rigidity and harshness had to be, and was, dissolved gradually by the tender approach of the Bridegroom Christ. He was the one who stirred me to the desire for love and union in the first place, and he it was who would dissolve my heart in the tenderness of his transformative, merciful touch. My own perpetual struggle against my human frailty and limitation, in the desire to live and love as the saints did, had to be eased under the touch of the gentle yoke of Christ, so that I would accept the path he marked out for me: one of littleness and ordinariness, filled with the hidden heartbeat of love that was content to be naked and poor, without any works to show for itself, without anything but the gra-

---

[*] "The thirst of God..." This is the light in which we see our lives unfold, the true source of Thérèse "little way" and the wellspring of Mother Teresa's entire life of love. As Joseph Langford wrote: "St. Thérèse and Mother Teresa: two sisters in spirit, who are like two mirrors who mutually reflect each other, one revealing what at first glance is not obvious in the other... St. Thérèse and Mother Teresa are the two witnesses whom God chose to reveal his Thirst for love, the vocation for all humanity to love and be loved, and the 'Little Way' open to all. ... Mother Teresa has always understood her vocation as modeled on her patron saint, St. Thérèse of Lisieux.... St. Thérèse intuitively felt that the infinite desire of the Lord to love and to be loved by His people—which was the foundation of her little way of confidence, abandonment and love, as well as her insatiable zeal to increase divine love in souls—had its origin and source in the mystery of the thirst of Jesus." But as will become clear, as well, this thirst is but the effect of the ardor of the divine life, purely gratuitous and eternally fulfilled in the intimacy of the Father, Son, and Holy Spirit, which so tenderly want to stop at nothing until we, too, their beloved children, share in their life and their joy.

tuitous love of the tenderest Father and most passionate Bridegroom. This led me straight to the heart of the "little way" of Thérèse of Lisieux, who rebelled ever so gently against the so-called "heroic greatness" of the reformers of her Order (John and Teresa), while holding to the spirit of their love and their deep contemplative vocation, and deepening it. But reading the life of Thérèse, one can still see Jansenistic tendencies clinging, which she did everything she could to shake off as she came to realize them —attaining complete transparency in her message of the merciful love of the Father in the last months of her life.[*] To walk with her on her path of discovery of God's love for his littlest ones is to walk our own path of healing and growth, our own path of discovery of the way in which God relates to us, and desires for us to relate to him.

And then Teresa of Calcutta, who took Thérèse of Lisieux as her namesake, carried this revelation to its final form, its most mature expression in the revelation of the *thirst* of Christ, and, in him, of the heavenly Father. She became a living icon of the tender mercy of God, which shines upon us like a dawn illumining our darkness with incredible tenderness.

Meeting God's unqualified acceptance of us banishes our fears and renders our defenses needless, allowing them to fall away one by one. God's loving gaze...frees us to journey to our depths, and to make peace with those parts of ourselves that we feared admitting. We become more sincere, more vulnerable and open, and more tender in turn. The more we are in touch with God's pleasure in loving us, the more we ourselves become pleasing. As Mother Teresa reminds us, in words reminiscent of her own journey, our task is to *believe unswervingly in God's delight* and to remember it in times of trouble:

You are precious to Him. He loves you, and He loves you so tenderly that He carved you on the palm of His hand. When your heart feels restless, when your heart feels hurt, when your heart feels like breaking, remember, I am precious to Him, He loves me. He has called me by name. I am His.

Being in Mother Teresa's presence gave the poor of Calcutta, and those of us who watched from afar, a glimmer of what awaits us in the kingdom, in that ocean of delight that is the Father's heart. She has granted us a foreshadowing of what it will be like to rest in the Father's loving gaze, and to spend our eternity in his cherishing.

---

[*] It is also significant that, at the heart of her life, little Thérèse reacted strongly against an act common in her time: to offer oneself as a victim to divine Justice, and thus to suffer the punishment and pain due to others before God. She saw the generosity of spirit here, but turned away from the false undercurrent; indeed, she swam in the opposite direction, offering herself as a "victim to Merciful Love," with the intention of receiving herself all the pent-up love in the Heart of Jesus which others would not receive. What a beautiful spirituality! To open wide my being to receive as much love as possible, to receive all the love God desires to give, both for myself and for others...to receive the immense outpouring from the very One who wants nothing else but to pour out his entire being in love, to fill me abundantly with his joy!

... God's thirst for us [is] unconditional and unchanging, even when we find ourselves lost in the struggle with sin. Far from diminishing God's yearning for us, our brokenness unleashes in him yet deeper wellsprings of tenderness and mercy. God's mercy is more than passive acceptance of us, more too that ready pardon should we return. God's thirst for us is a relentless, never-regretted resolve to be with us *in our wandering*—to seek us out and bring us back, and once we have returned, to shower us with blessings greater than those we had lost.[3]

At the risk of overemphasizing the differences between the earlier Carmelite reformers and the later spirituality of Thérèse of Lisieux and Teresa of Calcutta (and remembering that it is the *same God* and indeed the *same message* that they all proclaim, with a symphony of harmonious voices in breathtakingly beautiful agreement!)[*], one could say that the tendency to portray sanctity as for the *elite,* for the few heroic, became a manifestation of the possibility of holiness for *all,* and particularly for the littlest and weakest of God's children. It is beautiful to see, indeed, how the divine truth "purifies itself" as it continues to unveil its inner essence to receptive human hearts throughout history. Implicit assumptions are gradually brought into the open, and show themselves to never have been an authentic part of the true message, to have been simple accretions or even "projections" into what the authors never intended to portray. Brought out and surrendered to the divine light, these heart-obscuring assumptions thus make way for the light of divine truth to shine into us—for the real *essence*

---

[*]This beautiful unity of thought and life, finding the seeds of all that is beautiful in Thérèse and Mother Teresa already present in John of the Cross, is well expressed by Jean Vanier:

"Christians struggled for many years under the power of an Almighty God, fearful of this Law-giver and of the punishments they would receive if they did not obey him, and hopeful of the rewards if they did. Then the pendulum swung. Fear of authority was replaced by a negation of authority. Jesus became Emmanuel, God-with-us, the gentle and kind friend, who blesses everything and who makes few demands. It was a positive swing but something was lost in the transition: Jesus lost his divinity, his sacredness, the flame of love that purifies, hurts and burns in order to lead us into something totally new: the ecstasy of love and a peace that surpasses all human understanding.

"It is important to come back to the true face of God, the God of love, a love that burns and purifies and leads to the Wedding Feast; that *is* the Wedding Feast. ... [Our world needs to recognize] a humble, little John (he was even physically small), a John who suffered pain and poverty, a John of humble origins. [We should recognize] how John met and loved Teresa of Avila and how this beautiful woman brought him hope, encouragement, and inspiration and a new flame of love. ... John feared and fought against a cheap god, a god of the imagination and of human dreams, a god who was an idol rather than a reality, a god who blesses our mediocrity and weaknesses rather than calling us to growth. John sought the real God, the flame of love that burns and quenches the deepest yearnings of our wounded hearts. The God revealed by John is not a God to be feared: God is a Lover. Jesus, the Word made flesh, is a gentle and demanding Bridegroom: we are the bride. God seeks us like the Hound of Heaven, to bring us poor mortals into the friendship and ecstasy of love." (Foreword to *The Impact of God* by Iain Matthew, xi-xii. See the end notes.)

of the message of truth and love to show itself—and to conform another part of our hearts to the loving goodness of our Father and to the path of love that he marks out for us.

For me, this path led from a world-denying, harsh embrace of a vocation of prayer, solitude, and suffering (tending towards inhuman rigidity), which was manifested in my continual failed attempts to enter a strict monastery (Carmelite or Carthusian); and it led through the dissolution of a desire that the "gift" that I felt implanted within my heart would be manifested in a community, into something more humble, hidden, and real than any of this. It led through countless mistakes and mis-steps along the sure and certain path of God's love, marked out for me at every moment, and guiding me surely to the place he desired me to be...indeed, making each moment rich with love, beauty, and transfiguring intimacy. With the stripping away of all of my desires, dreams, hopes, and expectations, I could only stand naked before God, accepting his love in utter poverty in each moment. It led to the embrace of the joyful experience of being weak, humble, and incapable—to a "descent" into the joyful poverty of total destitution and apparent failure (though all lovingly and providentially orchestrated by God to fulfill his plans for me). In other words, this path gave birth to the joy of finding, precisely in the little ordinariness of my life, my true vocation. Indeed, even more importantly, I discovered and experienced the primacy of simple intimacy with God, simple repose in the gaze of his love, to be so much more important and fundamental than any vocation.

Only from this primal belovedness, this sheer and naked encounter with the God who loves me, can my embrace of the particular contours of my life and vocation unfold, and do so freely as expressions, incarnations, and renewed means of that deeper and abiding truth of encounter and intimacy. I myself found, in my increased daily suffering and incapacity, in apparent "failure" of all my hopes and dreams, and in increasing chronic illness joined to an interior experience of spiritual destitution and loss, the true spontaneity of love and prayer for which my heart longed, and to which I had felt called since I was young. I at last accepted what I had in fact desired all along, but did not know where to find: the path of utter littleness and poverty, of vulnerability, in simply being a child of God like any other, who prays for his brothers and sisters, and seeks to satiate the thirst of Christ, with his own life offered humbly in prayer and solitude, in silence and word, in solitude and togetherness, in suffering offered in atonement for the world and in the joy that engulfs all suffering within itself, and redeems it.

+ + +

So what exactly is the point in all of this? It is quite vulnerable to share these mysterious workings of God in my life of faith and prayer, but I do so in the conviction that no human experience, however intimate, is of significance for the individual alone, but also occurs within the inseparable unity of the Body of Christ, and casts ripples into other hearts whether for good or for ill. As Saint Paul wrote, "If one member suffers, all members suffer together; and if one member is honored, all rejoice together" (1 Cor 12:26). In addition, I recognize that, for God, there are no such things as coincidences. Looking at the lines of divine providence inscribed in the circumstances and events of my life, even those that I find most incomprehensible or difficult to appreciate, I can begin to discern a loving plan. This is a loving plan unique to me in my irreplaceable identity as God's son, an identity like no other person; it is a plan to redeem me, sanctify me, and unite me to the Trinity in the fullness of nuptial intimacy for which I was created. But it is also a plan that is realized—with different contours and unique expressions—in the life of every person. For we all share a common vocation and destiny, a call to participate in the same love and communion of the Father, Son, and Holy Spirit, both in this life and in the next.

More specifically, I recognize in the path on which God's providence has led me an experience of a very specific *education*. All that I have written in my previous books, and what I intend to write here, comes from an incredible indebtedness to God and to others, who formed me to speak of his love in a way that I could never do on my own, but in a way that grips me, in my utter poverty and need, with the abundance of divine light poured out in darkness. The "tracks" on which my railroad car has run, you could say, have been very narrow; and whenever I have tried to sway from them either to the left or to the right, God has hemmed me in by inexplicable and unexpected means. And this poverty, in which all I can do is let go of all possession and control, all comprehensive oversight, and surrender to the current of love that holds me, possesses me, cares for me, and flows through me...this poverty is something that I hope to cherish ever more deeply.

In all of this, it is like there is a word that God has wanted to speak, a word of healing for the wounds that are hurting so many hearts in the Church and the world today, and also a word of deepening and renewal, that the central mystery of the Gospel, and of human life itself, may become more apparent, more tangible, and more real for the children of God, whom he seeks so ardently and so tenderly.

And I am happy to offer this humble service to the truth of Christ, to be a "servant of the servants of God" by letting God point the way back to the center that is continually in danger of being forgotten. May my words, as imperfect as they are, help you to live more deeply and radically in and for the love of God, in the sanctity that is the vocation of every person, and in the witness of love for which our broken world is thirsting. And finally, may you come to know "the breadth and length and height and depth, and to know the love of Christ which surpasses knowledge, that you may be filled with all the fullness of God" (Eph 3:18-19).

The words of this book are one more little effort, very weak and imperfect, to give voice to this great mystery, so that, as Christ said: "Your joy may be complete" (Jn 16:24).

WEEK I

Responding to the Invitation of the Bridegroom

DAY 1
THE PASSIONATE THIRST OF GOD

Therefore, behold, I will allure her,
and bring her into the wilderness,
and speak tenderly to her.
And I will betroth you to me for ever;
I will betroth you to me in righteousness and in justice,
in steadfast love, and in mercy.
I will betroth you to me in faithfulness;
and you shall know the LORD.
(Hosea 2:14, 19-20)

The language of the Bible is a language of relationship. From the earliest history of humanity marked out for us in the book of Genesis to the final pages of the book of Revelation giving a glimpse of our eternal destiny, we see God's plan to draw us *into intimate relationship with himself*. This means that, in order to understand the authentic beauty of Scripture, of the history of salvation laid out before our gaze—as well as the very meaning of our own lives on this earth—it is necessary to understand the *nature* of this relationship. What kind of relationship does God establish with us? How does he seek to relate to us, and how does he desire us to relate to him?

These questions get to the root issue for each one of us: *who* is God? Is he a relentless taskmaster, a harsh judge, a distant patriarch, a master over his slaves? Is he an egoist who clings to his prerogatives and uses his creatures to minister to his own wishes and self-gain? This is what the evil spirit, symbolized by the serpent in Eden, tried to convince Adam and Eve of at the beginning of human history. But it was a lie; and it is *still* a lie when we believe it today, however subtly. Whenever we flee from the face of God into sin and selfishness, we are not liberating ourselves unto freedom; we are descending into slavery, far from the love of our Father who only desires our good and happiness. For he created us out of his abundant generosity for no other reason than to share in the happiness of his own eternal life, already in this world and forever in the renewed creation at the consummation of history.

This is the true nature of relationship that God desires to have with us, one that manifests his own inner being as Love—as Trinity—in the everlasting communion of the Father, Son, and Holy Spirit. *This* is the truth written all over the Bible, growing in an ever increasing crescendo throughout the Old Testament until it bursts forth with radiant clarity in the New. But this truth is also written all over our human existence, and in our very bodies as man and woman, as children, spouses, and parents. For the relation of God to us is not adequately understood as that of Master and servant, as Lord and subjects, or even as Creator and creature. As John Paul II says, "The paradigm of master and slave is foreign to the Gospel." Nothing but *intimacy*, a deep intimacy that mirrors the most intimate of human relationships that we experience in this life, while also infinitely surpassing them in depth and ardor—nothing but intimacy can truly express the depth of communion that the God of heaven and earth desires to have with each one of us.

A love aflame with desire, burning with ardent *thirst,* this is the love that God has for us, for *me.* It is a love that longs for me with tenderness, seeks for me with passion, looks upon me with delight, and reaches out to touch me, hold me, and caress me with gentleness. It is a love that restores, through sheer grace, what my own sin and foolishness has destroyed, plunging to the depths of the darkness in my suffering heart in order, there, to affirm my hidden beauty, to set it free and restore it, so that in God, in union with his love, I may be beautiful as I was meant to be. This alone is the kind of love that can do justice to the nature of God that is revealed to us in the pages of the sacred text, and is presented to us throughout history in the preaching and life of the Church.

Yes, the language of the Bible is the language of *family,* and the God revealed to us therein is a God thirsting to establish a relationship of intimate love with each one of his children. From the first pages of Genesis, when God creates humanity as male and female, husband and wife, and commands them, "be fruitful and multiply" (Gen 1:28), to the climax of the book of Revelation, in which the Bride cries out to the Bridegroom, "Come, Lord Jesus!" (cf. Rev 22:17-21), we see that God delights in the family, and relates to us as members of his own family. Of course, this participation is imperfect, weak, and incipient at the beginning of history, and only grows gradually over time as God educates humanity in his ways and enters into a series of ever more intimate covenants with us. This climaxes in the covenant wrought through Jesus Christ, in which all of God's activity in the world and in history reaches its definitive fulfillment, a fulfillment that is only awaiting its final consummation with the conclusion of history.

Yes, God's relationship with us is one that is both *paternal* and *spousal,* and also brings forth in us the fruitfulness of *parenthood.* He wishes to relate to us, and to truly be, our Father and our Bridegroom, even if he is so in an infinitely more real and profound manner than the imperfect way these relations are manifested in the context of human relationships in this world. And through this union of breathtaking communion, we are rendered transparent to his light, living with his very life, such that it passes through us—through our own freedom joined to his freedom—into the world and into the hearts of our brothers and sisters.

God has impressed upon us, in both body and spirit, this orientation towards *intimacy through self-giving.* And this is manifested primarily in the three fundamental relationships of *child, spouse,* and *parent* (with *friendship* being, as it were, the common thread of all love in the simple mutual affirmation of persons). This vocation to love lies at the origin of our very existence—received through the conjugal gift of man and woman and the growth of life in the womb of the woman's body. And such a love is also the foundation of our experience of self and of reality—in the gaze and smile of our mother, whose very love awakens us to consciousness and grants us an intuition of the Love that lies at the very origin of the universe and is the deepest meaning of all things.

Coming from Love, sustained by Love, enfolded in Love, and called to enter ever deeper into Love in reciprocal love and total self-surrender. This is the marvel of human existence, a marvel gravely wounded by sin at the beginning of time and by every personal sin committed since, and yet a marvel affirmed and redeemed by God in Jesus Christ at the fullness of time. And this gift of redemption, of the "re-giving" of our very humanity anew, restored and ennobled in Christ, seeks only to be appropriated by us, to touch us and enter into us, renewing us to such a degree that the wounds of sin are healed and we become partakers in the very nature of God's own life and love. This is the reason that we were created in the beginning, and it is the reason that, lost as we are in sin, God became flesh to redeem us: so that we may live the very life of God, as God himself lives it, and may do so, not as the result of our own efforts or merit, but on the basis of the free gift of God given in Christ Jesus.

We have been created, redeemed, and chosen to share in the intimate life of the Trinity, to be partakers in the very inner life of God. Nothing, absolutely nothing in the universe finds meaning outside of the love of the Father, Son, and Holy Spirit. Rather, all finds its purpose in the light of his loving self-communication and its fulfillment in returning to him anew, through the heart of man and woman surrendered to him in reciprocal love.

To be a beloved child of the heavenly Father, a spouse of Jesus Christ, the divine Bridegroom, and to be radiant with the fecund love of the Holy Spirit! This is my vocation and my destiny. This is the reason for which I was made by God. This is the reason that, lost as I was in sin and selfishness, covering over my nakedness in shame, fear, and guilt, he came to me —naked himself in vulnerable love upon the Cross—to reopen me to the flow of acceptance and reciprocal self-giving, to being loved and loving, that in this way I may enter anew into intimacy with his own life.

And what is unveiled to me in this naked vulnerability of God upon the Cross, in the gaze and voice of Jesus Christ in his Passion? Here God has become flesh for me—the second Person of the Trinity, the eternal Son, has become a man and married himself to my own humanity, my own experience, my own flesh, even my own darkness. And he has done so precisely so that he can unveil to me anew his own inmost Heart...yes, the Heart of his Father, who, through adoption, is my Father too. So what does he reveal? As Teresa of Calcutta expressed it: it is God's *infinite longing to love and be loved.*

This is the kind of God that I have, and the One with whom I am invited to enter into deep relationship. It is a God who not only desires me to be happy, to find fulfillment in his love, but who also *thirsts for me*, who yearns for me, moved as he is by the beauty that he sees in me, a beauty that he himself created and redeemed. Shall I refuse him this gift of myself, turning away to veil my nakedness in shame, in the million possible distractions? Shall I remain in the lies of the evil one, insinuated into me to keep me far from the Father who loves me, from the Bridegroom who seeks me? Or shall I step forth from the trees of the garden, throwing off the fig leaf of fear, in order to be looked upon by his cherishing love, to be approached by him, and to give myself to him who, in this sacred space, gives himself, in all his ravishing beauty, to me?

DAY 2
THE HEART OF ALL REALITY:
TRINITARIAN LOVE

Allow me to share a quote that summarizes what I have said in the previous reflection, condensing the theme that lies at the heart of this book and providing a beautiful "compass" for our reflections. The following words come from Father Joseph Langford, who is perhaps the foremost exegete and promulgator of the spirituality (or as he would say the "secret fire") of Mother Teresa of Calcutta. He writes:

> No one I know enjoyed weddings more than Mother Teresa. She who saved every grain of rice so that nothing would be wasted, happily "wasted" whatever it cost for her orphan girls to have a proper trousseau on their wedding day.
>
> For Mother Teresa, the intimacy of human marriage was a reflection of the union God wished to forge with all mankind, and with each individual soul. While the gods of other religions wished to be feared, served, or simply worshiped, the God of Israel longed to relate to his people *in love,* to the point of making love his central command, the core of his Covenant, and the first hint of how serious was his thirst for our return of love: "You shall love the LORD your God with all your heart, and with all your soul, and with all your might" (Dt 6:5).
>
> Since we are created in the image of God, our human longing for intimacy is a reflection of God's own nature, and a sharing in the divine impetus to love and be loved. Time after time, the prophets turn to this motif in describing the inner life of Yahweh, and the intimacy he desires with his people:
>
>> Ezekiel, speaking of God's relationship with the people of Israel, is not afraid to use strong and passionate language (cf. 16:1-22). These biblical texts indicate that *eros* is part of God's very Heart: the Almighty awaits the "yes" of his creatures as a young bridegroom that of his bride. (Benedict XVI, Message for Lent, 2007)
>
> Because we are fashioned in his image, there is a stirring in the human soul that longs for union with God, and for communion with one another. The longing to merge in love, as Father and Son in eternal union, is written in our very nature. No one needs to teach an infant to embrace his parents. No one ever needed to show another culture how to hold and hug their loved ones to themselves. The innate, spontaneous drive to embrace those we love points to the full merging and eternal union with the Godhead for which we were created, and which is symbolized in every human embrace.
>
> This mystery of God's thirst for union, lived out in the Trinity's eternal embrace, is written in the depths of all being. Not

only humanity, but all creation exists *for communion.* Every entity is drawn to, and exists for, another. From the heart of God to the heart of man, from the spiral of the galaxies drawing their countless stars in a single dance to the entwined double helix of DNA, the Trinitarian mystery of communion is reflected and played out in all that is.

The kind of intimacy God offers us, even here on earth, not only approaches our highest experience of human intimacy, but surpasses it. No matter how close human spouses may come, they can never truly dwell one within the other, inseparable, their souls forever merged. While the soul was created for, and longs for, this ultimate kind of union, it is only symbolized and prepared for in marriage. The true inter-dwelling of lover and beloved takes place only in our relationship with God: "You...in me...and I in you" (Jn 17:21).

After all, we never truly *feel* the love of another human being —we only experience our own love for them. Only God's love is capable of penetrating and being perceived directly by the human soul—and, not uncommonly, even to the point of overwhelming the senses. The common experience of the saints is that our union with God, even here on earth, knows no bounds—save those we ourselves set. The great Spanish mystics Teresa of Avila and John of the Cross paint as close a picture as can be of the full panorama of blessedness and bliss that await us in God, in the full interdwelling of Creator and creature, even in this life. As the Mystical Doctor proclaims in his *Spiritual Canticle:*

> O you soul, then, most beautiful of creatures, who so long to know the place where your Beloved is, that you may seek Him, and be united to Him, you know now that you are yourself that very tabernacle where He dwells, the secret chamber of His retreat where He is hidden. Rejoice, therefore, and exult, because all your good and all your hope is so near you as to be within you; or, to speak more accurately, that you can not be without it, "for lo, the kingdom of God is within you." So says the Bridegroom Himself, and His servant, St. Paul, adds: "You are the temple of the living God." What joy for the soul to learn that God never abandons it, even in mortal sin; how much less in a state of grace! (*Spiritual Canticle,* 8)

Those who have discovered this blessedness, as have Mother Teresa and the saints, gladly give up not only selfishness and sin, but every other lesser good, to possess this "pearl of great price." Like the merchant of fine pearls in the gospel story (Mt 13:45-46), so overjoyed at his good fortune that he never thinks of the cost, the saints experience their sacrifices not as deprivation, but as a small price for such an immense reward. The saints have been the truest and the greatest lovers in human history, those who have gone the furthest in the pursuit of love, all the way to its divine Source—and they have marked out a path for us, living to the full the divine union for which we all exist.[4]

How breathtaking this is... Let us, today, try to open our hearts to truly interiorize the import of these words, to let them touch our hearts deep within. Here, the love of God can unveil itself, stirring into flame our thirst for intimacy, our thirst for intimacy with the very Source of all love, the very Consummation of all intimacy in the heart of the communion of Father, Son, and Holy Spirit. And indeed, this thirst is already within us, and has always been within us, at the core of our humanity fashioned in God's image and called to his likeness. And not only that, but God already thirsts for us, and seeks us out, infinitely more deeply, constantly, and ardently than we have ever thirsted for him. He comes and initiates the gift. He is already at work in us—in me—to convert my heart to him, to ravish me with his beauty, and to attract me into the joy of his embrace.

For this reason he has created me, and for this reason he redeemed me in Christ, who became man to be close to me in the flesh, and suffered and rose from death to take all that is my own into himself and into the very life of the Trinity. Let us not fail to wonder at this gratuitous and undeserved gift, poured out into our lives from the opened Heart of Jesus Christ on the Cross and in the Resurrection. Let us rather, stirred by wonder and gratitude, simply cry out, "Jesus, I trust in you!" opening our whole being to welcome the gift of grace—of God's own life as Trinity—pouring into us. And as we accept this gift every day, as we surrender to its currents surging through us, our own reciprocal response of cooperation will be born, sustained, and brought to fulfillment.

At the beginning of these reflections, therefore, I would like to emphasize the *primacy of receptivity*, of a wonder-filled acceptance of the love of God bestowed upon us in each moment and circumstance of life. This is an attitude both *filial* and *spousal*, the attitude of childlike and virginal receptivity to the gift of God and his love. It is the attitude of prayer. Everything else that we shall explore in coming reflections will be held within, and never unfold outside of, this primal receptivity, this primal experience of being seen, known, and loved by the God who has created us and chosen us for himself. Indeed, to the degree that we repose in this already-given gift of love, in the delight of God who looks upon us in Christ, and, in looking, loves, we can walk the path of love ourselves, in healing, transformation, and total surrender, throughout all that this entails in the sorrows and sufferings of this life—and in all its joys!—until we are taken home to eternal rest in the bosom of the Trinity.

DAY 3
THE BRIDEGROOM'S TENDER INVITATION

Arise, my love, my fair one, and come away;
for lo, the winter is past, the rain is over and gone.
The flowers appear on the earth, the time of singing has come,
and the voice of the turtledove is heard in our land.
The fig tree puts forth its figs, and the vines are in blossom;
they give forth fragrance.
Arise, my love, my fair one, and come away.
O my dove, in the clefts of the rock, in the covert of the cliff,
let me see your face, let me hear your voice,
for your voice is sweet, and your face is comely. (Song 2:10-14)

The Bridegroom revealed to us in these words is one who truly *feels*, who is deeply *moved* by love for his bride, in the tenderest spaces of his heart and in his whole being. And he calls her forth—he calls each of us forth—from her hiddenness in fear and sin, that she may step forth from the clefts of the rock into the light of his loving gaze, that he may see the beauty of her face and hear the loveliness of her voice. In other words, this love of the Bridegroom, who is Christ, is *thirst*.

It is important to emphasize this, not only because so few people recognize it, but because this is so central to who God is and how he loves. God is a God not merely of *agape*, of self-sacrificing love, but of *eros*, of ardent longing. Indeed he is the One in whom *agape* and *eros* are inseparably united, a single and indivisible love: the desire for the well-being of the beloved and the longing for union with them; the outpouring gift of self for the other and the openness to receive the other into oneself.

God's love is thirst because it is ardor, passion, affection, tenderness. Thus, even though God—being infinitely perfect in himself and lacking nothing—cannot suffer, he can nonetheless, as Saint Bernard says, *suffer-with*. He can open himself to be *moved* by us in com-passion (in co-suffering), feeling with us our own pain, as well as feeling, in himself, the way that our sins and infidelities—as well as our love, our receptivity, our gratitude—affect him. How, in fact, could it be otherwise? If the ability to be touched and moved by others in vulnerable love is a perfection, a virtue—indeed the heart of all love—then it must exist in God, not in a lesser way, but in a fullness infinitely more rich and abundant than it exists among human persons!

Yes, in his love for us, God has made his very being, as it were, a *longing-for-us*. And he has done so without reserve and irrevocably. This is what love is, in its inner essence, after all: vulnerability before the other, to receive and to give. Thus God does not, and never will, relate to us in any other way than in vulnerable longing, in humble invitation, in uncompromising self-outpouring, and in pure acceptance of us in all that we are. Let us pray that we can hear his plea, filled with tender longing and also touched with deep sorrow at our betrayal and our apathy: *"They do not know me, so they do not want me,"* as Christ lamented to Mother Teresa of Calcutta. We hear this same voice in Scripture, "They have forsaken me, the fountain of living waters, and have hewed out cisterns for themselves, broken cisterns, that can hold no water" (Jer 2:13); and in the liturgy: "My heart had expected reproach and misery. And I looked for one that would grieve together with me, and there was none; and I sought one that would console me, and I found none."[5] Mother Teresa comments on these words so beautifully, and we can take her invitation with all seriousness:

> Tell Jesus, "I will be the one." I will comfort, encourage and love Him. ... Be with Jesus. He prayed and prayed, and then went to look for consolation, but there was none. ... I always write that sentence, "I looked for one to comfort Me, but I found no one." Then I write, "Be the one." So now you be that one. Try to be the one to share with Him, to comfort Him, to console Him. So let us ask Our Lady to help us understand.[6]

Saint Thérèse saw the same:

> ...this same God, who declares He had no need to tell us if He is hungry, did not hesitate to *beg* for a little water from the Samaritan Woman. He was thirsty.... But when He said, "Give me to drink," it was the *love* of His poor creatures that the Creator of the universe was asking for. He was thirsty for love.... Ah! I feel it more than ever before, Jesus is *parched,* for He meets only the ungrateful and indifferent among His disciples in the world, and among *His own disciples,* alas, He finds few hearts who surrender to Him without reservations, who understand the real tenderness of His infinite Love.[7,8]

In speaking about the thirst and lament of Christ, of God, it is important to clarify that we do *not* mean that God is needy, that he is imperfect or scared or needs our help, or that he seeks us for his own fulfillment, or that he relates to us as a clingy lover, a narcissistic user, a controlling parent, or any other faulty human analogy. This is a danger that can be felt or seen in certain other writings about the thirst of Christ, even beyond our own projections, focusing on satiating his thirst or consoling his heart. Such false understandings can be deeply harmful, so it is important to emphasize anew that God's thirst is far beyond and far different than all of this. *God's thirst is born not of his need but of our need.*

His thirst is free, gratuitous, lighthearted, joyful, playful, and serene. It is a gift born from the fullness of joy, of delight, which desires to share itself with us, so to turn our sorrow into joy, our loneliness into communion. Thus God's thirst, even the thirst of the man Christ, is abundance. It is but another name for his overflowing generosity, his abundant joy in the everlasting playful intimacy of Father, Son, and Holy Spirit. Here we see more deeply how in God eros and agape are one.

In all of this, we see how prayer is *the encounter of God's thirst with our thirst.* We are thirsting for God, created as we have been precisely for union with he who is all beauty, goodness, and truth. And yet he is also thirsting for us, tender love and ardent mercy that he is, the magnetism of intimacy that seeks to draw his precious creatures into the same eternal joy that is his as Father, Son, and Holy Spirit. And if this is true, then his love is not a mere willing, but a movement of the heart, an affection, a tender surging of delight and desire, as well as, when confronted with evil, apathy, and sin, an experience of inexplicable, divine sorrow, pain, and lament.

And thus his mercy is not a mere forgiveness bestowed from on high, a mere legal act of dismissal of guilt, but an ardent pursuit of us even in our darkest place, even in the lostness of sin, in order to gather us up in his arms and to bring us home. His mercy is thus not opposed to his justice, but one with it; it is God's own fidelity towards himself, towards his infinite goodness as Father, as eternal Love. And, when faced with human misery and sin, with a broken and shattered world, mercy alone can restore justice. Mercy, as love poured out into poverty and brokenness, can alone restore what is broken and draw human hearts back into right relationship with God. And this restoration, this right relationship, is precisely what justice is (thus the meaning of the term "justification," in which, through faith and baptism, we are reconciled with God and admitted into his own inner life of love).

If we stand, therefore, in a world so broken, so filled with ignorance of God and even rejection of him, it is very appropriate that we begin these days of reflection by stilling our hearts and *listening*. Let us listen to the lament of Christ longing for love, Christ on the Cross crying out, "I thirst," and thus revealing to us the *depths of longing in the heart of God to love and be loved*. Only this can reveal to us the true nature of our heavenly Father, the true love of our divine Bridegroom, and the breath of the Spirit who seeks to fill us with himself.

Indeed, in this listening to Christ, we can hear our own lament, our own desire, our own hope, voiced by him, taken up and offered to the Father. We can hear the voice of all humanity gathered together in Christ and made a single prayer of pure love:

> When the hour had come for him to fulfill the Father's plan of love, Jesus allows a glimpse of the boundless depth of his filial prayer, not only before he freely delivered himself up ("Abba . . . not my will, but yours."), but even in his last words on the Cross, where prayer and the gift of self are but one: "Father, forgive them, for they know not what they do," "Truly, I say to you, today you will be with me in Paradise," "Woman, behold your son" - "Behold your mother," "I thirst." "My God, My God, why have you forsaken me?" "It is finished;" "Father, into your hands I commit my spirit!" until the "loud cry" as he expires, giving up his spirit.
>
> All the troubles, for all time, of humanity enslaved by sin and death, all the petitions and intercessions of salvation history are summed up in this cry of the incarnate Word. Here the Father accepts them and, beyond all hope, answers them by raising his Son. Thus is fulfilled and brought to completion the drama of prayer in the economy of creation and salvation. The Psalter gives us the key to prayer in Christ. In the "today" of the Resurrection the Father says: "You are my Son, today I have begotten you. Ask of me, and I will make the nations your heritage, and the ends of the earth your possession." (*Catechism,* par. 2605-2606)

Let us therefore listen deeply, and, in listening, allow our own true voice, our own heart's deepest and most hidden longings, to come forth, and to express themselves vulnerably before Jesus. Let us listen, in turn, to his own voice echoing in the silence of our heart, revealing to us his ardent thirst of love, for all of humanity and for us, uniquely and specifically. Here two voices will come together, at the foot of the Cross of Love, and speak in a dialogue of love, in which both voices begin to assuage the thirst of one another, and birth the joy of intimacy.

DAY 4
THE THIRST OF JESUS

I would like to offer one more reflection on the theme of thirst—both that of God and of our own hearts—before proceeding to the next theme. Indeed, it is all-important to be in touch with this thirst of God and of our own hearts, since it is the fuel that drives everything, in the universe and in our own lives. All is driven by *desire*, from the innermost heart of God to the humblest of human actions. Thus to be in touch with this desire, so often buried over by fear, is to be enabled, little by little, to let it be grasped by the desire of Christ, and to be liberated by him so that, in God, it may find definitive fulfillment.

"Thy will be done on earth as it is in heaven!" That is what this means, does it not? Let thy desire, a desire of pure love, pour forth into our frail hearts, to heal them and to set free their desire to be wedded to your desire, that you may desire in us and we may desire in you. Only in this way can the fullness of God's will be done on earth, in us and in the whole universe, as it is done in heaven, in the bosom of the intimacy of the Father, Son, and Holy Spirit. But to do this, desire must first be accessed; fear must first be recognized; and vulnerability must first be accepted, opening our fears and desires to the gaze of the One who, in his desire for us, draws near.

I would like to help us get nearer to both the desire of Christ and our own desire by reading large sections from a letter of Teresa of Calcutta (how beautifully present she is for us in these reflections!). Indeed, I would like to allow her to lead us deeper, into the depths of the thirst of God revealed in Christ Crucified, Christ hanging on the Cross and crying out for our love, as we stand nearby like the beloved disciple John, with the Virgin Mary and Mary Magdalene. In this proximity to the fire of God's love revealed in the Crucified Christ, we can allow him to lead us home to the truth of our own hearts, and, even more, into the Home of his Heart, thus carrying us from the painful longing of Good Friday to the radiant joy and abiding intimacy of Easter Sunday.

But first, let us start from the beginning, as if starting to pray for the very first time, as if encountering the love of Jesus for the very first time. Let us ask, then: what does it mean to pray? What does it mean to experience the love of Jesus? What does it mean to love him in return? Let us allow Mother Teresa to lead us:

> My dearest Children,
>
> Jesus wants me to tell you again, how much is the love He has for each one of you - beyond all that you can imagine. I worry some of you still have not really met Jesus - one to one - you and Jesus alone. We may spend time in chapel - but have you seen with the eyes of your soul how He looks at you with love? Do you really know the living Jesus - not from books, but from being with Him in your heart? Have you heard the loving words He speaks to you? Ask for this grace, He is longing to give it. Never give up this daily intimate contact with Jesus as a real living Per-

son - not just an idea. How can we last - even one day living our life without hearing Jesus say "I love you" - impossible. Our soul needs that as much as the body needs to breathe the air. If not, prayer is dead - meditation is only thinking. Jesus wants you each to hear Him - speaking in the silence of your heart.

Be careful of all that can block that personal being in touch with the living Jesus. The hurts of life, and sometimes your own mistakes - [they] make you feel it is impossible that Jesus really loves you, is really clinging to you. This is a danger for all of you. And so sad, because it is completely opposite of what Jesus is really wanting, waiting to tell you. Not only He loves you, even more - He longs for you. He misses you when you don't come close. He thirsts for you. He loves you always, even when you don't feel worthy. Even if you are not accepted by others, even by yourself sometimes - He is the one who always accepts you. My children, you don't have to be different for Jesus to love you. Only believe - you are precious to Him. Bring all you are suffering to His feet - only open your heart to be loved by Him as you are. He will do the rest.

You all know in your mind that Jesus loves you - but in this letter Mother wants to touch your heart instead. Jesus wants to stir up our hearts, so not to lose our early love... Why is Mother saying these things? After reading [Pope John Paul II's] letter "I Thirst," I was struck so much - I can not tell you what I felt. His letter made me realize more than ever how beautiful is our vocation. How great is God's love for us in choosing [us] to satiate that thirst of Jesus, for love, for souls - giving us our special place in the Church. At the same time we are reminding the world of His thirst, something that was being forgotten. I wrote to Holy Father to thank him. [His] letter is a sign... to go more into what is this great thirst for Jesus for each one. It is also a sign for Mother, that the time has come for me to speak openly of the gift God gave [on] Sept. 10th - to explain fully as I can what means for me the thirst of Jesus.

For me, Jesus' thirst is something so intimate - so I have felt shy until now to speak to you of Sept. 10th - I wanted to do as Our Lady who "kept all these things in her heart." Jesus' words on the wall of every MC chapel, they are not from the past only, but alive here and now, spoken to you. Do you believe it? If so, you will hear, you will feel His presence. Let it become as intimate for each of you, just as for Mother - this is the greatest joy you could give me. Jesus Himself must be the one to say to you "I Thirst." Hear your own name. Not just once. Every day. If you listen with your heart, you will hear, you will understand.

Why does Jesus say "I thirst"? What does it mean? Something so hard to explain in words - if you remember anything from Mother's letter, remember this - "I thirst" is something much deeper than just Jesus saying "I love you." Until you know deep inside that Jesus thirsts for you - you can't begin to know who He wants to be for you. Or who He wants you to be for Him.

[Our Lady] was the first person to hear Jesus' cry "I Thirst" with St. John, and I am sure Mary Magdalene. Because Our Lady was there on Calvary, she knows how real, how deep is His longing for you and for the poor. Do we know? Do we feel as she? Ask her to teach. Her role is to bring you face to face, as John and Magdalen, with the love in the Heart of Jesus Crucified. Before it was Our Lady pleading with Mother, now it is Mother in her name pleading with you - "listen to Jesus' thirst." Let it be for each ... a Word of Life.

How to approach the thirst of Jesus? Only one secret - the closer you come to Jesus, the better you will know His thirst. "Repent and believe," Jesus tells us. What are we to repent? Our indifference, our hardness of heart. What are we to believe? Jesus thirsts even now, in your heart and in the poor - He knows your weakness, He wants only your love, wants only the chance to love you. He is not bound by time. Whenever we come close to Him - we become partners of Our Lady, St John, Magdalen. Hear Him. Hear your own name. Make my joy and yours complete.[9]

DAY 5
NUPTIAL SPIRITUALITY:
RESPONDING TO JESUS' THIRST

I would now like to tie together the insights from the previous reflections in order to focus specifically on the central theme of this book: *a nuptial spirituality*. First, let me define these terms, so it will be clear precisely what we are talking about (even though the very reality of which we are speaking is a matter of the heart, and thus not something that can be comprehended and classified by the mind!). By spirituality I do not mean some "intellectual framework" applied to my life, a kind of paradigm through which I interpret everything; nor do I mean a particular emphasis which, based on my own preferences or insights, I elect for myself (for example, "I prefer a Carmelite spirituality as opposed to a Jesuit one," etc.). The only thing that deserves our conviction, the obedience of our lives, is not a perspective, an emphasis, but the *truth*. We should give all, everything that we are and have, in the ardent desire to receive and respond to the Gospel in its wholeness, in its entirety, and in its true depth. And as we do so, with our eyes not on ourselves but on Christ, on the Trinity revealed in and through him, "spirituality" happens spontaneously: it is simply the *incarnation of the Gospel in the contours of our unique life, in our time, place, and relationships*. Thus spirituality is true to the degree that it is not a self-enclosed system, but simply the en-fleshing of the Gospel, of God's love revealed in Christ through the Paschal Mystery and drawing us to participate in the inner life of the Trinity. Spirituality is true to the degree that it is simply another fulfillment of the words at the beginning of the Gospel of John: "And the Word was made flesh" (Jn 1:14).

By the word *nuptial*, I refer to that love which is characterized by the *reciprocal and total gift of self between two persons*. The most common example of this in our experience is, obviously, the love of man and woman that leads to marriage and family life—and thus can just as well be called "spousal" love. I am using the two terms more or less interchangeably. Nuptial also refers to the intensity with which the *desire for union with the beloved* is manifested in such love, as opposed to forms of love in which such desire is either not expressed at all or expressed in a lesser degree, for example in the love of neighbor in which the theme of charity and service takes the forefront, or in friendship or siblinghood in which the desire of union, though present, is not so pronounced or so intense.*

---

*I would like to note, however, that *all* love bears, at least in seed, a *nuptial* character, in that it is oriented towards a gift of self that is both *total* and *unitive* (and also *generative*), even though this is manifest in a diversity of different ways while this temporal life lasts. In heaven, all love will be rendered transparent to, and fully manifest, this inclination to totality and intimacy. In this life, the vocation of celibacy or virginity takes its stand precisely in *anticipating* such "category transcending" love, a love that, precisely by being "only all for Jesus" (as Mother Teresa says), is also totally for each one of God's children, and not afraid of being tender, intimate, and close, from the heart of the love that enfolds and permeates all things.

Even earthly spousal love is a dim (but beautiful) reflection of the nuptial form of relationship that God—in the Bridegroom Christ—desires to have with each one of us. For he loves us with *totality*, with the gift of his self, whole and entire, in the Paschal Mystery and in the Eucharist (and in prayer and in each moment of life, too!). And he wants to receive all of us, unreservedly, in response, as I quoted Saint Francis saying in the introduction: "Hold back nothing of yourself for yourself, so that he who gave himself totally to you may receive you totally." And this total reciprocal gift of persons is oriented towards the *complete mutual belonging* of the two to one another. Yes, love's mutual belonging is manifest both in the service—in the tender attentiveness that seeks the other's good—that each person offers to the other, as well as in the gratuitous intimacy that they cherish. The intimacy holds the service and sustains it, while the service manifests, strengthens, and deepens the intimacy. And the link between the two is *gratuity*: the sheer for-its-own-sake-ness of the way that Lover and Beloved relate to one another, in which each thought, desire, choice, and act is an affirmative "Yes" to the beauty and value of the beloved person. This is similar to what I have said elsewhere about the *amor complacentiae* (love of complacence) holding in itself, and being manifest within, the *intentio benevolentiae* (benevolent desire) and the *intentio unionis* (unitive desire). In other words, the disposition of contemplative delight in the beloved gives birth to, and sustains, the pursuit of what is truly good for the beloved as well as the impulse to ever deeper intimacy with them in truth.

But this is not adequate unless we add another element. In all true love of a mature depth and expression, there is another dimension that comes to the fore. It is *sharing in the subjectivity of the other person, such that their desires, pains, experiences, and their very life, become one's one*. This is what John Paul II in his Theology of the Body refers to as "intersubjectivity," which will be our definitive experience in the new creation at the end of time, but which is anticipated in all true love in this life. And it is above all anticipated with God, who comes so close to us, sharing in our life and sharing his life so fully with us, that he can affirm that we "abide in him" and he "abides in us." And this is not just an ontological matter—a matter of being—but also a matter of *experience*. After all, subjectivity refers precisely to experience, to the inmost experience of my own "I" in its unrepeatable relationship with reality. It is my inner resonance at each moment, my secret world of experience, that is directly accessible to me alone.

But love, in some way, makes it accessible, a "shared reality" through empathy, compassion, and the mystical co-experiencing made possible in the Body of Christ. This opening up of one's inner subjectivity, the intimate experience of the "I," to be shared in by another is indeed one of the deepest acts of love and vulnerability, and makes possible the deepest intimacy. As Christ himself said to his apostles at the last supper: "No longer do I call you servants, for the servant does not know what his master is doing; but I have called you friends, for all that I have heard from my Father I have made known to you" (Jn 15:15).

We can thus define a *nuptial spirituality* as that in which I respond to the invitation of Christ to participate in his own subjectivity, and to allow him to totally pervade my own: that we may live in one another in mutual indwelling, sharing a single life of love, communion, and devotion, and together bearing fruit from this union. That sentence is quite rich, and deserves a pause for reflection (and digestion!). Let me try to unfold a bit. A nuptial spirituality is one fueled by *the ardent desire to respond to the thirst of Christ*. As Sister Miriam James Hiedland says concerning the love of Teresa of Calcutta: "It is not a sterile, sanitized version of charity but a fierce, noble pursuit of the divine Lover himself."[10] This is a beautiful definition of the essence of spousal love, at least in the dimension of its driving force. It is that ardent devotion of heart and mind, indeed of one's whole being, that seeks to give all at every moment to and for the Beloved, to be all his and for him, and, in him, to be for all those whom he loves. It is the confluence of *eros* and *agape* in a single passion of love, a single thirst. And this thirst is ever renewed and reborn from a receptive presence, a deep attunement, to the Heart of Jesus as it reveals itself to me.[*]

But in the same way as my nuptial love is present to and devoted to Jesus in this way, he is present to and devoted to me. For the love is *mutual*, the gift is *reciprocal*. So just as I give my life and my being wholly to the One whom I love, so he gives himself totally to me. He shares in all that is my own, even and especially that which is most intimate. Every moment, experience, desire, and fear is important to him, precious and cared-for. And he expends himself at every moment to draw nearer to me, to unite himself to me more intimately, and to seek my authentic good in all circumstances and all things. And as I receive this loving devotion of Christ anew and more deeply every moment, my own loving devotion is awakened and sustained in response.

Yes, *this* is the dance of nuptial love, of spousal mysticism, of conjugal spirituality with Christ. Call it what you will. It is accessible to each one of us, regardless of our vocation. For it *is* our true and deepest vocation. It is at the heart of our call to return into the intimacy of the Trinity: through nuptial union with Jesus Christ, the eternal Son, we are drawn into the full experience of childhood before his Father and ours, and experience the complete permeation of our being and life with the Spirit of their shared Love. Here all our longings for relationship and communion are super-fulfilled. Here our capacities for childhood, siblinghood, spousehood, and parenthood are fulfilled in their very Origin, in our direct and unmediated union with the Trinity himself.

Thus, to be entirely transparent, a *nuptial* spirituality leads into, and gives way to a *Trinitarian* spirituality, a sharing in the very manner of living and loving proper to the Trinity. It opens the way to seeing the entire universe bathed in the light of the relations of the Persons of the Trinity, and called, through redeemed man and woman united to God, to participate in these relations through love: sharing in the reciprocal surrender and

---

[*]There is a beautiful paradox here: both *eros* and *agape* grow side by side, each enhancing, purifying, and deepening the other: longing for intimacy with the Trinity and total devotion to him and to the salvation of others. They fuel, renew, and flow into each other, in a kind of circumincession. And both, always, spring from the primal and abiding experience of being loved. "We love, because he first loved us" (1 Jn 4:19).

mutual indwelling of the Father, Son, and Holy Spirit.*

This nuptial spirituality, in conclusion, is the meeting of two thirsts—our thirst and the thirst of God. These two thirsts are *devoted* to one another, and give drink to one another precisely through love. As Teresa of Calcutta said: "We are here to satiate the thirst of Jesus, to proclaim the love of Christ—the thirst of Jesus—for souls by the holiness of our lives. ... We are here to satiate the thirst of Jesus...that is why we must be holy."[11] It is precisely holiness, as an expression of pure love and total gift, that satiates the thirst of Christ for love and for intimacy with us. Thus this nuptial spirituality is the manifestation of mature thirst, thirst come to full expression. It is not so much like the "romance" of early and immature love, but rather the mature fruit of total commitment, complete reciprocal gift, and abundant fruitfulness.

---

*This insight leads us to something deeply important. Particularly in our fallen world where human love is (at first) more immediately tangible to us than divine love, we are in danger of gauging or measuring God's love against the image of human love. Thus a "nuptial" spirituality could be understood as a projection of human spousal love onto God, or just this kind of love taken to its highest measure. Thus I want to emphasize that this passage from *using the nuptial image to illustrate mystical union with God* and instead to *direct participation in the inner life of the Trinity* is a real maturation, not only of vision but of life. It is a different kind of love altogether, infinitely deeper and superior to spousal love, even while fulfilling all that is good, true, and beautiful in every kind of human love and in all the thoughts, affections, desires, and capacities of the heart. A person who comes to know the depth and beauty of the Trinity, and of participation in his life through intimacy and love, sees very clearly how truly dim and partial a reflection all human loves are. It despises them not, but gauges them all in God and by God, and not vice versa. The burning radiance of the life of Father, Son, and Holy Spirit is the origin and consummation of all, and in its light we can see and relate accordingly to all things, and indeed can do so with lightness, freedom, and joy because we see how very small indeed they are, though precious in the eyes of their Creator, and destined to participate eternally in the unmediated fullness of his life.

DAY 6
A SECOND CONVERSION

From that time Jesus began to preach, saying, "Repent, for the kingdom of heaven is at hand." (Matthew 4:17)

Often, it is the painful circumstances of life, and our own wounds and hurts, growing into bitterness, which keep us from responding wholeheartedly to the invitation of our divine Bridegroom. This is understandable, since with our limited human vision we often cannot see the good that God is always bringing forth out of suffering, even out of evil. To us it appears as a failure, a hindrance, or even as a place from which God has chosen to be absent. But, without neglecting to recognize that evil *is* evil, and that it should never exist and hurts the heart of God deeply, we must affirm even more vigorously that *God has made himself intimately present in the heart of all evil and suffering, in order, through his redeeming presence, to bring about an even greater good.*

This is true of the whole trajectory of world history, which, as members of the single human family, we are parts of, participants in. And it is also true of the most small and seemingly insignificant experiences and circumstances of our daily lives, and in the unfolding of our unique path. God, who is Love and Mercy, makes himself present in all the places of poverty and suffering in our lives and in the world with the outpouring of his goodness. He is attracted to us in our poverty, in our pain; he delights in us in the slightest stirrings of desire or hope, the slightest conformity of our heart to truth and beauty. Indeed, he is drawn to us, reaching out with both longing and delight, even when we are lost in sin or sunk in bitterness, to break the shackles of our suffering from the inside, and to make loving encounter possible anew, and the intimacy born of encounter.

Thus his call to "repent" and "believe" is ever renewed, more frequently than the sun that rises every morning. And, in this call to conversion to him—to laying our vulnerability before his gaze and surrendering ourselves into his hands—he offers us a call to deeper intimacy, to a deeper experience of his love for us and to a more total and radical love for him who is so worthy of our love. I would like to share a very pointed example of God's intimate presence at the heart of human suffering and even the greatest moral evil, to show, to illustrate, how truly God is at work bringing forth good in the midst of evil, light in the midst of darkness. Hopefully in this way we can open ourselves anew, more deeply and totally, to the light of God present in our own life.

Takashi Nagai was born in the Shinto tradition of Japanese religion, and then, through encountering the scientific "enlightenment" that swept through his country in the early 1900's, lost faith in divinity and came to believe, rather, in science as if it were a religion. But grace sought him out and gradually reopened his heart, closed by unbelief and by sins that, in this atmosphere, threatened to swamp the nobility left in his heart. After boarding with a Catholic family in Nagasaki, where he worked as a doctor and soon-to-be radiologist, he gradually embraced the faith in its fullness, receiving baptism and the sacraments. He wed Midori, the daughter of the parents who had taken him in, and began to manifest, in his ministry to the ill—both in the hospital and on the blood-stained battlefields of Japan's imperialistic warfare—the compassion and charity of Christ.

In addition to all that he had received from God, however, and to all the vigor of his response, there was yet another conversion awaiting him. This was not a conversion from unbelief to faith, but, for lack of better words, a conversion from committed faith to radical faith, from integrity to sanctity, from the acceptance of Christ in faith (and the desire to live according to his life) into the total and unconditional surrender of one's self into the orbit of his divine love. This "second conversion," from fidelity to sanctity, came about through the paradoxical gift of poverty and suffering —indeed a suffering and loss that is hard for most of us to even imagine. Working as a radiologist in the hospital in Nagasaki, near the so-called "Catholic sector" where the small population of believers was condensed, he was witness to the tragedy of the atomic bomb dropped by the U.S. at the end of World War II. Being on the far side of the hospital when the bomb was dropped, he survived (but not without a miraculous intervention of Saint Maximilian Kolbe, who instantaneously healed a severed aorta in his temple). However, the loss surrounding him was incredible, over seventy thousand dead, and most in a split-second, incinerated in the destructive and radioactive blast.

Nagai found the remains of his wife, a few bones, ashes, and a mangled rosary, a couple days after the incident. Here was the depth of poverty, a massive wasteland of sheer death where a city used to be; even the abiding beauty of nature was extinguished, and the sky itself painted black like an ominous sign of divine wrath. But this is not how Takashi Nagai saw and experienced this event. No, for grace was at work in his heart, bringing him, precisely through the darkest of nights, to a level of faith and surrender that was unattainable by his own efforts. His first response after finding his wife's remains indicates this transformation: he thanked God that he had granted Midori to die praying, to pass in dialogue with the One whom she would be in dialogue with for all eternity.

Soon Nagai became the locus of what would be a profound rebuilding —not only physical but spiritual—of the shattered city of Nagasaki. Bedridden himself because of leukemia due to the radiation he had absorbed from his work and research, he wrote a bestselling book on the atomic bomb in the light of faith, *The Bells of Nagasaki*, which also became a movie within a year. (And this was all in the non-Christian country of Japan!) He radiated peace, serenity, and charity to the many who came to visit him each day, and continued to write until the end of his life. He stayed close to his mother-in-law and his son and daughter to the end (who had survived the bomb by being taken outside the city), living in his little hut next to their home.

What had been the turning point for him? What had shifted within his heart, his spirit, when he looked out on the wasteland that had once been his home, and found, not despair, not anger, not rebellion, but faith, trust, surrender, and...yes, gratitude? The bishop asked Nagai to speak in the ruins of the cathedral about the attack, only a short period after it occurred, in order to help people process what had happened and to begin the process of rebuilding. In his words then he unveiled the shift that had happened for him, and thus began a shift in the city itself. He said that God had allowed the atomic bomb to be directed to land exactly where it did: over the Catholic sector of Nagasaki, when it had been originally intended for another city, and then, as a second plan, for a different sector of Nagasaki. Why? Because he chose the believers, who clung to him and were ready to offer their lives to him, to be a *hansai*, a "sacrifice," in order, as he said, to atone "for the sins of all the nations during World War II" and "so that many millions of lives might be saved."[12] Reading deeply within the lines of his own personal history and the history of his people, he was able to see the loving hand of divine providence working all for good, to atone for sin, to heal wounded hearts, and to make all knew within the orbit of redeeming grace.

This is what Takashi Nagai's prayer, witness, and words helped to occur within the city of Nagasaki. Through finding new life himself—through accepting the path of the love of Christ in the poverty of total surrender—he was able not only to find abiding peace and joy himself, but also to mediate it to thousands of others. As one of his biographers expresses it:

> When Nagai addressed the A-bomb mourners at the Nagasaki funeral Mass, he used the startling word *hansai*, telling them to offer their dead to God as a whole burnt sacrifice. Many were shocked and even angered by this. Sensitive Nagai examined his conscience about this in a book he wrote not long before he died. He concluded he was right in urging people to accept the deaths as *hansai*. His proof? The peace of heart this acceptance brought. Nagai had become a Word of God man, discerning major matters according to the words of Scripture. He concluded that the *hansai* insight was authentic because it brought him and many others "the fruits of the Holy Spirit." For Nagai, Galatians 5:22 said it all: "The fruit of the Spirit is love, joy, peace, patience, kindness, goodness, faithfulness, gentleness, self-control; against such there is no law." Jeremiah 6:16 says: "Stand by the roads, and look, and ask for the ancient paths, where the good way is; and walk in it, and find rest for your souls." Nagai, standing at the crossroads of death, averred that *hansai* spirituality had brought great peace.
>
> If you speak Japanese and have attended the A-bomb anniversaries in both Hiroshima and Nagasaki, I think you will have observed a great difference. I had noted this over a number of years, and while attending the two ceremonies on the fortieth anniversary in 1985, I heard some regular participants express it this way: "Hiroshima is bitter, noisy, highly political, leftist and anti-American. Its symbol would be a fist clenched in anger. Nagasaki is sad, quiet, reflective, nonpolitical and prayerful. It does not blame the United States but rather laments the sinfulness of war, especially of nuclear war. Its symbol: hands joined in prayer.[13]

I would like to share a quote from Takashi Nagai, so that you may taste something of the joy that he found, born from the darkness of his own and his people's passion, redeemed by the Passion and Resurrection of Christ:

> Sometimes I feel that if I write another page, I'll collapse with exhaustion. But I finish it, and I feel ready for more! Actually, I can write far more swiftly now than years ago when I was writing the thesis for my doctorate. Then I wrote because I had to. I had to keep talking myself into continuing, like the bike team behind a long-distance runner. Now I write, well, like a boy doing what he likes doing. You know, if a boy wakes up and it's a sunny day, he says: 'Wow, a great day for baseball.' If he wakes up and it's raining, he says: 'Wow, a great day for catching eels.' Even though I cannot move a foot away from bed, there's a song deep within, 'Let's go to it', set to the kind of music boys hear in their hearts.
>
> There are some people who write haiku poetry to make a living. You know what I think? We should make our living become haiku poetry. You might toil in a clattering factory or on a tossing fishing boat or be battling to make a living in a dingy shop. There are people who have written inspiring haiku poems in such unpoetic situations. And we, if we really want to, can make any occupation, and twenty-four hours of each day, into a poem. Of course, first we have to create a heart that is both serious and light! We have to gaze below the surface of things, search out the hidden beauty that is everywhere and discover the glorious things all around us. Then each day becomes a haiku poem.
>
> There are some people who do their job because they have to. They get the job done, but they pay a high price in terms of freedom and joy. Children, on the other hand, play all out in their games because they know freedom and joy. And didn't someone tell us we have to become like children?[14]

What, after all of this, can we draw out as the fruit of this reflection? There are obviously many things, Takashi's life is so rich in meaning. Even refraining from speaking of the freedom born of wonder and the spirit of play, which is so central and important in life, indeed which is the very heartbeat of the life of God and of our participation within it, there is much to say. I would like to simply return to the beginning of this reflection and to point out, at the beginning of these weeks of contemplation, the reality of *ever-renewed conversion*. Yes, Takashi had converted to God and his Church years earlier, turning his life over to the love of Christ; and this conversion was authentic. But through renewed circumstances, providentially used by God to bring forth abundant fruit, he was called still deeper into the following of Christ: into the poverty of total surrender and the intimacy possible only in complete sanctity, the utter transformation of the human person achieved through the activity of divine grace. Yes, through all this Takashi received a transformation which surpassed anything that his own efforts at conversion could have accomplished, even though it also elicited his acceptance, his surrender, to the One who approached him. And by responding to this inviting grace, he found a joy and peace deeper than he had known before.

At the heart of our deepest weakness and need, when our own resources run out, when we cannot see a way forward, when we feel "torn open" by circumstances or by desire, grace comes. God comes. He reaches out to touch the veil we keep over the inmost recesses of our heart, inviting us to pull it back, indeed, to let it be torn by his touch and by our consenting surrender. And he does so *from within,* from his habitual abode at the core of our being, where he wants to meet us: in our innermost solitude alone before him. In this sacred solitude, made totally poor and dependent by his grace, we can at last stand before him naked and unveiled, in complete trusting vulnerability. And here before him, bathed in the light of his affirming and cherishing gaze, a gaze that both sees beauty and creates it, and gazing with our interior gaze upon him in response, intimacy is born. This is the truest and deepest meaning of conversion, conversion come to full blossom: the total surrender of myself into the hands of the divine Beloved, and my acceptance of the gift of his very self-communication to me. Here the depths of the poverty of love and the vulnerability of surrender is sealed as the most profound and total intimacy in mutual belonging.

The words of Christ quoted at the beginning of this reflection, "Repent, and believe in the Gospel," therefore, remain true for each one of us every day. They continually resound for us, inviting us to open our hearts to God more deeply, to recommit ourselves to his love, and to set out anew with the dawning of each new day upon the great adventure of discipleship —this great path into nuptial intimacy with Christ, and, in him and through him, participation in the innermost life of the Trinity. Yes, God desires everything, for he has given everything. He seeks nothing less than total belonging and total communion. Thus to turn anew to him is to embrace, as if for the first time, with wonder and gratitude, this beautiful drama of total acceptance and self-giving, and to live it in intimacy with him, until the eternal Day dawns and we find everlasting rest in the home that has been prepared for us, and, indeed, has been present to us, holding us, at each step of the journey.

DAY 7
WALKING INTO THE ARMS OF LOVE

In the last reflection I spoke about the reality of conversion as a daily renewed attitude and action. In what does this consist? The contours, of course, are unique for each one of us, as God leads each of us in an unrepeatable way conformed to his specific plan for us. But it is also true that the nature of relationship, of intimate love, is one, since it springs from the bosom of the undivided Trinity, is manifest in our world and in the lives of all, and seeks to incorporate us into itself. So too, the word of God's self-revelation, and his very gift of self, is one: in Christ and in the Church, through the Spirit. Thus, this word distills into the life of each one of us as a *unique* word, spoken to us like it is spoken to no other, spoken to us as if we were the only one, and yet it is a universal word binding us all together in the single, undivided truth and love.

We can speak of certain traits of this invitation of love from God, this word and gaze of love, and thus also of the disposition of conversion (in Greek *metanioa,* a change-of-mind, or a renewal of spirit). Conversion, in its inner essence, consists in the continual re-opening of my heart and life to God's gaze of redeeming love, which shines into me to bring out into the light all that is hidden in darkness, and to call me forth from sin into love, from solitude into communion, from isolation into relationship, from fear into confident trust, from enclosure in myself into surrender into the embrace of the One who loves me. We can see conversion throughout the Gospels, in the lives of all those who responded positively to the person and the message of Christ, letting their lives be changed by their encounter with him. But one story in particular comes to mind concerning the experience of *continual* conversion, daily conversion, and not only the first moment in which we make an about-face to *begin* living for God in faith. It illustrates, indeed, quite vividly the "school of trust" that is walking with the Lord, the response to which is our conversion and commitment and fidelity to the gaze, the voice, and the call of God. Let us read the passage together now:

> Then he made the disciples get into the boat and go before him to the other side, while he dismissed the crowds. And after he had dismissed the crowds, he went up on the mountain by himself to pray. When evening came, he was there alone, but the boat by this time was many furlongs distant from the land, beaten by the waves; for the wind was against them. And in the fourth watch of the night he came to them, walking on the sea. But when the disciples saw him walking on the sea, they were terrified, saying, "It is a ghost!" And they cried out for fear. But immediately he spoke to them, saying, "Take heart, it is I; have no fear." And Peter answered him, "Lord, if it is you, bid me come to you on the water." He said, "Come." So Peter got out of the boat and walked on the water and came to Jesus; but when he saw the wind, he was afraid, and beginning to sink he cried out, "Lord,

save me." Jesus immediately reached out his hand and caught him, saying to him, "O man of little faith, why did you doubt?" And when they got into the boat, the wind ceased. And those in the boat worshiped him, saying, "Truly you are the Son of God." And when they had crossed over, they came to land at Gennesaret. And when the men of that place recognized him, they sent round to all that region and brought to him all that were sick, and besought him that they might only touch the fringe of his garment; and as many as touched it were made well. (Mt 14:22-36)

Here we see how Peter, who has already chosen to follow Christ, is nonetheless asked to "step out" anew to draw even nearer to the one who loves him. He has until now been seeking security in the boat, to which, as a professional fisherman, he is so accustomed. But now, as it totally fails him, tossing about on the waves to the point of sinking, he looks out and sees Jesus approaching him, walking on the waves as if they are solid ground, secure and safe. In this moment, with his gaze intersecting with the gaze of Love that meets him from Christ, Peter's heart is moved— moved to desire a deeper security, an unchanging security that depends upon nothing but the sustaining love of God incarnate in Christ. Indeed, he desires to cast away all of his fading securities and to stake everything upon the pure love of God, precisely in order to draw closer to this love that has so deeply touched him, forgiven him, and stirred his heart into a life that he didn't even know was possible. And so he himself makes the offer, born not of a legalistic obligation, but precisely from the womb of encounter and relationship: "Lord, if it is you, bid me come to you on the water." In this very offer of Peter, he is in fact responding to the prior offer of Christ, unspoken but true, whose very approach on the water summons Peter forth to meet him.

And the Lord's response is so beautiful: "Come." So short, but full of abundant meaning. "It is I, Peter. I am here...for you. I come to draw closer to you, laying my own Heart vulnerably open for you to receive me, to welcome me. But I desire you also to open yourself vulnerably to me; to stand before me naked and defenseless; to allow me, in turn, to receive you, as I wish to be received by you."

And Peter walks, with his gaze fixed upon Jesus. He is sustained by this mutual gaze: his gaze upon Christ and Christ's gaze upon him. This gaze of love, of mutual beholding in trust and desire and surrender, is the solid ground for his feet, even upon the crashing waves of the greatest storm. But whenever Peter turns his gaze away, he allows himself to become distracted, frightened, and then loses the awareness of Christ's sustaining gaze and his presence. And so he begins to sink. To give in to fear is to cease to walk on water; to be distracted by everything that the human heart cannot control is to begin to cling to fading securities again. But to fix one's eyes on Christ is to look beyond, to look within, and to find the invitation of Love in everything and beyond everything: inviting to deeper love and intimacy with the One who is the Bridegroom of our heart.

This is what is asked of us each day, regardless of what is going on in our life, and indeed, precisely in the midst of it. For all of our circumstances, whatever they may be, are providentially arranged by God for our good and for the good of all—just as the experience on the stormy lake that night was directly arranged by Jesus to summon forth in his apostles deeper faith and surrender, and just as the experience of Takashi Nagai and the people of Nagasaki was cradled in the provident plan of God, working all things for good for his precious children. How in *my* life is God calling me to walk on the water deeper into intimacy with him? How is he asking me to open my vulnerability, to surrender it, to be received by him? How, in turn, is he asking me to welcome his own Heart, laid open before me as a gift? This act of trust, of surrender—this step into the poverty of vulnerability that finds no security but in the love of God, and no fulfillment except in intimacy with him—leads to such tremendous miracles of grace!

And we thirst for precisely this...for precisely the depth of love that God desires to pour into us. So let us not be afraid to walk out to him, our gaze fixed on him and his gaze fixed on us, and to fall into his welcoming arms, received by him in our vulnerability so tenderly and so lovingly. And in being received by him in this way, we will be opened to receive him anew, too, in the ineffable grandeur of his beauty and goodness. We will receive him anew into the boat of our lives, into the boat of the Church herself which he desires to visit ever anew, and which he will support, renew, and guide with his presence. Yes, he will "get into the boat" with us, calming the waves and bringing peace and security, and indeed leading the boat securely to its destination...home to the Father.

WEEK II

TRANSFIGURING LOVE

DAY 8
LIBERATED BY BEAUTY, GOODNESS, AND TRUTH

The law of the LORD is perfect, reviving the soul;
the testimony of the LORD is sure, making wise the simple;
the precepts of the LORD are right, rejoicing the heart;
the commandment of the LORD is pure, enlightening the eyes;
the fear of the LORD is clean, enduring for ever;
the ordinances of the LORD are true, and righteous altogether.
More to be desired are they than gold, even much fine gold;
sweeter also than honey and drippings of the honeycomb.
Moreover by them is thy servant warned;
in keeping them there is great reward. (Psalm 19:7-11)

I spoke earlier about the *primacy of receptivity,* of the priority of God's gratuitous gift, which stands at the origin of human activity and impels it forward to its authentic end. Joseph Ratzinger (Benedict XVI) has some beautiful words on this. In his book, *Introduction to Christianity*, he writes:

From the point of view of the Christian faith, man comes in the most profound sense to himself, not through what he does, but through what he accepts. He must wait for the gift of love, and love can only be received as a gift. It cannot be "made" on one's own, without anyone else; one must wait for it, let it be given to one. And one cannot become wholly man in any other way than by being loved, by letting oneself be loved. That love represents simultaneously both man's highest possibility and his deepest need and that this most necessary thing is at the same time the freest and the most unenforceable means precisely that for his "salvation" man is meant to rely on receiving. If he declines to let himself be presented with the gift, then he destroys himself. Activity that makes itself into an absolute, that aims at achieving humanity by its own efforts alone, is in contradiction with man's being. Louis Evely has expressed this perception splendidly:

The whole history of mankind was led astray, suffered a break, because of Adam's false idea of God. He wanted to be like God. I hope that you never thought that Adam's sin lay in this ... Had God not invited him to nourish this desire? Adam only deluded himself about the model. He thought God was an independent autonomous being sufficient to himself; and in order to become like him he rebelled and showed disobedience.

But when God revealed himself, when God wished to show who he was, he appeared as love, tenderness, as outpouring of himself, infinite pleasure in another. Inclination, dependence. God showed himself obedient, obedient unto death.

In the belief that he was becoming like God, Adam turned right away from him. He withdrew into loneliness, and God was fellowship.

This whole thing indubitably signifies a relativization of works, of doing; St Paul's struggle against "justification by works" is to be understood from this angle. But one must add that this classification of human activity as only of penultimate importance gives it at the same time an inner liberation: man's activity can now be carried on in the tranquility, detachment and freedom appropriate to the penultimate. The primacy of acceptance is not intended to condemn man to passivity... On the contrary, it alone makes it possible to do the things of this world in a spirit of responsibility, yet at the same time in an uncramped, cheerful, free way, and to put them at the service of redemptive love.[15]

To speak of the primacy of God's grace is in no way to condemn the human heart to passivity, nor to diminish the importance and capacity of our will, our choice, in directing our lives according to truth. As the book of Sirach says, "It was he who created man in the beginning, and he left him in the power of his own inclination" (15:14). Thus, as Saint Augustine explained, "God who created you without you, will not save you without you" (*Sermo* 169, 13). Rather, as Ratzinger emphasized, human activity—knowing that it is infinitely indebted to the undeserved and ever-present gift of God—can spring forth with greater freedom, confidence, and joy than if it was born of a fearful and burdensome sense of responsibility before a difficult task to be borne alone. Nothing, and I mean *nothing*, is ever borne alone. For God is with us, and has given us everything, even to the point of giving his very self. He is more interior to us than we are to ourselves, and more intimately upholds us, cares for us, and elicits our freedom than we can possibly imagine.

And thus, in responding to God's gift and call, both in the external manifestations of his revelation in the law, the prophets, and the Gospel (condensed in the teaching and life of the Church), as well as in the interior workings of his grace in our heart, stirring up our conscience to recognize and accept the truth and the good, we find the path to authentic *freedom*. Despite what our contemporary world would have us believe, human freedom is not arbitrary; it is not a simple capacity to choose without any external forces to hinder us from exercising our own freedom and self-determination. Rather, human freedom has been given by God from the very beginning as a capacity for truth and goodness, for beauty and love. Indeed, freedom has an interior correspondence with truth, like the point of a compass always searching for true north, which will grow ever clearer and more discerning to the degree that we listen to it and obey it (and thus obey God who speaks to us in the inner sanctuary of our conscience, in the sacred space of our intellect, will, and spiritual affectivity).

But what do I mean, specifically, by the "good," and by "truth"? In our relativistic world, wounded by materialistic secularism and atheistic humanism (how many -isms!), we can be swayed, even unconsciously, by false conceptions of the good and the true. The narrowness of our secular society, indeed, can be traced back precisely to the rupture from an authentic understanding of truth and goodness (and ultimately from the God who is the source of truth and goodness). These have become, for our society, relative categories, depending upon the wishes and the will of each individual person, and thus not shared between people and between nations. The result of this, however, is chaos, unhappiness, and division, not unity in harmony and love. For there can be no common good built on mere "tolerance," but only on the shared pursuit of objective values, of universal goodness and truth. And the beautiful fact of reality, assured to us by God and his Church, is that truth is indeed eternally valid, everlastingly objective, since it is simply the very *order of things* as fashioned by the creative hands of a loving God, as a manifestation of the innate truth of his own eternal life as Father, Son, and Holy Spirit.

And thus goodness, too, is wholly objective, being the *end* to which God has ordained us, as he has each creature, to its authentic fulfillment in accordance with the truth of reality. Even natural goods that seem wholly irrelevant to morality are in fact not—in other words, goods that don't directly call for a strong ethical response such as pleasant or utilitarian goods, for example food and drink or working for a wage, since they summon forth a response born of virtue, born of prudence, justice, temperance, and fortitude. Nonetheless, there are certain goods that bear a specifically "weighty" ethical value, thus calling for a response of particularly transcendent obedience and respect, of care and affirmation (such as the conjugal act, or the dignity of human life, or the right of each person to the free exercise of religious belief and personal determination). In both values, or rather, in all values, with all of their particular nuances and their unique "word" within the creative plan of God, human freedom is invited to a response of love and affirmation that reflects and participates in the love of God himself, which is precisely a delight before and an upholding of what is good.

I have spoken of goodness and of truth; but this little analysis would not be complete without mentioning *beauty*. In fact, these three so-called "transcendental properties of being," truth, goodness, and beauty, are inseparable from one another. *Truth*, being the foundational "what-ness" of reality, its unchanging essence, summons forth our responsiveness under the guise of the *good*, both the appealing good and the ethical good;* but all

---

*There are three kinds of "goods," or dispositions towards seeking a good, all legitimate in their place, though also calling for an "order," an integrity in lived expression. There is the just good (*bonum honestum*), the useful good (*bonum utile*), and the pleasurable good (*bonum delectabile*). The latter two are directed towards, and seek to remain always within, the primacy and directedness of the *bonum honestum*, so that all of our desires and actions are just, and ordered towards justice: right relationship with God, with others, and with the whole of creation, in a disposition of ethical responsiveness, of affirming tenderness, of love. (See John Paul II, *Memory and Identity,* 34-36.) In our contemporary society, one of the profound wounds that makes true ethics so unintelligible to many is the blindness of *pragmatism,* which cannot conceive of the "disinterested" nature of much human action as a gratuitous response to the obligatory word of objective reality, born of givenness, of God's creative Love. If all my acts are "in order that" I may receive some benefit from them, then I gauge morality on a scale of possible benefits rather than on the basis of the innate intelligibility of reality as fashioned by God. In fact, in order to answer all of the profound moral disorders of our age —from abortion, to same-sex approval and practice, to contraception, to euthanasia, to rebellion against the authority of God and the Church, etc.—the most important thing is precisely a rediscovery of *wonder* before reality as God's sacred gift. This wonder awakens the desire to conform to this reality, to cherish it, to care for it, and to let it be what, according to his loving designs, it has always been meant to be.

true goodness, all good truth, radiates forth to strike our hearts, and to move them in response, as *beauty*. To understand and reverence one of the three calls forth a response also to the other two, and vice versa. And this is not all, but all three are but manifestations, under a different aspect, of the single and indivisible reality of Love: of the Trinity's eternal Love lying beyond all creation and yet also as the creative origin and foundation of the whole created order and of our own existence within the world.

DAY 9
APPROPRIATING THE GIFT OF REDEMPTION

And behold, one came up to him, saying, "Teacher, what good deed must I do, to have eternal life?" And he said to him, "Why do you ask me about what is good? One there is who is good. If you would enter life, keep the commandments." He said to him, "Which?" And Jesus said, "You shall not kill, You shall not commit adultery, You shall not steal, You shall not bear false witness, Honor your father and mother, and, You shall love your neighbor as yourself." The young man said to him, "All these I have observed; what do I still lack?" Jesus said to him, "If you would be perfect, go, sell what you possess and give to the poor, and you will have treasure in heaven; and come, follow me." When the young man heard this he went away sorrowful; for he had great possessions. And Jesus said to his disciples, "Truly, I say to you, it will be hard for a rich man to enter the kingdom of heaven. Again I tell you, it is easier for a camel to go through the eye of a needle than for a rich man to enter the kingdom of God." When the disciples heard this they were greatly astonished, saying, "Who then can be saved?" But Jesus looked at them and said to them, "With men this is impossible, but with God all things are possible." Then Peter said in reply, "Behold, we have left everything and followed you. What then shall we have?" Jesus said to them, "Truly, I say to you, in the new world, when the Son of man shall sit on his glorious throne, you who have followed me will also sit on twelve thrones, judging the twelve tribes of Israel. And every one who has left houses or brothers or sisters or father or mother or children or lands, for my name's sake, will receive a hundredfold, and inherit eternal life. But many that are first will be last, and the last first." (Mt 19:16-30)

Man cannot live without love. He remains a being that is incomprehensible for himself, his life is senseless, if love is not revealed to him, if he does not encounter love, if he does not experience it and make it his own, if he does not participate intimately in it. ... The man who wishes to understand himself thoroughly—and not just in accordance with immediate, partial, often superficial, and even illusory standards and measures of his being—he must with his unrest, uncertainty and even his weakness and sinfulness, with his life and death, draw near to Christ. He must, so to speak, enter into him with all his own self, he must "appropriate" and assimilate the whole of the reality of the Incarnation and Redemption in order to find himself. If this profound process takes place within him, he then bears fruit not only of adoration of God but also of deep wonder at himself. How precious must man be in the eyes of the Creator, if he "gained so great a Redeemer," and if God "gave his only Son" in order that man "should not perish but have eternal life." (*Redemptor Hominis*, 11)

The gift of redemption flowing from the Paschal Mystery of Christ, as I said, comes to the human person as both a *gift* and a *task* which elicits human freedom. It comes first of all as a gift, as a gratuitous outpouring of healing love on behalf of God's own generosity. We see this in the precious words in the quote above. Christ's call to the young man is not merely a task, an obligation, but both a *gift* and a *promise*. It is a gift of love and election: Looking upon you, I love you, and, loving you, I choose you for myself, beloved. And it is a gift of promise: If you would be perfect, if you wish for fulfillment and happiness, only surrender all things and follow after me; I will care for you and lead you unto the end.

And precisely as a gift, Christ's love and call also stirs man and woman into action, into a vibrant and heartfelt responsiveness to the gift of grace, to God's own activity which precedes, enfolds, accompanies, and brings to fulfillment. How sad, indeed, it is to turn away from this prevenient gift! How sad to look into Christ's loving gaze, cherishing and beckoning, and then to turn away, refusing the invitation! But to respond...how beautiful this is. How beautiful to receive that gaze of love, that gaze that pierces to the depths of the heart, to the core of our being, and, in piercing, stirs awake what sin has put to sleep, bestowing light and courage and desire. This gift given through the gaze and the word of Christ is for each one of us. He meets us in different ways on the paths of life; but he meets us nonetheless. And he wants to meet us ever anew and ever more deeply, until we are totally transformed in him. This ever-renewed gaze and call unfolds throughout time in a deepening relationship which is both maturing prayer and maturing fidelity, until the bond between Christ and the one he has chosen is so deep and pure that nothing can tear it asunder.

Gaze and call. Gift and task. In authentic Catholic theology and life, the gift of redemption is not something "once-and-done," but rather a gradual process of transfiguration of human heart and life. Or more accurately, redemption has been fully accomplished in Christ on behalf of all humanity, who has already risen from the dead and sits at the right hand of the Father; but it is still working itself out in each one of us, seeking to incorporate us into Christ in such a way that we find new life in him, the eternal life which he gained for us.

The path of fidelity to God's saving grace, therefore, leads from the first gift of *justification*—the gratuitous forgiveness of sins and adoption into the life of the Trinity—to the gradual unfolding of this life in the gift of *sanctification,* which culminates in the definitive state of *salvation.* The first comes from without and requires only our assent of faith, our "yes," which consents also to the sacramental regeneration given in Baptism which mediates this newness of life to us through water and the Spirit. But this "yes," then, in fidelity to the seed of divine life received, cooperates with its interior dynamic in order to "cast off the new man" and to "put on the Lord Jesus Christ" (Eph 4:22; Rom 13:14), to be inwardly transformed by God's activity and by the human cooperation elicited by it.

In this way, the inmost wellsprings of the heart's thought, feeling, and choice can be so purified, and so united to God, that from their very first movements these spontaneously and habitually conform with the nature of God's own life and purity (without thereby ridding us of creaturely limitation and the obvious capacity for misjudgments and mistakes). And through the wellsprings of the inner heart, of the "inner person," action too, in all the details of life, is renewed; while, on the other hand, the inner person cannot be renewed except that external action and life conforms to the law of God and his guiding will for his children.

Thus we see the path marked out for us, which John Paul summarizes in this way:

> The call "Follow me!" is an invitation to set out along the path to which the inner dynamic of the mystery of Redemption leads us. This is the path indicated by the teaching, so often found in writings on the interior life and on mystical experience, about the three stages involved in "following Christ." These three stages are sometimes called "ways." We speak of the purgative way, the illuminative way, and the unitive way. In reality, these are not three distinct ways, but three aspects of the same way, along which Christ calls everyone, as he once called the young man in the Gospel.

The first of these ways, or dimensions of our transformation by grace, is the *purgative*, which consists in turning away from sin and clinging in fidelity to God's commandments and to his will. "Observance of the commandments, properly understood," as John Paul said, "is synonymous with the purgative way: it means conquering sin, moral evil in its various guises. And this leads to a gradual inner purification. It also enables us to discover values." Purgation, in the literal sense, refers to fire purifying, burning away impurities and disorders in human life and conduct, and in the hidden spaces of the heart. This is brought about both by human obedience to God's self-revelation and to the light of conscience which speaks of him, and, even more fundamentally, by the interior activity of God through grace, in prayer and the sacraments and the circumstances of life by which he purifies us and prepares us to be pure as he is pure, to be united to him in the transparency of love. But we are getting ahead of ourselves.

John Paul said that this gradual purification paves the way for the discovery of "values." This means that an obedience to the light of God's law, which may at first feel burdensome, since we do not yet *see* the interior intelligibility and radiant beauty of the law—namely the values that the law protects and to which it points—will gradually give way to a more direct responsiveness to such values. This responsiveness does not dismiss the law or reject it (why would it?); rather, it fulfills the law even more deeply and thoroughly, by a deep attunement to those values expressed in the law, as well as those which surpass the regulation of the law itself but stand on the furthest end of the righteousness to which the logic of the law awakens the longing of the human heart.

The ability to correspond with such values cannot come through mere human activity alone, but through God's grace making human fidelity—indeed interior newness of heart—possible. Thus in place of sinful vice, the disordered inclination to what is evil, virtue grows up and flourishes. As the pope says, concerning the growth of the *illuminative* way: "Values are lights which illumine existence and, as we work on our lives, they shine ever more brightly on the horizon. So side by side with observance of the commandments—which has an essentially purgative meaning—we develop virtues." Virtues are a spontaneous facility and constancy in recognizing and doing good. They are a habitual capacity of the human person, in all of his faculties of mind, will, and affectivity, for responding to what is beautiful, good, and true in reality, as it presents itself in the multifarious circumstances of life.

In other words, virtue consists in the disposition, abiding and spontaneous, free and joyful, to encounter, to be moved by, and to respond to the values inherent in reality, particularly those values bearing a specifically ethical character. Through virtue we come to live in a habitual "contact" with the world as God has created it, and with God himself as the Author of reality. And this effects a liberating change in our own interior disposition, such that we become conformed to reality, conformed to God in a kind of connaturality, a oneness that makes us more and more like him. This is the purity of heart that allows us to see God, just as the seeing of God makes us pure of heart.

John Paul continues:

> With the passage of time, if we persevere in following Christ our Teacher, we feel less and less burdened by the struggle against sin, and we enjoy more and more the divine light which pervades all creation. This is most important, because it allows us to escape from a situation of constant exposure to the risk of sin...so as to move with ever greater freedom within the whole of the created world. This same freedom and simplicity characterizes our relations with other human beings, including those of the opposite sex. Interior light illumines our actions and shows us all the good in the created world as coming from the hand of God.

This is the freedom and simplicity by which I allow my heart to be moved in beauty, goodness, and truth by the light of God that is present within the whole creation and in each one of my brothers and sisters. And as my heart is harnessed more and more by the sweet attraction of this light —both in creation and in unmediated contact with God himself—I enter more and more into the experience of the *unitive* way. "This is the final stage of the interior journey, when the soul experiences a special union with God. This union is realized in contemplation of the divine Being" and of the mystery of the Trinity, "and in the experience of love which flows from it with growing intensity. In this way we somehow anticipate what is destined to be ours in eternity."

And in this blessed state, we "can find God in everything, we can commune with him in and through all things. Created things cease to be a danger for us as once they were... Creation, and other people in particular, not only regain their true light, given to them by God the Creator, but, so to speak, they lead us to God himself, in the way that he willed to reveal himself to us: as Father, Redeemer, and Spouse."[16]

DAY 10
MYSTICAL LOVE AT THE HEART OF ALL LIFE

He who has the bride is the bridegroom; the friend of the bridegroom, who stands and hears him, rejoices greatly at the bridegroom's voice; therefore this joy of mine is now full. (John 3:19)

In the previous reflections, I have tried to provide a basic groundwork for our understanding and responding to the great gift of the Gospel, of the call of Christ issued to each of us in the uniqueness and concreteness of our life. The most important thing in all that I have said, however, is that God's gift is *light*, that it is oriented, from the beginning to the end and in every moment, to granting us a participation in his own eternal life as Father, Son, and Holy Spirit, a life of love and intimacy in everlasting joy. Thus all of the ethical life, all of the pursuit of goodness, beauty, and truth, even all the most simple and subtle questions of the education of conscience, of the discerning choice of goods, of the sensitization of the heart to beauty—all of this finds its meaning, not merely as some ascetical program of growth in healthy humanity, but *as a response to the loving call of God in Jesus Christ*.

Indeed, in the "three ways" that I spoke of previously, there is also a traditional distinction made between the *ascetical* life and the *mystical* life (the transition of which would occur primarily during the end of the purgative and during illuminative stage). The *ascetical* life refers to that period of growth in which human activity is experienced as primary, in which our own efforts at repentance, fidelity, prayer, and maturation in virtue take the foreground, and God's activity seems more hidden, more intangible, subtly eliciting, guiding, and upholding. The *mystical* life refers to the period in which, as the heart matures, God's direct activity becomes more evident, more tangibly taking the lead and effecting what human effort alone cannot achieve. Gradually, grace grows in its effects within us, and the divine presence comes to enfold our consciousness and to manifest itself within our existence.

Faith, hope, and love come to irradiate even the natural operation of our faculties such that these faculties function primarily on the basis of God's presence within them—on the basis of the abiding disposition of trust, desire, and surrender as a living participation in the life of the Trinity —than merely on their own natural operation. This degree of personal transformation indeed grants a taste, however imperfect, of the destiny that awaits us in eternity, when our freedom shall be fully liberated through everlasting nuptial union with God, face-to-face and in unmediated embrace.

This distinction between the ascetical life and the mystical life, however, can obviously be taken too far, for God is present and active as the primary force of the spiritual life from the very beginning, and human activity is still present even in the highest experiences of the life of holiness and mysticism. It would perhaps be more accurate to say that, as the life of holiness matures, human activity and freedom are taken up ever more deeply into the activity of God, such that they become more simple, more spontaneous, and more unified. Rather than being moved so much by rational discernment or consideration, our choices and acts are stirred into being by God himself who has so deeply grafted our own faculties to his that he is able to live and act within us, and us in him. I will speak much more of this later, as we are getting way ahead of ourselves. The basic point here, which we will see played out in a number of different areas, is the gradual unification of the human person with God, in which the human spiritual faculties of intellect, will, and affectivity (as well as the lower faculties of emotion, bodily feeling, etc., in a different way) are irradiated by the light of the theological virtues of faith, hope, and love.

Understood as God's own manner of living and loving, these virtues are not proper to our natural humanity (unlike the cardinal virtues of prudence, justice, temperance, and fortitude), even though we have the God-given capacity and openness to receive them, but they are rather granted to us by the direct gift of God in grace and baptism. They are bestowed upon us by God in the gift of redeeming grace, by which he adopts us into his own life as Trinity, and grants us to begin to share in the mystical nature of his own eternal Being.

Thus faith is not merely a human act of trust, a human assent to the trustworthiness of God who reveals himself (though it is certainly this); it is, further, a *living contact* with the very One who reveals himself, in which the mind is placed in a mystical, intuitive, non-conceptual contact with the very uncreated Mystery of God, and with the substance of the truths of faith taught by the Gospel and the Church. This substantial contact with reality through faith is so true, so real, that it grants a true *knowledge*, a true living contact, with the Beloved of our heart and with his work in the world, even beyond what can be expressed in concepts or grasped by mind or feeling.

Thus hope is not merely desire for the things promised to us by God, and an abiding constancy in holding firm to him in the midst of all that would beset and distract us on the way; it is, further, a contact, a possession, of the very realities for which we hope, already present to us in fullness, even if behind the veil of mortality and temporality. As the Letter to the Hebrews says: "Faith is the substance of things hoped for and the possession of things not seen" (11:1, *alt. trans.*). Hope is already full possession of the reality for which we long, even if it is hidden by the veil of mortality and awaiting the security of definitive consummation when the shadows of this life pass.

Finally, love is not merely a choice of the human will to give oneself to God, to surrender to his invitation and to follow him in fidelity, to serve him and one's neighbor; it is also a living participation in the very substantial love of God, it is his own manner of loving present and active within us and eliciting our own love in his likeness. As Jesus himself says in the Gospel of John: "With the very love with which the Father has loved me, I have loved you; abide in my love... Love one another with the very love with which I have loved you" (Jn 15:9, 12). As Saint Hilary says concerning the gift of the Spirit manifest in faith, hope, and love:

> We receive the Spirit of truth so that we can know the things of God. In order to grasp this, consider how useless the faculties

of the human body would become if they were denied their exercise. Our eyes cannot fulfill their task without light, either natural or artificial; our ears cannot react without sound vibrations, and in the absence of any odor our nostrils are ignorant of their function. Not that these senses would lose their own nature if they were not used; rather, they demand objects of experience in order to function. It is the same with the human soul. Unless it absorbs the gift of the Spirit through faith, the mind has the ability to know God but lacks the light necessary for that knowledge.

The unique gift which is in Christ is offered in its fullness to everyone. It is everywhere available, but it is given to each man in proportion to his readiness to receive it. Its presence is the fuller, the greater a man's desire to be worthy of it. This gift will remain with us until the end of the world, and will be our comfort in the time of waiting. By the favors it bestows, it is the pledge of our hope for the future, the light of our mind, and the splendor that irradiates our understanding. (*Treatise on the Trinity*, 2.1.33)[17]

We will come back to this, as the three theological virtues are the basis of the mystical life, and the growth of mystical prayer and experience is wholly dependent upon the growth of these three virtues (as well as, in a secondary way, upon the growth of the gifts and fruits of the Spirit that incarnate and express the activity of these virtues—i.e. of God himself—in our concrete humanity).[*] But the essential point that I want to bring to the fore here, at this point in our reflections, is precisely *the transition from living fundamentally on the basis of my own human discretion to living on the basis of the guidance of God*. This is an essential dimension of faith. Indeed, perhaps it is *the* most central result of the choice to follow in the footsteps of Christ. It is the holy de-centering from self to the Beloved. It is the sacred poverty of letting-go, in which open hands and open heart are the only adequate gift offered to the God of Love, who, precisely in this poverty, finds the freedom to act within human heart and life.

We see this vividly in the accounts of all those who "left everything and followed" Christ in the Gospels, as well as in the lives of the saints and disciples of Jesus throughout history. Even if they were led to God and to Christ through rational thought, through study leading to intellectual conviction (for the Gospel, particularly in its Catholic fullness, is profoundly rational and convincing even on a human level), the step from intellectual conviction to faith is a large one. For faith is a *letting go of control of my life into the hands of the One who approaches me and invites me*. Thus my mind lets go of its autonomy in judging, and submits itself to the greater wisdom. My heart lets go of any hope for "expertise" in the realm of prayer, holiness, or communion with God, and instead consents to dependent

---

[*] "The moral life of Christians is sustained by the gifts of the Holy Spirit. These are permanent dispositions which make man docile in following the promptings of the Holy Spirit. The seven gifts of the Holy Spirit are wisdom, understanding, counsel, fortitude, knowledge, piety, and fear of the Lord. The fruits of the Spirit are perfections that the Holy Spirit forms in us as the first fruits of eternal glory. The tradition of the Church lists twelve of them: 'charity, joy, peace, patience, kindness, goodness, generosity, gentleness, faithfulness, modesty, self-control, chastity' (Gal 5:22-23)." (*Catechism of the Catholic Church*, 1830-1832)

poverty in total reliance on the Love that, precisely as Love, is enough. And this is a beautiful transition, a radiant and fruitful surrender, for through it my mind is now harnessed in service of a greater mystery, which it can never exhaust but only reverence, adore, and honor. Thus my affectivity, too, is bowed before the ineffable mystery that approaches me and unveils itself before me, such that it lets go of all clinging and possession, in order to be moved and led in the purity and intensity that are proper to God's beauty and his love. Even my will is surrendered, letting go of its own foresight and control and guidance, not thereby to become passive, but to be elicited in total commitment to and subjection to the guiding will of God manifest in Christ and communicated through his Church.

And this total surrender of faith—which carries in itself hope and love, as these three virtues are inseparable, and in fact one, different aspects of a single mystery and life—this total surrender of faith does not rob the human person of their desire for freedom and happiness, but rather opens up precisely the only path to its deepest and most authentic fulfillment.*[18] This is because, from the beginning of history, man and woman were created in openness to the gift of grace and communion with God: fashioned for everlasting intimacy with the Trinity. Our very nature in all its givenness, even its apparent autonomy, is in fact crying out for the affirming, redeeming, and transfiguring gift of grace, of participation in God's own inner life!

This is how the human person can only fully find himself through the "sincere gift of himself," as Vatican II said (*Gaudium et Spes,* 24). This is how the service of Christ is true liberation; this is how incorporation into the Church as God's family, and into the very family of the Trinity that is the essence and foundation of her life, is the only ultimate path to fulfillment of our nature and our humanity. Here our capacity for knowing is unsealed; here our ability to feel and be moved; here our orientation to love and to communion through self-giving.

For here our desire and capacity for relationship—for friendship, for childhood, for spousehood, for parenthood—is taken up, healed, and transformed to find a fulfillment that is not possible on the basis of nature alone, even as by grace nature itself is healed and made new. For here we find this capacity for communion fulfilled in relationship with God himself: as a child of the eternal Father, who looks upon us with such tender love; as a spouse of the Son incarnate, Jesus Christ, who is our true and eternal Bridegroom; and in transparency to the fruitfulness brought by the Spirit of Love, who renders our whole being transparent to the redeeming

---

*These three virtues explicitly lie at the heart of Mother Teresa's spirituality, in her repeated insistence on relating to God with 1) loving trust, 2) total surrender, and 3) joy. Loving trust is faith illumined by love; total surrender is love born of faith; joy or cheerfulness is the fruit of mature hope, and indeed the splendor of all three virtues together. And this disposition, totally Marian, totally Christic, is one of complete freedom and childlike boldness, the "little way" available for all, born of radical, uncompromising, unhesitating confidence in the goodness and love of our Father and our Bridegroom. It gives birth to profound union with God, and co-action with him at every moment: "Today I will do whatever Jesus wants. And you will see that oneness. That surrender to God, to use you without consulting you [i.e. totally freely]. That accepting is a great sign of union with God. Holiness is that total surrender to God. *Totus tuus.* Completely yours. *Totus tuus.* Completely surrendered. That accepting whatever He gives. That giving whatever He takes. You need much love to be able to see the hand of God."

light of God pouring out through us into the world and into the hearts of our brothers and sisters. And on the basis of this mystical intimacy with the Persons of the Trinity, a whole new depth of human communion is also made possible, a new purity of love and closeness of togetherness, born of a new order of communion between person and person in the likeness of the very Persons of Father, Son, and Holy Spirit.

Indeed, the Lord Jesus, when He prayed to the Father, "that all may be one. . . as we are one" (John 17:21-22) opened up vistas closed to human reason, for He implied a certain likeness between the union of the divine Persons, and the unity of God's sons in truth and charity. This likeness reveals that man, who is the only creature on earth which God willed for itself, cannot fully find himself except through a sincere gift of himself. (*Gaudium et Spes*, 24)

DAY 11
THE HEART OF VIRTUE

The virtues, capacities of our humanity fostered by grace and human cooperation, are best understood not as self-enclosed dispositions existing in isolation, but rather as an abiding state of vulnerable relationship ever-renewed in love. This does not mean that they are not *mine*, truly belonging to me in my unique personhood and my incarnate nature; for they certainly do. They are a transformation of the person who I am, to be more deeply conformed to reality, and, above all, to Christ himself. But virtues are not *mine* in the sense of being a *possession*; I do not *have* them. Rather, they are a part of me, an expression of my being as it lives in relationship with the world of objective values, with God, with self, and with others. And thus the virtues grow most deeply, most richly, not by my focusing on them and seeking to make them grow, but by my disinterestedly responding to the call of love in each moment and circumstance, with my eyes directed outside of myself.

This does not mean, of course, that it is wrong or unhealthy to "cultivate" the virtues; this is a perennial theme throughout the life of the Church and of humanity itself. Whenever I become aware of a vice within me, and I desire the good, then I wish to fight against this vice and to grow in the corresponding virtue. All of this is good. This is, indeed, the authentic meaning of *asceticism*, as the training of my nature to correspond more wholeheartedly—more joyfully, freely, and spontaneously—with the call of reality, and above all with the call of God. But it would be wrong to fail to recognize that there is also a danger here. For in the very effort to grow in the virtues, I may incline away from the childlike dependence on God that is the heart of all virtue. I may indeed end up complicating my interior life with a lot of self-watching, self-criticism, self-praise, and self-combat, rather than living what is of *true* importance: fleeing into the merciful arms of Jesus with all that I am, and giving everything to him without reserve.

This is another of the many reasons why *prayer* is of primary importance in the life of faith, even more so than action. My actions each day are meant to be enfolded within, and to spring forth from, an abiding dialogue of filial love with my heavenly Father, and from the disposition of vulnerable openness before him. In this vulnerable openness, I allow him to look upon me in all that makes up my heart, my experience, and my life in this world. And I welcome this gaze, knowing that it is one of love, even as it pierces "to the division of soul and spirit, of joints and marrow, and" discerns "the thoughts and intentions of the heart" (Heb 4:12). It is a gaze of love because it does not criticize or condemn, but rather shines light on what is wrong and evil to purify it, and affirms what is good to foster, strengthen, and mature it.

And above all, this gaze looks to delight, to rejoice in who I am in my inmost being, pure and gratuitous in the radiance of the divine creativity; only from this primal gaze of gratuitous love, and quite spontaneously from it, does God also seek to elevate and transform me so that my whole being, my very existence, may conform to what he sees in me and what he has destined me, eternally, to be. Indeed, for God to look is for him to love; and he is able to do this because, for him, what he sees is always eternally valid. He sees all of my past, present, and future laid out before him as if a single moment, and yet he sees each single moment in its unique fullness. He sees all in the light of my eternal destiny, where I shall stand before him, purified, healed, and transfigured, irradiated wholly with his light and sharing freely in his life.

To surrender myself, in all my misery, sin, and suffering, in all my longing, hope, and desire, to this gaze of God, therefore, is to enter into a gaze that is simultaneously affirmative and transformative, that bridges over the gap between who I am and who I shall be. For God, through the power of redemption, they are already one. And as I enter into this gaze and live in its light, by the path that it marks out for me, the gap begins to close in my concrete life as well.

And through this prayer, this living in the light of prayer, I am freed of the temptation to focus more on my own efforts than on the grace of God. And yet this does not mean passivity, laziness, or refusing to offer the vigorous and wholehearted cooperation that God desires. No, prayer and activity are not opposed to one another, except with a superficial glance. For it is precisely prayer that teaches me to engage in the right way in the struggle for virtue, for holiness, for radical belonging to God and total love for others. Because it teaches me to see everything in the light of God's ever-present and already-victorious love, it enables me to live and love, not as a burdensome task borne alone, but in the wonder-filled playfulness of a child who knows that he is seen, loved, and cared for. I can embrace my life as a great adventure, a beautiful story being written by God, in which I am asked to participate, with my hand cradled within his own.

+ + +

After this important clarification about the playful attitude with which God desires us to embrace the life of faith, prayer, and growth in virtue, we can begin to look, briefly, at the nature of the central virtues. It is important to emphasize, before we begin, that the playfulness of spirit that faith begets seeks to be expressed, not only in certain moments of leisure or reprieve, but at the very heart of our daily responsiveness to values, and in our efforts to pray and grow in virtue. Play is not a "break" from the more serious things in life, but rather like the atmosphere in which all unfolds: the atmosphere of faith.

It is but the expression of trust in God and in his ever-present love, in his provident hand that "works all things for good for those who love him" (Rom 8:28). And it is born from a deep contemplative gaze that sees and embraces even the responsibilities of life—indeed particularly the responsibilities—lightly and with a disposition of surrender to God, but also recognizes that, before all and above all, we were created for gratuitous play and wonder-filled intimacy for its own sake. Here we see again what Takashi Nagai said about having a disposition that is "both serious and light." The gift of faith opens new horizons, a new way of living the gift of existence and the responsibility to exercise freedom in obedience to truth and for the sake of love, which is central to the dignity of the human person.

It is understood and felt as a great "drama," like a classical novel, which is appreciated in all of its details, in all of the effort and sacrifice and ever-renewed fidelity that the protagonist is called upon to exhibit, precisely because—in the eyes of its Author—it is a beautiful piece of art. The same spirit of play that springs up in reading a good story (and even deeper) should spring up in our living of our own lives in the sight of God. But this is only possible when we *truly* live in the sight of God, in prayer continuously exposing ourselves to his gaze and letting it show us the truth of our existence and the path for our feet. These fatherly eyes will show us, little by little, that however marred human existence and this world are by sin and suffering, it is still, in his eyes, a marvelous story, a space of intimacy, and a playground in which he wishes for his children to rejoice and play.

And yet this play is not a mere past-time that distracts from the more serious things of life; rather, it is the very lifeblood of the whole of existence. It is the wellspring of mature responsibility, and the inner disposition of reverent humility, and the malleability of true receptivity to God's healing and transforming touch. Thus play is gratitude. It is wonder, and lightness, and flexibility; it is humility and surrender and letting-go; it is trustful reliance on the care of God more than on our own efforts, and, in this, the uncalculating obedience to his guiding hand that relies on him, and not on oneself, for the good fruit of obedience and for the fulfillment of all things born of gratuitous love and intimacy.

DAY 12
FAITH, HOPE, AND LOVE
AS THE LIFE OF GOD IN US

The human virtues are rooted in the theological virtues, which adapt man's faculties for participation in the divine nature: for the theological virtues relate directly to God. They dispose Christians to live in a relationship with the Holy Trinity. They have the One and Triune God for their origin, motive, and object.

The theological virtues are the foundation of Christian moral activity; they animate it and give it its special character. They inform and give life to all the moral virtues. They are infused by God into the souls of the faithful to make them capable of acting as his children and of meriting eternal life. They are the pledge of the presence and action of the Holy Spirit in the faculties of the human being. (*Catechism of the Catholic Church,* par. 1812-2813)

The four cardinal virtues are so called because they are the "hinges" of the life of the other virtues. (*Cardo* is Latin for hinge.) Prudence, justice, temperance, and courage are the fonts of the other virtues, the heading under which they can be classified (insofar as it is actually important or helpful to "classify" virtues in this way). But if what I said earlier is really true—namely that virtue is best understood not merely as a self-enclosed disposition but rather as a living relationality with reality—then another insight becomes beautifully apparent for us. It is that these "hinge" virtues are in fact hinged in something deeper: in our filial relationship of total reliance on God, and in our spousal reciprocity with him. Yes, the true *fountain* of all that is good in the human person and in human nature, and particularly of our radical renewal through the Redemption wrought in Christ, is *grace*.

Grace itself alone can fully restore our wounded nature to its full integrity—and indeed raises it to an even higher level than it had at the beginning—and can foster in us those capacities that make us able to truly share in the very life and love of God. We are not capable of this based on our own desire or capacity, even as our very capacity is oriented towards this. In other words, our whole created being, our very nature, is crying out for the gift that can only be received by grace, as free gift from God. That is part of the import of the quote I shared earlier from Joseph Ratzinger. I as a human person come most fully to myself not by what I myself choose and do based on my own self-determination, but by what is given to me, and which I can only freely accept: the gratuitous love of God and a free participation in his life through grace.

And yet, as this gift is received, it becomes ever more truly *my own*, such that I begin to live through and in this gift bestowed freely upon me, eliciting and setting free my own freedom. For the life of God is dynamic, rich, ever flowing like a river or ever dancing like a flame, in the mutual self-giving between Father, Son, and Holy Spirit. And I am caught up into this dance through adoption and espousal, through grace, such that I too can learn to freely dance with the Persons of the Trinity, participating in their own freedom through my own graced liberation. This is the significance of the *theological virtues*, the dispositions of faith, hope, and love.

These virtues, unlike the cardinal virtues or any other virtues, are not inherent as capacities in us through our nature or humanity; rather, they are freely given to us by God from the outside. They are, in fact, God's own life, his own manner of living and loving, grafting itself into our humanity in all of its faculties and experiences. And to the degree that we welcome and acquiesce to this awesome gift of God's life within us, we come to live the life of God, with God, in God, and through God. We become "partakers of the divine nature" (2 Pet 1:4), and not only in a substantial way that is impossible to experience or live consciously; rather, we are called to partake in this nature, and to live the life of God, in an increasingly personal, relational, and conscious way.

This is the origin of Christian prayer, as well as of the sacramental life in its fullness. And in a specific way, it is the root of what is usually called *mysticism*. Mysticism, properly speaking, refers to our participation in the *mystery* of God's life—the life of the Trinity—through faith, prayer, and the sacraments. As the Catechism expresses it:

> Spiritual progress tends toward ever more intimate union with Christ. This union is called "mystical" because it participates in the mystery of Christ through the sacraments—"the holy mysteries"—and, in him, in the mystery of the Holy Trinity. God calls us all to this intimate union with him, even if the special graces or extraordinary signs of this mystical life are granted only to some for the sake of manifesting the gratuitous gift given to all. (par. 2014)

This is deeply clear and profoundly encouraging. This means that the breathtakingly beautiful things that we read about in the lives of the saints and in their writings concerning their experience of God *are also intended for us*, even if the "special graces or extraordinary signs" are meant only for them. (We will see this in the final reflections of this book.) What they experienced "fleshed-out" in mystical experience is meant to be lived, and truly experienced, by *all* of us, even if in a more subdued, "ordinary" way, in the humble home and holy sanctuary of faith, hope, and love, and in life transfigured by divine grace. Yes, it is our vocation and destiny to share in the innermost life of the Father, Son, and Holy Spirit, and God desires this to become a lived reality—*the* lived reality of every moment—already now in this life, even while it presses on to consummation in eternity. Thus, however humble and hidden it may be, the life of holiness is never "ordinary" in the sense of being mundane, profane, constrained, or narrow in the limits of the pettiness and superficiality that suffocates our sinful world. Rather, we are called to live the same ardent intensity of love, the same total surrender, the same complete intimacy with the Trinity, even if the manner of experiencing it is unique for each one of us, stretching thin the veil of this mortal life to allow us to glimpse the beauty of eternity to a greater or lesser degree, depending on God's loving intentions for us.

Let us return now, however, to our explanation of the meaning of "mysticism." More specifically, mysticism usually refers to the trajectory of maturing prayer, in which the three theological virtues of faith, hope, and love begin to transfigure and renew the operation of our spiritual faculties of intellect, affectivity (or memory), and will, and overflow even into our imagination and our bodily senses. In other words, mysticism is the process whereby the human person is gradually transformed by the activity of grace operative through prayer, the sacraments, and the experiences of life. And the wellspring of this transformation lies in faith, hope, and love, grafted into our faculties and illumining them from within. To the degree that we allow these virtues to manifest and grow within us, and live on the basis of them, we enter into a living communion with the very uncreated life of God (for these virtues *are* God's life). But here it becomes rather misleading to keep insisting on focusing on the *virtues*, and much more important simply to focus on *God*. To keep looking at faith, hope, and love as the "stuff" of the spiritual life is similar to looking at the biological processes of the body as the "stuff" of authentic sexual intimacy. The focus, rather, should be on *persons*, on the way that persons relate to one another in mutual self-giving, in tender attunement and reciprocal delight.

Thus the teaching of the Church and of her spiritual tradition on faith, hope, and love simply indicates the *disposition* with which to welcome the approach of God, and the manner in which to draw near to him as our one true Beloved. As I have said elsewhere, these three virtues—of faith, hope, and love—can be understood as trust, desire, and surrender, though they are also richer in depth and import than this.[*]

Faith is the trusting acceptance of all that God desires to give and to reveal about himself and about reality, and thus also acceptance of the path along which he desires to lead me throughout my life. It is therefore assent to all that Scripture reveals and all that the Church teaches, but it is also a holy hospitality for God's gift in all the specificities of my unique existence, and the welcoming of his call as it comes to me anew each day. It is the root of my response, in other words, to the gift and the call of God in Christ and through the Holy Spirit.

But faith is not complete without hope and love. Hope can be understood as desire—as the God-ignited desire for those things that he has promised to us, and our trust that we will indeed receive them. Thus hope is an incarnation of faith, its application and expression in our relation to the good things God has offered to us, which take time to grow to maturity, and above all to our eternal destiny in everlasting intimacy with the Trinity and with the whole of renewed humanity. Hope thus reaches out beyond sight to make contact with what God has promised, and indeed with what he has given which cannot yet be experienced to the full (like his own life present within us).

And faith and hope together flow into love, just as, in the deepest sense, love stands at the origin of the other two virtues, and is their abiding wellspring. Love is the total surrender of the heart to the Beloved, the letting-go of my very self into his welcoming embrace—which surrender is also, simultaneously, a welcoming of the gift and surrender of himself to me. Thus love is the fulfillment of faith and hope, their full blossoming and highest expression. For it is the consummation of the movement of the

---

[*]See *Loving in the Light of Eternity: Love and Intimacy as the Heart of All Reality*, the two reflections, "Pulling Back the Veil: Faith, Hope, and Love," and "The Sweet Unveiling of Love."

theological virtues, and of the Christian life itself. For it is the expression and root of exactly what I expressed earlier as a *nuptial spirituality*, of our wholehearted response to the thirst of God in Christ, and the dynamic movement of mutual self-giving and abiding intimacy with the Trinity that this makes possible.

Faith, hope, and love—trust, desire, and surrender—these are in fact three inseparable aspects of a single reality, somewhat in the way that the faculties of mind, will, and affectivity are three aspects of our indivisible heart or spirit. Manifest in different ways at different times according to the call of the moment and the gift of God, what is most important is that they are really nothing but *our way of living according to the very life of God himself*. For God's own life is the consummation, for all eternity, of the disposition, of the living activity, that is manifested in time as faith, hope, and love: as the human person's response to God's gift, and our sharing in God's own life through this gift. For the Father, Son, and Holy Spirit relate to one another in a ceaseless dance of trust, desire, and surrender.

They abide before one another in a gaze of perfect security, a gaze that is given and received in perfect safety and complete vulnerability since it is a gaze of reciprocal tenderness: a gaze of trust born of love (thus the origin of faith) that cannot harm or violate, but only affirm, cherish, and delight. So too, they abide before one another in the dynamism of ardent desire, the very intensity of the divine longing to love and be loved, finding its fulfillment right at the heart of the Trinity, before creation has even been fashioned (thus the origin of hope as desire). God's own life is eternally blessed and complete; he has no need of creatures for his fulfillment. Rather, he has created us out of an overflow of love, out of the benevolent desire that we may share in his own life for all eternity. But in himself, God is perfect; the intimacy between Father, Son, and Holy Spirit is everlastingly complete. Thus this trusting gaze of cherishing tenderness (faith) and this ardent desire to love and be loved (hope), is eternally fulfilled in the total surrender of the divine Persons to one another (love), in which is forever sealed the intimacy between them in complete mutual belonging.

Yes, in God there is no need for trust—since all is absorbed totally in the divine light and in the fullness of unmediated union—and there is also no need for hope—since the reality desired is always already possessed in its fullness in love. But this does not mean that we cannot trace faith and hope, as interpersonal dispositions that allow us to share in God's life and to relate to him as he relates to us, back to the inner life of God. Rather, it means precisely that we *need* to do this. Only then can we understand how faith, hope, and love are the beginning of eternal life already on this earth. As John of the Cross says, the light of faith, hope, and love that we experience in this life is *identical* with the light of glory in which we see God face to face in the next life. This light is only *appropriated* to our temporal state, transmuted, as it were, into our concrete humanity, so that, like a leaven in the dough, it may transfigure us from within, little by little, until "the whole loaf is leavened" (Mt 13:33). Then, through this gift of God's own life bestowed upon us and alive within us, we will be prepared to live in the light of glory, in the very mutual self-giving and total intimacy that is the life of God, for all eternity.

DAY 13
THE CARDINAL VIRTUES AS INCARNATE LOVE

Human virtues are firm attitudes, stable dispositions, habitual perfections of intellect and will that govern our actions, order our passions, and guide our conduct according to reason and faith. They make possible ease, self-mastery, and joy in leading a morally good life. The virtuous man is he who freely practices the good. The moral virtues are acquired by human effort. They are the fruit and seed of morally good acts; they dispose all the powers of the human being for communion with divine love.

Four virtues play a pivotal role and accordingly are called "cardinal;" all the others are grouped around them. They are: prudence, justice, fortitude, and temperance. "If anyone loves righteousness, [Wisdom's] labors are virtues; for she teaches temperance and prudence, justice, and courage" (Wis 8:7). These virtues are praised under other names in many passages of Scripture. (*Catechism of the Catholic Church,* par. 1804-1805)

Prudence, justice, temperance, and courage were neglected in our last reflection, were they not? I intended to speak of them, but I got carried away in trying to express the ravishing beauty of God's life manifest in us through faith, hope, and love. Therefore, before moving on to the next topics I want to address—namely the path of healing and transfiguration, as well as the reality of infused or mystical contemplation—I would like to devote a few words to these four cardinal virtues. In particular, since there are other books that explain them, and the Catechism has good definitions of them, I would like to bring out into the open something that is not often recognized or explained. Namely, I want to point out how the inner form of the cardinal virtues can be traced back precisely to faith, hope, and love. Or, perhaps better said: the natural virtues are not self-enclosed human capacities, but are intended to find their ultimate fulfillment in being "vessels" that are filled with the very life of God.*

Let me explain. Prudence is often called the "mother" of the virtues, since it is the one that directs all the rest, like a compass directs all of our other actions in trying to travel from one destination to the next. As the Catechism says: "Prudence is the virtue that disposes practical reason to discern our true good in every circumstance and to choose the right means of achieving it; 'the prudent man looks where he is going' (Prov 14:15)" (par. 1806). The ability to discern between our true good and false goods (or between evil) is at the foundation of the capacity of choice, as is the ability to discern the best way to approach, receive, or attain such good. Put this way,

---

*Even if it is certainly true, as the Catechism says, that the human virtues are "acquired by human effort," it is equally true that all human effort is secretly buoyed up by grace—even in a pagan's striving for virtue, God is hiddenly present—and also that virtue finds its *consummation* in yielding all human capacities totally to the divine presence and activity. As the Catechism says: "they dispose all the powers of the human being for communion with divine love."

prudence is a virtue that resides in the mind (reason or intellect), particularly as it relates to our discernment of concrete created realities or specific decisions. This is what it means that it is a virtue of the "practical reason."

However, we can dig deeper under the surface of the virtue of prudence and realize that a fully divinized prudence (like we see in the saints), is not merely an educated practical reason, but a disposition of the whole human being towards true love in every moment. The full maturity of prudence lies in *zeal*. For the adequate response to every good is *love*. The good stirs desire, and desire is at the root of love, which pursues the good in order to attain it. Thus we can say that prudence (insofar as transfigured by grace) is precisely the concrete place, in us, in which faith and hope intersect in love. It is the place in which the trusting receptivity of faith and the firm desire of hope illumine us to see and embrace God's presence and call in each moment. It is, in short, having eyes for the Beloved. It is the ability to see the path he marks out for us, illumining our way as the Lamp of Love. "The eye is the lamp of the body. So, if your eye is sound, your whole body will be full of light; but if your eye is not sound, your whole body will be full of darkness" (Mt 6:22-23). Prudence, thus, is not a form of caution or fearfulness, not an excuse for pusillanimity or compromise; and in its mature form it is not even a facility at reasoning to a good conclusion in given circumstances. It is, rather, a connaturality with the good, a harmony between my being and the beauty and goodness of God placed in each created reality, and speaking to me out of given circumstances to call me closer to him, and into fostering his own goodness in the world for my own well-being and that of others.

Said another way, we could recognize prudence as the perfect path of harmonization between *charity* and *humility*. It recognizes the truth both of God and of myself, of his all-surpassing beauty and desirability (charity), and of my own nature, being, and circumstances in seeking him (humility). Prudence thus does not seek to live based on abstract ideas, nor on the basis of an unrealistic striving not proper to or possible for me in my uniqueness, nor on the basis of a fearful self-protection. On the contrary, it lives the ardent desire of trusting love to the full, and with radiant vigor, and expresses it properly in my own unique situation and life—the song of my unique story!—in harmony with the life of the Trinity and with the whole communion of saints.

Prudence is thus truth, a *feel for truth*. And this feel is not a dry awareness, nor merely a matter of the intellect, but an illumination of the mind, a spontaneous conformity of the affection, and an impulse of the will: all toward the authentic good marked out by God in everything. It is to "live the truth in love" (cf. Eph 4:15), or to "love in the truth" (cf. 2 Jn 1-6), to live with eyes wide open the realistic path of love proper for *me* in the sight of *God,* and to do so on the basis of God's own gaze and in radiant openness to the communion of life and the ministry of charity for all of the children of God and to satiating the thirst of God himself.

Allow me to say a little on the other three cardinal virtues too, recognizing the limits of space in this given reflection. Prudence, being the root of the other three cardinal virtues, has the most to be said for it. In fact, justice, temperance, and courage can be seen as specific expressions or applications of the virtue of prudence, which in turn is a manifestation of faith, hope, and love. Justice, as the Catechism says, "is the moral virtue that consists in the constant and firm will to give their due to God and neighbor" (par. 1807). Thus it is charity and humility as incarnate in our seeking equality, harmony, fraternity, and proper relationship in all of our dealings. It is the aliveness of our heart to feel with and for all of our brothers and sisters what is authentically good for them, and to hurt at the injustices present in society, and to burn with longing to alleviate them. Thus the full maturity of justice lies in *merciful love*. It is also expressed in the virtue of religion, in an ardent piety, in that we thirst to render justice to God, to love, adore, reverence, serve, and cherish him as he deserves. Clearly, it is precisely love, the nuptial love of which we have spoken, which fulfills this aspiration of justice in its fullest expression. For God is worthy of nothing less than total love and utter surrender!

Temperance, on the other hand, is an expression of everything that I have said above as it relates to my relationship with my own appetites and desires. It is prudence, it is humility and charity, as it distills into the order that virtue brings to my daily life in all of its needs, desires, and wishes. As the Catechism says: "Temperance is the moral virtue that moderates the attraction of pleasures and provides balance in the use of created goods. It ensures the will's mastery over instincts and keeps desires within the limits of what is honorable. The temperate person directs the sensitive appetites toward what is good and maintains a healthy discretion" (par. 1809). It is thus a lack of prudence, a lack of humility and charity, a lack of faith, hope, and love, to abuse these desires in disordered self-indulgence, in possessiveness that robs my neighbor of his due (injustice), or in acts that harm me in my integral wholeness or harm my neighbor in theirs. Indeed, the fullness of temperance lies not just in self-restraint, but in the *love of poverty*, in nakedness of spirit to the fullness of love born of reciprocal gift in each moment.

Finally, courage is the flame of hope's desire, the trust of faith, and the surrender of love as manifested in my confrontation with fear or hesitation, in my endurance of suffering, hardship, or obstacles to the fulfillment of my desire for the true good, and above all for union with the divine Beloved. In this sense, courage or fortitude sustains the path of fidelity to God's call, from the first steps to the end; it is manifested, most radiantly, in an eagerness and joy in responding to the invitation of God's love, and in the total gift of myself to him without counting the cost. As the Catechism says, "Fortitude is the moral virtue that ensures firmness in difficulties and constancy in the pursuit of the good. It strengthens the resolve to resist temptations and to overcome obstacles in the moral life" (par. 1808). The fullness of courage lies in *bold confidence* in God, a confidence that expects everything from his abundant goodness with the simplicity and lightness of children.

And as Father Mark Toups said, "Courage is not the opposite of fear. The opposite of fear is *communion*. The only answer to your fear and anxiety is the knowledge that Jesus is here, intimately present with us. He will personally walk with each of you." Here we come right back to the *relational* nature of the virtues, which are nothing but an expression of the vividness of our communion with the God who loves us and walks with us at every moment, and of the integrity of our walking with him. When such an intimate relationship is truly alive, all of the virtues grow and flourish quite spontaneously, fueled as they are by the tenderest trusting receptivity, the most ardent and holy longing, and the most unconditional loving surrender.*

---

*As a conclusion to this section, I would like to quote the wonderful book on Christian ethics by Servais Pinckaers, O.P., and draw a "jam-packed" point from it. He gives the definition: "Christian ethics is the branch of theology that studies human acts so as to direct them to a loving vision of God seen as our true, complete happiness and our final end. This vision is attained by means of grace, the virtues, and the gifts, in the light of revelation and reason." (*The Sources of Christian Ethics*, 8)

This definition is exactly correct. But is also inspired me to create a definition of my own, the "interior" side of this "exterior" definition, as it were. I have chosen completeness over succinctness, as it is precisely meant to expound upon the seed above. By comparing the two and, especially, by breaking down the component parts of the following definition, much can be gleaned about the nature and meaning of life as a whole, and about ethics within it. It is a summary that is meant to reward revisiting and contemplation, and indeed to grow with the human heart as it matures throughout life. Here is the definition:

"Christian ethics is the branch of theology that studies human freedom, in both intent and act, as it journeys to union with the loving will of God as revealed in his creative handiwork—given in nature and in revelation, in man's reason and conscience, in the objective values of the world, and in man's inner orientation toward the beauty, goodness, and truth that bring him and his fellow man happiness. This journey is sustained and completed by grace and the gifts of the Holy Spirit, especially the theological virtues, fulfilling natural human capacities and virtues in direct participation in the life and love of God himself. For this is man's true and final end, both individually and communally: the consummation of humanity, the image of God, in God's likeness, in an interpersonal communion of knowledge and love, human and divine, brought to full flower."

DAY 14
THE GOD WHO ACTS

I have spoken first (in week 1) about the ardent desire in the heart of God to love and to be loved, to pour himself out in the whole of his being into us, and to elicit our reciprocal surrender, thus forging with us profound nuptial intimacy. I have spoken second (in this week 2) about the "human substratum," as it were, of our transformation by grace, about virtue as human capacity and divine gift, as well as about the trajectory of transformation in its rich unfolding. But I want to emphasize now how these two meet and come together in the most vivid way. I have tried to make it very clear that, no matter how much the life of faith and following in the footsteps of Christ calls forth our freedom in a vigorous responsiveness, *the primary actor is always God.* He it is who initiates, who is primarily at work, who leads the way, and indeed who can bring to completion within us a work that so far surpasses not only our capacity but also our comprehension. In this respect, all that he requires is openness, the acceptance of a bride to the gift of the Bridegroom, and her surrender which springs forth within her in response to his proximity and his touch.

Indeed, those who have most deeply experienced God speak of him precisely in this way: as vigorously active, as always initiating, as vibrantly alive, as perpetually seeking out his children in order to enter into communion with us and to draw us deeper into the depths of his own loving heart. Our own frail and miniscule efforts are as nothing in comparison with the breathtaking beauty and intensity of the divine activity. And we need only speak our "yes," only consent to God, and he will rush in with tenderness yet with ardor—with flaming tenderness of love!—to do what he, in his eternal goodness, so deeply desires to do. As Jesus said to Angela of Foligno: "Make yourself into a capacity, and I will make myself into a Torrent."

This primacy of God's gift, presence, and activity is also *determinative* for prayer. What I mean by determinative is that it is *the* condition for the authenticity and fruitfulness of prayer. A prayer is good to the degree that it *allows God to act*, and lacking to the degree that—through human stubbornness, sin, and unwillingness—it hinders his free activity in us. In other words, prayer is good to the degree that it is *Marian*, participating in the virginal and bridal "yes" of Mary, who opened wide her whole being, body and spirit, and her whole existence, as a space of receptivity for the gift of God—which is God himself!—and for his loving activity. It is also, in this way, also *Christic,* participating in the disposition of the eternal Son before his Father, receiving the torrential outpouring of paternal love and delight that is gushing from the Father for all eternity. It is this same torrent that flowed into the heart of Jesus Christ as a man—the God-man, the incarnate Son—at every moment of his life, and, from here, flows forth ceaselessly into us. See, filial and bridal love! This is what God desires for us, and the disposition which allows him to accomplish his marvels in us, unto the most breathtaking consummation of intimacy!

To recognize this also cuts through a lot of "stuff" that distracts and preoccupies our hearts in prayer and the Christian life. So many "am I doing it right's?" and "I don't know how to do that's" and "I don't know where this is leading's" give way here. If God is supremely active, then he will not fail to show us all that we need to know, and indeed to show us an abundance in his desire to communicate his own loving vision to us. And so too, he will not settle for anything less than our total transformation in him and the consummate intimacy that this makes possible, while this intimacy in turn is what transforms us. As faltering and imperfect as our prayer may be on the human level, as apparently dull and ordinary, it is not so from the perspective of God. For God *always* shows up, and always acts with power: the power that is nothing but the surging tenderness of infinite Love!

Let us therefore simply try to "show up" ourselves, as deeply and vulnerably as we can. Let us yield up to God the most vulnerable and hidden secrets of our heart and our life—laying ourselves naked before his gaze in order to receive his gift. This is ultimately all that he requires.

+ + +

Let me bring this reflection full circle by quoting some vivid words from Father Iain Matthew's precious little book on John of the Cross. I said that those who have experienced God most deeply—the real, living, infinite God revealed to us throughout history and most fully in Jesus Christ —experienced him as *supremely active in a love that ever seeks out to touch, heal, transform, and unite in intimacy.* Let us use the concrete example of how this was the case for the Spanish Carmelite, this humble man so ravished by the Trinity. The God whom John encounters

> is not prissy, stale, or exhausted; his God is new, daring, vital. Flame, fire, blazing, burning—the basic image is meant to say something.
>
> John makes it explicit. Where God is concerned, 'love is never idle; it is in continual movement.'
>
> The Spirit that John knows is 'an infinite fire of love,' able to set the heart 'blazing more intensely than all the fire in the world.'
>
> His presence is 'fiesta' in the soul, 'like a song that is new, always new, wrapped round with joy, and love.'
>
> With such a God, the journey does not narrow into dainty, stuffy elegance; it opens out into broader landscapes, where issues are more real, and more is at stake. Love grows geometrically (two, four, eight, sixteen); it spirals upwards with increasing velocity.
>
> Rapture, and infinite breadth: these characteristics depend on a third, the most fundamental. As the poem [*The Living Flame of Love*] throbs with the activity of Another, so, permeating the pages of the commentary, is an awareness of a self-communicating God, a God whose plan is to fill us with nothing less than himself.
>
> This is God's 'language,' in which speaking is doing, and his action is himself. The flame is a person, 'the Spirit of your Bridegroom,' the breath of Christ. The work pulses with God's eagerness to belong to other persons. Nothing less would satisfy 'the liberality of his generous grace.' He gives, and what he gives is

himself.

So John's magnificat responds to a Spirit-flame who does not wait to be approached. He hovers over to enter, presses in, and once in, burns through until he finds the deepest core of the human person.

... To this [union in love] his language has been geared: bride and Bridegroom, married intimacy, the Bible's symbol of the Christ who 'loved the church and gave himself' (Eph. 5:25). Now, as we sound John's experience at its most authentic, we find this to be the reality he knew: a God who is pressing in to give *himself*.

He does not give in a general way only, like rays of sunlight shining above a mountain, but leaving me-in-particular shadowed in the valley. John's God enters to confront the person as if there were no other. It seems to her that God has no other concern, 'but that he is all for her alone.' God comes in strength, capable of reconciling opposites, 'giving life for death's distress.' His embrace is as wide as Good Friday to Sunday, and nothing in the person is too much for him. He finds in the soul, not a burden, or a disappointment, but a cause for 'glad celebration.' John dares to place on the lips of his God the words:

'I am yours, and for you, and I am pleased to be as I am that I may be yours and give myself to you.'[19]

Why would we wish to refuse such a loving and tender invitation? Why would we reject such a tender gift pressing upon us, seeking to enter into our inmost depths, to heal, give life, and carry to the ecstatic happiness of total intimacy and perfect love? But God awaits our "yes," and himself works so tenderly and lovingly to elicit our freedom, so that his outpouring and our acceptance may both be full and free, as all love must. For in this way true mutual self-donation, and the fullest blossoming of communion, comes to flower.

Yes, if this is truly the God who loves us, then openness to his approach, and surrender to his love, is nothing but embarking upon the most spectacular adventure. There could be nothing more beautiful, or more fulfilling, than letting him have his way, this way that leads into the inmost recesses of our hearts where he wishes to consummate a spiritual marriage with us, and straight also into his own heart, where we shall share, in this life and for all eternity, in the intimacy that is his as Father, Son, and Holy Spirit.

WEEK III

THE ARROW OF LOVE

DAY 15
THE ARROW OF LOVE:
ONE ALONE, YET ALL THINGS

The Greek term for sin is *hamartia*, meaning "to miss the mark." It invokes the image of archery, in which the arrow, intended to strike a bull's-eye, instead flies off from its intended mark and lands elsewhere. This is indeed a quite accurate way of "imaging" sin, from the first betrayal of Adam and Eve in the Garden of Eden to all of our infidelities to God's law and grace in the present day. To choose sin is to choose wrongly; it is to turn aside from the path of life, from the *end* toward which we are directed as persons created in the image and likeness of God, and instead to seek fulfillment in something that cannot satisfy. It is to hurt the heart of God, who desires our happiness so ardently, and to harm ourselves, other persons, and often the very fabric of the created order. Thus repentance, too, is simply to "realign our sights" upon the truth, goodness, and beauty to which we are meant to be ordered. And sanctity is to "hit a bull's-eye," not on the basis of our own efforts or expertise, but because of the transforming grace of God at work within us.

Indeed, this image of the arrow is quite apt in many ways. For, as I have said over and over throughout my writings, the Heart of Christ is the Convergence-Point in which all lines intersect. Jesus, raised up on the Cross and in the Resurrection, draws all of humanity, and indeed the whole creation, to himself. What has been scattered afar in sin, disintegrated and fractured, is gathered together into harmony, unity, and peace, by the Divine Magnet in whom we are all made one. Here the singular *uniqueness* of each person, intimately united to Christ in his incomparable love, is brought to fulfillment and consummation. And yet in this same space such uniqueness is opened wide to *universal communion*, to the world-cradling embrace of love that makes all persons one in a unity that reflects and shares in the life of the Father, Son, and Holy Spirit.

This intersection of personal singularity and universal communion—both fulfilled and consummated in the Convergence-Point of Christ—is, in a way, the very essence of Catholicism. It is a sharing in the very uncreated life of God, who is the union of Singularity and Unity: as three distinct Persons sharing in a single Intimacy of the divine life. Each Person, in this intimate communion, is not narrowed, neglected, or made in any way anonymous, but is rather cherished, affirmed, and allowed to be fully who he is, in his unique personhood; and yet this occurs not in isolated self-affirmation, but in the reciprocal gaze of love between Lover and Beloved, in which the Name of each is lovingly spoken by the other, and they rejoice together, without fear and in total vulnerability, in the Intimacy that they share.

There's another sentence that needs to be unpacked and reflected upon. But let me move forward in our reflections at this point, beginning to speak about the next theme I would like to address. In the Introduction, I spoke about my indebtedness to John of the Cross, who fathered me into the life of faith in a beautiful way, and, I trust, still does. Well, it can be said that this "straight arrow" of love is the best way to understand the significance of John of the Cross's insights in the Church. Alone, without being complemented by a more affirmative and ecclesial spirituality, John's writings are inadequate, incomplete, and can even be harmful. But for the specific word that God asked him to speak, he excels in depth. Ravished by the beauty of the divine Bridegroom, John's whole life was consumed with one desire: to enter into the deepest possible intimacy with the Trinity already in this life, and to live this intimacy fully for all eternity.

He was that arrow that cared for nothing but to go straight to the heart of God, without the slightest distraction, delay, or hindrance. To fly straight to God by the most direct route, and to let go of all else in the process. In this way, he also educates us in the essence of a true and holy desire for God, a desire in which God not only takes first place in our life, but is our All in all, the only desire that engulfs all other desires within itself. Thus John beautifully shows us the essence of *purity of heart*, which, as Kierkegaard says, is to "will one thing." Indeed, it is to desire and seek one thing, with *all* the faculties of one's humanity and with one's every moment. All things should be cast recklessly into this conflagration of love that consumes all in order to transfigure it into an offering to Christ, to the Father, pure and holy to share in his own life in the most total and intimate way.

The path that John of the Cross marks out for the person who thirsts for God, therefore, is one of *negation*. It is the stripping away of every slightest thing that could encumber the heart on its journey to God, the most subtle and hidden disordered attachments to created things, to the fallen self, or to the deceit of the evil spirits. Indeed, John even wants to throw off good things, to cast everything away in order to be found alone with God alone, to live in a world in which God alone exists, naked with the naked heart, in a nuptial union more intimate and total than any created image can even begin to comprehend or suggest. And while this desire is, in itself, very beautiful and pure, it is also something that needs to be manifested *according to the incarnate nature that God actually gave to us as human persons*. This "arrow" of longing into the heart of God, in other words, is the inner trajectory of our entire life, the flame that burns and consumes at its sacred center; and yet it is meant to be manifested in a life that enfolds, affirms, embraces, and sanctifies *all created things*, taking them up gratefully and lovingly in its path to God, bringing them with it into the divine embrace.

This is the emphasis that is necessary to "fill out" what is lacking or misleading in John of the Cross. For not only is a disordered and possessive choice for created things a sin before God—a clinging to creation against his intentions—but also an unhealthy rejection of creation and a failure to reverence and respond to the values inherent within it, a refusal of his "call" that is buried in creation seeking our response. Thus the naked longing for God beyond all things—naked to the naked God!—is the inner force that impels us forward each day, not only into the inner recesses of our own heart and into the heart of God beyond every created reality or earthly image, but also *to God at the heart of every created thing, and in particular every human person*. Thus we can receive and respond to God's beauty partially revealed in created realities with the same purity and ardor as we seek him *beyond* all created realities. Both are necessary, indeed equally necessary. God of course takes absolute priority, God beyond all, and yet this longing for God *cannot* be concretely manifested in silent prayer alone (even if here it reaches its highest apex), but also must pervade every experience, desire, and choice in our flesh-and-blood existence.

And God desires that it does precisely that. He wants us to find him both *beyond* everything and *within* everything. He wants us to descend into the inner sanctuary of our deepest solitude, where we stand naked before him in virginal receptivity, receiving his nuptial gift. He also wants us to open this solitude out to be touched and moved by his presence in the whole of creation (and creation's presence in him), and thus to take up creation into this inner space, so that, offered to him in the "priesthood of virginity," it too can find consummation, with us, in the embrace of the Trinity.

What is a conclusion we can draw from all of this? Among others, it is to point out the danger of *narrowness* in the spiritual life. There is a danger to emphasize, for example, solitude to the neglect of community, prayer to the neglect of activity (or vice versa), schedule to the neglect of spontaneity, bodily chastity to the neglect of love-manifest-in-the-body, pursuit of God beyond all things to the neglect of responsiveness to created values that speak of him. Thus there is a *paradox* in love: it is both a *straight-arrow* to the heart of God, casting all else aside to run to him, and also *an overflowing expansion from the center-point,* to take up all things, cherish and affirm them, and draw them back to the center. Yes, love is a straight shot to the heart of God, which also takes up *all* things into its movement.

So too love is ardent longing, the passionate pursuit of God in himself and God in all things; but it is also the patient and chaste receptivity to allow God to come, to communicate himself, in whatever manner he desires. What matters is that it is always *God* himself loved above all things and in all things, and also that *all things* are loved only in God and as he has given them to us. And in this love, rich and full as it is, is found true freedom and happiness. Every moment becomes a sacrament of his presence, from the deepest moments of prayer, silent and still with God, to the most vibrant encounters with created reality, with beauty, and with other persons in true intimacy. God is everything and in everything, and everything is in God. Whenever a heart comes to this place, then life becomes *ceaseless intimacy with the Trinity*, and the whole world is set ablaze with the fire of divine love, not to be destroyed, but to be affirmed, renewed, and consummated in the divine embrace of Father, Son, and Holy Spirit.

---

*What is primarily lacking in the spirituality of John, and other saints and doctors (to greater or lesser degrees), is a *positive recognition of the innate value of created reality*, and the importance—and indeed even the moral obligation—of giving it an adequate response. I wholeheartedly agree with their "diagnosis" of the roots of sinful, disordered tendencies within us (what John calls "appetites" or "attachments"), and how clinging to created reality apart from God blinds, dulls, drags down, diminishes, and harms the person. In our culture we are so accustomed to justifying our disordered inclinations, explaining them away, that we are content to remain stuck in the mud, to remain a bird meant to fly yet tied down by a cord. But a true encounter with the rav-

DAY 16
BAPTIZING THE JAILER

The insights from the previous reflection also greatly illumine for us the true path of healing and liberation. All authentic healing, whether from the wounds of personal sin or from traumas received throughout life, consists not in a fleeing from our humanity towards God, but rather in the liberation and ordering of our entire humanity in the integrity of a single movement towards God, and also towards all those things given and entrusted to us by God. The only thing from which to flee is sin and, in prudence, the near occasion of sin. All else should be swept along in the current of love, in the arrow shooting straight into the heart of the Trinity, and thus caught up into the divine conflagration that consumes, heals, and transfigures all things.

There is a beautiful passage in the Act of the Apostles that symbolizes this movement of true healing and liberation. Let us read it first, and then I will try to unpack its significance for our topic:

> The crowd joined in attacking them; and the magistrates tore

---

ishing beauty of Christ—and of our vocation to intimacy with the Trinity—stirs awake the ardent longing to be free of the slightest disorder in our desire, the most subtle sinful or possessive inclination, which would keep us from union with the divine Beloved. I part ways, however, in the focus on the *way of attaining to human wholeness and freedom from sin*.

Here my approach aligns more with Thomas Aquinas (and contemporary saints such as John Paul II), who emphasize the important, God-given meaning of the appetites as natural inclinations essential to our wholeness and well-being as human persons. I would add to this the value-responding philosophy of Dietrich von Hildebrand—and John Paul II, too—which recognizes the "divine call" that is present in created reality eliciting our response, and speaking to us of God himself. Even if there are different "layers" to created reality—from things that are merely subjectively satisfying (like taste and pleasure), to those that are objectively beneficial to us as persons (like healthy relationships, knowledge, culture), to those that are intrinsically valuable (like beauty, or the dignity of the person, or moral values calling for disinterested affirmation)—all things have their proper place in the plan of God. We find wholeness not through fear or flight, through perpetual war waged against our natural inclinations, but rather by *trustingly walking the path towards the healing and integration of desire, towards God and towards all things in God*. Here, also, we see the importance of humor, playfulness, and lightness of heart, which I truly believe is one of the greatest of virtues—born of filial trust in the Father and the willing surrender of all control of my life to him. In other words, playful lightheartedness is nothing but the breath of faith, hope, and love manifest in my concrete attitude towards my life as it unfolds within God's loving care.

In summary, then, as we will see more in coming reflections, our path should not lead merely *away* from a disordered clinging to created reality, but *toward* a healthy, affirming relation with all that exists, from the smallest to the greatest. The ardent longing for intimacy with God and perfect purity of heart before him should *coincide* and *harmoniously coexist* with a truly cherishing attitude towards all created things (all in their proper place within the hierarchy of being). This wholehearted, grateful, loving responsiveness to all things, to all being—both the divine Being and created being—was God's original intention for us in the beginning, and thus in it also lies true sanctity now, in this world, and the consummation of life awaiting us in eternity.

the garments off them and gave orders to beat them with rods. And when they had inflicted many blows upon them, they threw them into prison, charging the jailer to keep them safely. Having received this charge, he put them into the inner prison and fastened their feet in the stocks. But about midnight Paul and Silas were praying and singing hymns to God, and the prisoners were listening to them, and suddenly there was a great earthquake, so that the foundations of the prison were shaken; and immediately all the doors were opened and every one's fetters were unfastened. When the jailer woke and saw that the prison doors were open, he drew his sword and was about to kill himself, supposing that the prisoners had escaped. But Paul cried with a loud voice, "Do not harm yourself, for we are all here." And he called for lights and rushed in, and trembling with fear he fell down before Paul and Silas, and brought them out and said, "Men, what must I do to be saved?" And they said, "Believe in the Lord Jesus, and you will be saved, you and your household." And they spoke the word of the Lord to him and to all that were in his house. And he took them the same hour of the night, and washed their wounds, and he was baptized at once, with all his family. Then he brought them up into his house, and set food before them; and he rejoiced with all his household that he had believed in God. (Acts 16:22-34)

This passage is incredibly rich, both in itself and in the lessons it can teach us about personal healing. Of course, the exegesis I am about to offer is a spiritual and moral one (as opposed to literal or anagogical), but I think it fits in perfectly with the God-ordained meaning of the text. In fact, I share this symbolism in part because God used this passage in this manner to speak to *me*, such that I could hear more or less exactly what I am going to share with you in a time when I found it deeply consoling and helpful. So let us begin. Let us see Paul and Silas as a symbol of ourselves, or as our desire for freedom and wholeness. But look what happens! We are beaten down with rods and cast into a dungeon, our very legs bound in stocks. How often do we feel this way, as if no matter how much we desire to be free from sin, or free from the burdensome wounds that afflict us and keep us from the liberty and spontaneity in love that we desire, we are trapped in a dungeon and bound, such that we can hardly even move?

In the very inner prison, trapped as we are, what can we do but despair? Oh yes...there is more that we can do: pray to our loving God and praise him in the darkness, singing songs to him, as do Paul and Silas. And this prayer is simultaneously praise and petition, as we see so often in the Psalms. It is a plea for liberation from our bondage and the thanksgiving to God, in advance, for the surety of liberation that he, in his mighty love, is going to effect. It is very meaningful that the passage emphasizes that all the prisoners were listening to this song, and in particular the jailer, who had been charged with keeping them "safely." Notice something here. What could these prisoners, and in particular the jailer, represent? Are the prisoners not perhaps the dimensions of our being that we keep locked away in darkness, fear, and shame? And is not the jailer, in a very pointed way, the symbol of any shameful and difficult wound that we bear, particularly the one that most binds us, which seems to be the doorkeeper of our inner jail? Or to be more accurate: the jailer can represent a dimension of our being which is crushed under woundedness, "enlisted" to keep us shackled in false security, rather than joining us in the liberty of love. Thus, the jailer himself is good, even innocent, but he has been controlled himself by an impure force, a hurtful force, into locking up our inmost freedom from fully expressing itself and coming into the light.

Let us return to the story. In the dungeon, we can still praise God and pray to him. And as we praise God and entrust ourselves to him in the darkest part of the night—midnight—and in the inmost depths of the dungeon—the inner jail—he opens our poverty and nakedness to him little by little, unsealing our hearts for freedom. And his presence, his touch, shakes the very foundations of our being like an earthquake, to break open the bars that we ourselves by our own efforts could never tear asunder. He is Liberator, and by his own word he accomplishes for us the wondrous liberation for which our hearts desire. We need only trust, abide, and continue to worship and desire him in the night, and he will not fail to come.

But this is not all that the passage has for us. Notice, even after the prison is open, Paul and Silas do not immediately flee away. Rather, probably because they know the commands given to the jailer, they stay put. Thus whenever the jailer draws his sword to take his own life—having failed to keep "safe" the prisoners entrusted to his charge—Paul is able to call out for him to stay his hand. And then, together, they depart from the prison, jailer and prisoners together. Yes, not only this, but then Paul and Silas preach the word of God to him, and he and all his household are saved. In turn he, for his part, offers loving hospitality to them, washing their wounds and feeding them in his own home. Now if we recall the symbolism of this jailer, something amazing strikes us. Even when the prison doors of our suffering are thrown wide open, we cannot simply cast aside the dimensions of our humanity that seemed to hold us bound, that caused us such pain. For it is, in fact, not any legitimate dimension of our humanity which we must fear, but only the lies and deceptions under which it has been burdened, under which it, so to speak, "took orders." Rather, all the dimensions of our being beg to be taken out into the light of day, to be evangelized in the radiance of Christ, and to join us in praising God. In this way, what before was a place of suffering and slavery becomes a place where we experience the medicine of joy and renewal, of intimacy and security, a place in which Christ himself washes our wounds and feeds us.*

Jesus himself, when he burst the bonds of the grave, showed the way for us, for he kept the nail-marks in his hands and the open wound in his side, in his very Heart. He thus showed us that nothing is too broken to be renewed, nothing is too scarred to be made beautiful, nothing is too dead to be raised to the fullness of life. Indeed, when we are called to rise in

---

*This is yet another proof that the heart of Christian life is not fear, but *desire*, not a stripping away of our human capacities, emotions, appetites, or sensations, but their *ordering* and *integration* under the guiding light of God's truth revealed in Christ and poured out through the Holy Spirit. Perhaps Christ wants to minister to me, to fill me with his love, in the very place in my humanity that I seek so vehemently to reject or deny.

Christ, already in this life through conversion, healing, and the sanctity that grace brings, and in the next life unto the resurrection of the body, nothing —and I mean *nothing*—in our humanity is meant to be left behind. Perhaps I have, for example, struggled with sexual sin or wounds in the area of sexuality. When I heal from these, God desires not that I exclude this dimension of my humanity from my consciousness forever; rather, he desires that it is taken up into the light, rendered transparent in true purity and chastity, such that it glows with the redemptive light of Christ and becomes a witness of his goodness. Indeed, in a way it can be said that, within the designs of providence, the places of our woundedness are precisely God-ordained places through which he desires to shine some of his most radiant grace.*

The example of sexuality is very pertinent, since many persons still tend to think of chastity as a "freedom from sexuality," as an ability to ignore the sexual realm and act as if it didn't exist. But chastity is the fullest maturation of sexuality, harmonized anew with the inner voice of the person as a gift of love to God and to others. Indeed, as John Paul II said, "Purity is the glory of the human body before God. It is the glory of God in the human body through which masculinity and femininity are manifested " (TOB 57:3). Thus, sexual wholeness is not complete and full just by leaving behind sin, or escaping from the distracting presence of sexual feeling or desire; rather, sexual wholeness is complete whenever my whole being, body and spirit, spontaneously and freely responds to other persons, incarnate persons in their body, with a tender and cherishing gaze that is not even inclined to possess, to use, or to degrade, but rather moves my heart to cherish, affirm, protect, and care for them. The same can be said for all of the other vices, as well as all the other traumas and wounds that we can experience in this life. They too seek "to be baptized, and all their family." Underneath the struggle, a facet of our humanity is crying out to be liberated, evangelized, and harmonized with the deepest love of our heart as a gift to God and to our brothers and sisters.

---

*Let me be clear that I do *not* mean that I should carry with me the lies, confusions, or obsessions that burdened me when I sat trapped in the jail of woundedness. Rather, these should be totally broken and cast aside, to such a degree that "they neither are remembered nor come to mind any more" (cf. Is 65:17). What takes their place is pure light and childlike forgetfulness of the past, even as gratitude springs up for God's redeeming grace and presence through everything.

DAY 17
MY UNIQUE PATH OF HEALING AND INTEGRATION

(This reflection is a couple pages longer than the other reflections in this book, but I thought it necessary to make this point thoroughly and without summarizing, since it is so important. Just be aware it may take a little longer to go through, and may be good to receive it in two sittings.)

> *In the tender compassion of our God*
> *the dawn from on high shall break upon us,*
> *to shine on those who dwell in*
> *darkness and the shadow of death,*
> *and to guide our feet into the way of peace.*
> *(Lk 1:78-79; Canticle of Zechariah)*

The earth shakes and the prison doors swing open, as the dawn from on high breaks upon us, to guide our feet into the way of peace. This is the beautiful liberation that God brings. I am going to speak in depth soon of the transforming power of God's grace active in mystical contemplation—how his love *does things* within us far beyond our own comprehension, control, or experience. Indeed, God is *always* secretly at work in our inmost depths, like the seed germinating and growing in the soil though the farmer is unaware. We may only feel a little overflow from this inmost place, a sense of peace, or presence, or longing, or may in fact feel nothing at all but the faith conviction that he is and must be present and at work, for he is God, and there is no other.

I would like to add that, in this space, he also intends to speak into our hearts his clarity and his guidance concerning concrete matters of our existence. Again using the image from the previous reflection, he wants to shake us loose of the wounds that bind us, and to cast forth his light to lead us out of darkness. Thus it is important to open ourselves wide, in our very place of pain, to receive his direction and guidance for the path we are to walk. For there are many different ways in which I could walk, many different attitudes I could have towards my own path of healing or towards the dispositions and attitudes which are being healed. But it is often the case that only *one* is appropriate,[*] directly willed for me by God as an expression of his loving intentions for me and of the contours of my life fashioned by his "potter's" hands, molding my existence into a masterpiece of his love.

Let us give an example. Say that I have been raised in a paradigm of "success" and "achievement," in which I habitually (and quite obsessively, since wounds always have an obsessive character to them) gauge myself according to my "expertise" in a given area. To the degree that I feel qualified, I feel secure—again, since every wound seeks to give a false security where security should rather be found in God and in utter poverty and vulnerability before him. Thus, whenever I walk forward in my life or seek to embrace a new decision or expression of love, prayer, or ministry, this tendency to grasp for "expertise" or qualification, to prove that I am capable and prepared, kicks in with a vengeance. Say, for example, that this is

---

[*] I say "often" the case because in certain circumstances God leaves us free to choose between different options, both of which are good and fitting, and blesses our choice with his goodness and grace, molding himself around our choice.

manifested particularly in the area of intellectual knowledge and preparedness. I am inclined to read and study a lot to be prepared for teaching, say to fill myself to the brim with theological knowledge in order to teach children's catechesis! Or say I am beginning to experience a deep longing for intimacy with God in prayer, and my temptation is to "force-feed" myself the truths of the faith, rather than to open myself wide, in poverty, to receive the consolation of love that only *he* can give.

Now (leaving behind these two specific examples), as I find myself in this place of woundedness, opening my shackled heart to the liberating light of God, there are a number of different directions in which my path could lead. There are different ways in which God could "sanctify" my intellect, my attitude towards knowledge and preparedness. But there are two important things here: 1) The first is to open my heart to recognize the nature of true *wholeness*, which, regardless of my unique path, is one and indivisible, for it lies in the poverty and vulnerability of love. However God may wish to lead me, his deepest desire is simply to make me whole, to liberate and integrate all of my desires in the space of intimate relationship with himself and with the whole of creation, a relationship free of fear, of possessiveness, and radiant in childlike simplicity and carefree abandonment. 2) The second is to *discern the unique path that God marks out for me*, and to walk it without fear or doubt. In this second, the first is incarnate, while the first holds and gives meaning to the second.

Staying with the "tendency to intellectual control" example, I could, say, be called to become a college professor, even a theologian, and to place my intellect at the service of others in a very specific and engaging way. But in the process I could be stripped of all "expertise" and realize, deep in my heart and mind, my own poverty and littleness. My own mind, humbled by grace, could shift from an attitude of control to an attitude of wonder, and in this find healing and liberty. However, this could be the wrong path if God is calling me on another. Say, rather, that he calls me precisely to let go of all claim on expertise in the most radical way; he calls me to drop the pursuit of my scholarly degree before my studies are complete. And he calls me instead into a place of simplicity, poverty, and hiddenness, in which my reading and study are utterly reduced to commonplace reflection and prayer, to the simple daily contemplation of the mystery of God as revealed in Scripture and the teaching of the Church. In this renunciation of the scholarly path, and even anything that resembles scholarly study, research, or preparation, I am stripped naked to the very core of my being before God…and in this place find pouring into my little heart, utterly denuded in faith, hope, and love, a wisdom far surpassing anything I could have grasped through the other path. And this wisdom is the very opposite of expertise or qualification: it is the light of God pouring freely through my very poverty and littleness, the nakedness of my heart surrendered to him in simple and childlike trust.

The important thing to recognize here is that *I have a path of healing marked out by God himself, fitting to the contours of my own heart as created by him, and according to the transformation that he desires to effect within me.* What is important here is not, therefore, "what if's" about all the different things that I could do, but interior silence to hear, and to receive with vigor and conviction, the specific word that God desires to speak within me, and to walk the path that he marks out for me "without looking back" (Lk 9:62). For in this way, guided by his loving hand and entering into the poverty of total surrender before him, I can find the bond of deepest intimacy cradling me, and the wellspring of deepest fruitfulness surging up within me.

Yes, and through all of this, I can come more and more home to resting in the innermost truth of my own self—a self liberated through this path of healing and yet being beyond it, gazed and loved into existence by God, and in him always held. Liberated by love, I can relate to God, and to others, from this place of my authentic self, no longer defined by abstract ideals nor by all the false "self-definitions" that I have tried to place upon myself. I can simply be, in other words, who I am, not defined by anything but his love for me. I can walk naked and secure in all the circumstances of my life, because, within them all and beyond them all, I walk alone with God like Adam and Eve did in the Garden of Eden before sin.

+ + +

Let us now shift a little to look more deeply and explicitly at the path of healing and integration in its true nature, not as a discarding of our nature but as its healing and harnessing.[*] This will hopefully help to flesh out more deeply, in a more "objective," philosophical kind of way, the implications that I have expressed more personally in the last reflection and the first part of this one.

As I have said, all of the inherent desires and capacities of my humanity, according to God's intentions, are meant to find liberation and healing according to the radiant truth of love. No desires or capacities, even those that don't find concrete expression in my specific life (such as sexual capacity or parenthood), are meant to be castrated or eliminated from my humanity, but channeled into the energy of love, into the gift of self, into the liberty of my personal "yes" to God and all that speaks of God.

Thus, true purity of heart, born of the integration of the human faculties in harmony with what is beautiful, good, and true, comes about, in other words, not by way of a negation of the value of things, but rather by way of their super-affirmation. Any true mastery of the disordered inclinations within us is not meant to bring about a suppression of our contact with value, but rather to make possible the authentic orientation and liberation of our whole being in the orbit of the objective value of each reality. John Paul is very clear on this when he describes the human process of "self-mastery," by which he does not mean the mere control of our humanity by the force of the will. Rather, he means a holistic process in which disordered expressions of fallen desires are curtailed, while, at the same time, the deeper contact of our heart with the objective value of the same reality to which we had a disordered response matures and is set free. This brings about, even though gradually, an integration of our whole being, in all of our spiritual and bodily faculties, in contact with the reality as it is in the plan of God. And this mastery, therefore, really means the liberation of

---

[*]The following comes from my book *At the Heart of the Gospel: The Love in Whom All Lines Converge*, a section of a much longer treatment of the themes touched on here.

true personal spontaneity in response to the call of the objective good, which resonates fully in the subject of the person and wells up within them as the freedom of the gift. As he says in regard to our relation to sexual desire and the spousal meaning of the human body:

> [T]emperance and continence do not mean—if one may put it this way—*being left hanging in the void; neither in the void of values nor in the void of the subject.* The ethos of redemption is realized in self-mastery, that is, in the continence of desires. In this behavior, the human heart remains bound to value, from which it would otherwise distance itself through its [disordered] desire, orienting itself toward mere concupiscence deprived of ethical value… On the ground of the ethos of redemption, an even deeper power and firmness confirms or restores *the union with this value* through an act of mastery. … Thus, the ethos of the redemption of the body is realized through self-dominion, through temperance of the "desires," when the human heart makes an alliance with this ethos, or rather *when it confirms this alliance through its own integral subjectivity:* when the person's deepest and yet most real possibilities and dispositions show themselves, when the deepest layers of his potentiality acquire a voice, layers that the concupiscence of the flesh would not allow to show themselves. (TOB 49:5-6).

By "self-mastery" John Paul means not merely a form of willed self-control, but rather a dimension of the entire path of integration between body and spirit, between the impulses of the body and the "voice" of our deepest potentialities and desires. Thus, a better term, which he uses elsewhere is "self-possession," and which I would even prefer to call simply "integration." We could say that all three terms work together to illuminate a single reality, to illustrate its depth and wholeness: *self-mastery* allows the mind and the will to again gain their proper directive role in the human faculties, and yet not by repressing the rest of our humanity, but by joining with it and listening to it in self-possession; and this *self-possession* brings together in harmony and unity what has been fractured by sin and concupiscence; in other words, it *integrates* the human person, and it does so in response to the call and the gift of reality coming to the person from the outside, to which the full subjective richness of the person responds.

For that is the goal of the possession of self: to be gathered together in one's whole psychosomatic constitution, such that, rather than being subjected to the "slavery to sin" in which one's freedom is hindered by the movements of concupiscence (sinful desire for pleasure and possession), one instead rediscovers the "inner freedom of the gift" by which one can live one's own being as a gift from God, and can also freely make a gift of oneself to and for others. The *Catechism of the Catholic Church* describes it this way:

> The "mastery" over the world that God offered man from the beginning was realized above all within man himself: *mastery of self*. The first man was unimpaired and ordered in his whole being because he was free from the triple concupiscence that subjugates

him to the pleasure of the senses, covetousness for earthly goods, and self-assertion, contrary to the dictates of reason. (CCC, 377)

Though this state of complete self-mastery, of complete integration, will only find consummation in heaven, God has made it possible to recapture it and to experience it already in this life, by the wondrous gift of the redeeming and recreating grace of his love given in Christ and the Holy Spirit. It is a gradual path, and one calling for deep docility to God's healing touch in the depth of the heart, and in all the stirrings of our subjective consciousness and relation with all that is, but it can truly lead to a purity that tastes again something of the purity of the beginning, and indeed the purity of consummation that awaits us at the end of time. This path is twofold, both the healing from disordered movements rooted in concupiscence, and also the maturation of the desire and capacity for what is authentically beautiful, good, and true in the eyes of God. By the curbing of the disordered movements of concupiscence (namely, by self-mastery), the person gradually becomes capable of discovering and experiencing the true *value* of reality which concupiscence had hidden from sight.

The path to integration, therefore, passes *both* by way of the *renunciation* of the way of concupiscence which leads to sin, and also by way of a *super-affirmation* of the very value that concupiscence had twisted: in this case, the value of the individual person in the body, and of the body itself in its spousal and sexual meaning. Indeed, the value itself is meant to be what carries our entire response, from beginning to end, even if the awareness of this value is frail and weak at first, and only grows more and more visible and tangible over time. But from beginning to end, the value (given by God himself) is what provides the gauge, the trajectory, and the destination of our self-mastery and its corresponding integration of our faculties in the unity of our heart and life.

Indeed, the goal of self-mastery is not a perpetual suspicion of the spontaneous movements of our hearts, or even our bodies—a kind of continual rein placed on our being as if it were nothing but a wild horse destined to cause harm if allowed to express itself. Rather, as our being is healed more and more in an authentic and affirming contact with the value, these very spontaneous movements become harmonized with reality, they become ordered, they become beautiful, good, and true. And this is so because they become joined with the deepest aspirations of our being, fashioned in the image and likeness of God, and thus open to the transfiguration of grace. In a word, they become subservient to, or perhaps better, joined with, the "voice of the heart," and speak along with the heart the word of love it was fashioned to speak. Let me quote some earlier words by which John Paul beautifully expresses this movement. He says that this self-mastery truly matures

> when the person's deepest and yet most real possibilities and dispositions show themselves, when the deepest layers of his potentiality acquire a voice, layers that the concupiscence of the flesh would not allow to show themselves. These layers cannot emerge when the human heart is fixed in permanent suspicion, as is the case in Freudian hermeneutics. They also cannot manifest themselves if the Manichaean "anti-value" is dominant in conscious-

ness [i.e. seeing the body and sex as innately bad or dangerous]. The ethos of redemption, by contrast, is based on a strict alliance with these layers. (TOB 49:6)

Yes, a true wholeness in responding to values does not come about by the castration of any parts of our being, but by their healing and their integration. Thus, this path cannot come to maturity if the movements of our humanity, from the lowest to the highest, are cast into a state of continual suspicion, but only if they are allowed to live, and, in living, to grow to wholeness in union with the deepest voice of our inner being and our most profound capacity for love and intimacy. This movement of integration on every level of our being is what John Paul refers to as an "alliance," which is a kind of bond of communion, of harmonious agreement, between all the facets of our being, unified in the innermost core of our subject "I," and all harnessed in the single freedom of the gift.

Thus the goal of self-mastery is not a rigid control of our every experience and desire by the mind and the will, and certainly not a "successful" elimination of the very value (e.g. of sexual value and capacity) from consciousness; it is, rather, the harmonization of all the levels of our being such that, when in contact with this value, a "deeper and more mature spontaneity" is born within us. As John Paul says:

> At the price of mastery over these impulses [of mere concupiscence], man reaches that *deeper and more mature spontaneity* with which his "heart," by mastering these impulses, rediscovers the spiritual beauty of the sign constituted by the human body in its masculinity and femininity. Inasmuch as this awareness becomes firm in consciousness as conviction and in the will as the orientation both of possible choices and of simple desires, the human heart comes to share, so to speak, in another spontaneity of which the "carnal man" knows nothing or very little. ... The words with which Christ draws the attention of his audience—then and today—to "concupiscence"...indicate the road toward a mature spontaneity of the human "heart" that does not suffocate its noble desires and aspirations, but on the contrary liberates and helps them. (TOB 48:5)

All the levels of our being—from the judgment of the mind, the choice of the will, and the movement of affectivity, to the stirring of the emotions and the very sensations and responses of the body—are meant to become integrated such that they give a spontaneously adequate and integrated response to the value that speaks its word to us. Each part of our being, each faculty, plays its particular role within the orbit of our consciousness, at the service of the freedom of our personhood, at the service of the freedom of the gift springing from our inner "I." And when this integration reaches a certain degree, one need no longer live in continual fear of falling into sin, but can be carried with lightheartedness, trust, and a spirit of confidence by the invitation of objective values, and respond to them with the full and unreserved gift of one's heart, mind, will, affectivity, emotion, and body—in other words, with the full and adequate response of one's entire "I."

DAY 18
RESTING IN THE DIVINE GAZE

God pursues. God elicits. God gives. He is the initiator of all things in his tender generosity, from the very existence of the universe at the beginning of time to the very beating of my heart in this moment. If God did not look upon me with love in this very instant, I would cease to be. Indeed, prayer is in large part simply a matter of letting myself be looked upon with love by God, or rather looking back upon him so that I may see him who sees me, and experience his gaze.

"The gospel has eyes—'the eyes I long for so,' John calls them—and the point comes on the journey where the bride meets those eyes which had been looking on: 'It seems to her that he is now always gazing on her.'" How beautiful, and yet how vulnerable! Do we not feel so exposed, even uncomfortable, whenever we are going about our day without thought, and then glance up and realize that someone is watching us with an intent gaze? Of course for a human being this may be a violation, but for God it cannot be otherwise, since for anything to exist is identical with it being looked upon with love by God. And this is especially true of each human person.

"It has been said that 'a person is enlightened,' not 'when they get an idea,' but 'when someone looks at them.' A person is enlightened when another loves them. The eyes are windows on to the heart; they search the person out and have power to elicit life." This is the essence of the experience of prayer, in all of its manifestations: the reality of being looked upon with love by God. And this look is not apathetic or impassive, not careless or haphazard; no, it is a look of intense presence, of self-communicating generosity, and of gentle, non-forcing, and yet ardent desire to draw near, to give oneself and to receive the other in a reciprocal gaze of love. Yes, the gaze of God not only delights, wishes, desires, and affirms. It does all this, but it also does more. Just as for God to speak is to do, and to look is to love, so for him to gaze is for him to transform, to bring radiance and beauty. Our very existence, our very beauty as a person, is the fruit of this sustained gaze of love. And yet there are certain gifts, a process of transformation, which can only occur when this gaze is freely accepted, when our eyes open to meet the eyes that always look upon us.

'A person is enlightened when someone looks at them.' Chaos is enlightened when God looks at it. The 'Bridegroom' casts his gaze across the face of the abyss and sprays life across it. That is John's amazing understanding of creation: the universe, each element in it, each event in it, and the web of those events held together—all thought, all friendship, all history—are given being by the eyes of Another, eyes 'communicating' being to the world. Such a creation is flamboyant in its beauty, as the Word of God, glancing kindly but wildly, 'scatters a thousand graces' and floods the cosmos with traces of who he is.

There is a marvelous sense here of God's creative act being, not just a primeval beginning, but a present event. The event is as gentle, in a sense as precarious, but also as loving as the gaze of one who cares.

There is a marvelous sense too that the universe has a character to it. John says that when the Father gazes, he gazes through his Son. The Son is his face, smiling upon the world. 'God saw that they were good,' which was to make them good by 'seeing them' in his Son. Creation has a Son-like color, a Son-like shape which the Son alone could fill.

That is John's real interest: the Son does undertake to fill us. His eyes not only hold us in being; they hold us in friendship, a friendship made possible when he meets us with human eyes. Humanity is enlightened when the Son becomes flesh, looks at us, and draws us out of ourselves, raises us up to himself. In this the whole cosmos is renewed.

> 'This he did when he became man, lifting man up in the beauty of God, and so lifting up all creatures in him... In this raising up in the Son's incarnation and in the glory of his resurrection according to the flesh, the Father gave creatures not just a partial beauty; we can say that he entirely clothed them in beauty and dignity.'[20]

Breathtaking... The Father gazing upon us in and through his Son, with the vibrant presence of the Spirit. This is prayer. And this is the reality that transforms us, and in us the whole creation, lifting us up to participate in the very inner life of God, made beautiful in him with his own beauty which his gaze bestows upon us. There is indeed a passage in John's writing in which he gets carried away by this encounter of gazes, this enraptured look of beauty that bestows beauty, in which he sings forth in a kind of rhythmic outpouring his delight in the beauty of Christ and Christ's delight in his beauty:

> Let us go forth to behold ourselves in your beauty,
>
> This means: Let us so act that by means of this loving activity we may attain to the vision of ourselves in your beauty in eternal life. That is: That I be so transformed in your beauty that we may be alike in beauty, and both behold ourselves in your beauty, possessing then your very beauty; this, in such a way that each looking at the other may see in the other their own beauty, since both are your beauty alone, I being absorbed in your own beauty; hence, I shall see you in your beauty, and you will see me in your beauty, and I shall see myself in you in your beauty, and you will see yourself in me in your beauty; that I may resemble you in your beauty, and you resemble me in your beauty, and my beauty be your beauty and your beauty be my beauty; wherefore I shall be you in your beauty, and you will be me in your beauty, because your very beauty will be my beauty; and thus we shall behold one another in your beauty.

This is the adoption of the children of God, who will indeed declare to God what the very Son said to the Eternal Father through St. John: *All my things are yours, and yours are mine* [Jn. 17:10]. He says this by essence, since he is the natural Son of God, and we say it by participation, since we are adopted children. He declared this not only for himself, the Head, but for his whole mystical body, the Church, which on the day of her triumph, when she sees God face to face, will participate in the very beauty of the Bridegroom. (*The Spiritual Canticle,* 36.4c-5)

But what does this mean for us, in addition to what has already been said? It is really a confirmation of all that has been said. Even when we ourselves cannot yet see, God sees all, and, in seeing, loves. He sees us in his beauty and his beauty in us, and invites us to so yield to his gaze of love that we may grow into his beauty, enter into his beauty, being seen as beautiful and being beautified in him, in the same process becoming capable of seeing God's beauty and loving him for it, rejoicing in his beauty as it is in itself, as it is, too, in us. Yes, in loving us God bestows existence, life, beauty, and, to the degree that we consent to his gaze and his work, he brings healing and transformation and the newness of life that will find consummation in heaven...the life that is his own in the mutual gaze of enraptured delight between Father, Son, and Holy Spirit!'[21]

---

*I have included a poem in the end notes that delves deeply into the mystery of the divine gaze, first as lived in the intimacy of the relationship of the Father and the Son, and also as manifested in God's relationship with creation and with each one of us individually.

DAY 19
TRANSFIGURING CONTEMPLATION

> *What does it mean to be alone with Jesus? It doesn't mean to sit alone with your own thoughts. ... It means that you know that He is close to you, that He loves you, that you are precious to Him, that He is in love with you. He has called you, and you belong to Him. If you know that...you will be able to face any failure, any humiliation, any suffering—if you realize Jesus's personal love for you and yours for Him. (Mother Teresa)*[22]

Though the experience and progress of prayer throughout life is unique for each one of us, such that there are as many expressions of prayer as there are persons, it is also true that we all share, not only in a single human nature, but in a single God. And if we are all destined to be wed to a single divine Bridegroom, then it stands to reason that in our experience of him—admitting the unique resonance of his personal word of love to each one of us and the infinite variety and richness of his own radiant life—we can find a common thread. Yes, and underneath this thread, in the midst of these manifestations, we can discern a single face, a single God who, by the very many ways in which he communicates himself to us, reveals to us *who* he is, the nature of his own life and love.

I would like in this reflection, therefore, to speak about the way in which the divine initiative, the divine gaze, of which I have spoken above, becomes *present and tangible* in the heart of prayer. Traditionally, this is called "infused contemplation" or "mystical contemplation," emphasizing that it is something that depends entirely on God's initiative and gift, and is not dependent upon human activity even though it seeks human acceptance. And such a distinction is wholly valid. For experience itself testifies to this distinction. There is a form of contemplation, of prayer, in which I myself am engaged through the exercise of my mind, my will, and my affections; this is usually called *meditation*. Here I think, feel, and choose based on my own natural capacities in relation to, for example, a text of the Bible which I am reading. I may even be stirred by what I am reading in a wholly natural emotional resonance. So too there is *vocal prayer* in which I speak with God, either words given by Scripture or the Church—such as the Psalms, the rosary, or the Liturgy of the Hours—or words spontaneously from my heart (and this too is meditation, since my mind must be present, otherwise I am just rattling off words!). These are the natural forms of contemplation, of prayer, as opposed to the specifically "divine initiative" that becomes manifest in infused contemplation.

But we should not take the distinction too far. For even in the midst of these "natural" forms of prayer in which I am active, even intangibly and beyond our recognition, God is always present and active, gazing, loving, and transforming. His grace is even more present to me in prayer than I am present to him. And if I am stirred to desire, or moved by beauty, or awakened to repentance, or granted an insight, this is due to God's grace, poured out through his Spirit, into the heart of my prayer. Thus *all* prayer is "infused" (from the Latin *infusum*, that which is poured in), since *the principal actor in prayer is always the Holy Spirit*. This is true from the very first moment I begin to pray as a child, to speak the words of prayers my parents taught me, or begin to speak to God the silent words of my heart. Nonetheless, as prayer grows, it undergoes a transformation, or rather, God begins little by little to manifest himself in ways more vivid and more unmediated than he has before.

Even on a natural level, as prayer matures, the activity of our human faculties becomes more and more *simple* and *unified*. It does so in all relationships, doesn't it? As we grow in intimacy with another person and in deep knowledge of them, there is less need for concerted effort to get to know them, less need for prolonged conversation to dialogue between ourselves. Little by little our relationship becomes more interior, more profound, more rooted in the wordless communion of hearts that say in simple presence and gaze more than any words can say. So too it is with God. As my heart becomes acquainted with being with him, abiding in his presence and in the light of his gaze, I am opened more and more to let this gaze take over my time of prayer and the experience of my heart. So too, as I come to know God more deeply with my reason and understanding, the more discursive knowledge reaches out toward, and makes way for, *the wordless intuition of the heart*.

But so far this is all rooted in the natural process of human growth, knowledge, and relationship, which applies also to our communion with God (for God always respects our nature and the integrity of our being which he has given to us). Yet this does not mean that God is tied down! Rather, he is, as we saw, supremely active. And he *wants* to make himself present in prayer ever more vigorously, according to the unique way of communicating himself that he desires for me, and the precious and unrepeatable romance that he desires to unfold between his heart and mine. And so he comes. He *always* comes. But as my heart is prepared by his hidden grace, this grace can little by little come out from hiding, it can begin to make itself known and felt in a new way. His gaze, his touch, his delight, his embrace, immediately present to me without mediation, can pour forth into my subjective experience, ravishing and transforming my heart. And this is precisely why he does this, and wishes to do it: because he wants to be in deepest possible intimacy with me and in the most vivid way possible, down to the very roots of my conscious experience and in the whole of my transfigured being!

Thus we come to the "transition" into a new form of prayer, which again can take innumerable different expressions according to the unique plan of God for each person. Here mediation through reading, reflection, words, images, or imagination is surpassed, and *God communicates himself to the human heart directly, spirit to spirit*. He communicates himself in a way that touches and moves our faculties directly, without any exterior mediation or traceable cause. He may illumine our mind with a kind of knowledge that cannot be explicated in concepts, but is a kind of "obscure clarity," like the presence of another felt in the darkness. Or he may stir our will into inflamed desire, drawing us out in longing for him or infusing vigor and resolve into us where before we were filled with fear and uncertainty. Or he may awaken affection directly, communicating to us what he desires to communicate in a way that directly touches the heart. Or last of all, in the most mature stages, he may touch and communicate in the innermost sanctuary of our being—the heart of our heart, the inner heart of the spirit—with the fullness of his own Being: a divine "touch" of God upon the human spirit. This latter is the most radiant and ravishing experience possible in this life, and the words the saints use to describe it are bursting with ardor glowing from this encounter.

There are innumerable ways, infinitely rich and varied, and yet profoundly harmonious, in which God makes himself present in our experience, giving himself to us with his delighting gaze, his transforming touch, his peace-bestowing embrace. Though it may not appear so to our fallen minds, the path into intimacy with God—the path of prayer—is a greater and richer adventure than anything else. Traveling to every single city in the entire world throughout all the centuries of humanity would not offer even a fraction of the depth and breadth of what God has in store for us in prayer, the profound beauty and expansive richness to be found in Christ. As John of the Cross expresses it:

> O woods and thickets,
> planted by the hand of my Beloved!
> O green meadow,
> coated, bright, with flowers,
> tell me, has he passed by you?
>
> Pouring out a thousand graces,
> he passed these groves in haste;
> and having looked at them,
> with his image alone,
> clothed them in beauty.
>
> Ah, who has the power to heal me?
> now wholly surrender yourself!
> Do not send me
> any more messengers,
> they cannot tell me what I must hear.
>
> All who are free
> tell me a thousand graceful things of you;
> all wound me more
> and leaving me dying
> of, ah, I-don't-know-what behind their stammering.
> ...
> My Beloved, the mountains,
> and lonely wooded valleys,
> strange islands,
> and resounding rivers,
> the whistle of love-stirring breezes,
>
> the tranquil night
> at the time of the rising dawn,
> silent music,
> sounding solitude,

the supper that refreshes, and deepens love.

(*The Spiritual Canticle,* 4-7, 14-15)

Here we see how the person seeking God turns to created things, to the visible beauty of nature and the cosmos, and finds his image and glimpses of his beauty in them. And the human heart longing for God questions them regarding their Maker; it questions nature, it questions other persons, it questions the very fruits of culture and human thought. But they all direct the heart further, to the Beloved himself, who surpasses all things while beckoning the love-struck heart to the "ah, I-don't-know-what" that she longs for, present within and behind the stammering of creatures. And, at last, upon finding the Beloved and experiencing his love, his presence, the heart cries out in amazement at the discovery of all beauty, all fullness, all richness, present in him. He is the intimacy and quiet of a lonely wooded valley, and the sense of adventure and newness of strange islands (remember this was the 16th century!), and the vigorous yet serene surging of a river, and a breeze that whistles as it penetrates to the deepest part of the ear of the heart. He is a tranquil and quiet night, space of prayer and of love, and the radiance of rising dawn penetrating the night with its glow; he is silent music, speaking more deeply than any words or sounds, and sounding solitude, a communication born most deeply in solitary togetherness; yes, he is the supper of intimacy in bread and wine, Body and Blood, that deepens and refreshes love.

Let us now turn back to what was being said before. I said that there is great variety and richness in prayer, not only between different persons but throughout the life of a single person. This is how rich God is in his mystery, and how full he desires our journey into his love to be. And yet, his love and truth being one, this does not therefore by any means indicate that we can say nothing about it. On the contrary, even if we too can only stammer, we can try to help point out a little of that blessed I-don't-know what, to stir our hearts to seek him and to walk the path of love he marks out for us.

So what are some traits that we can point out? It often happens that the transition into this a new and deeper form of prayer—the primacy of God's self-outpouring activity—leads a person habitually away from their previous practice of meditation, for example reading Scripture or other books during the time of prayer. They find that they cannot pray in the way they used to, and instead are invited to lean into the new form of non-conceptual and non-graspable *knowing* and *loving*, poured into them by God himself. At first almost unnoticeable, so subtle and hidden is it, this form of presence to God, of God's presence to us, grows both in depth and intensity (even to the experience of ecstasy as the loss of bodily consciousness in total immersion in God). In another person's life, or in different times of prayer, this new, infused form of knowing and loving may fill precisely *the act of reading* or the activity of *human thought*, permeated with prayer. For example, I may be praying the doxology of the Liturgy of the Hours or the rosary (the "Glory be to the Father..."), and may feel my heart inflamed with longing for the Trinity and with a deep sense of understanding—a knowledge of his Three-in-One mystery that surpasses mere concepts—without any particular effort on my part. It is like I am reaching through the veil of the words to touch the face of the Beloved, or like he is reaching out to touch me. This too is infused contemplation, living within the activity of the human faculties. Finally, infused contemplation may be experienced as incapacity, as darkness, as a painful longing for God who feels absent, as a stretching of the heart towards the One who, in his more deeply known greatness, feels further away. This too—as long as the darkness is not due to sin—is God's activity, his presence-under-the-form-of-absence, which is so very, so intimately close to the one whom he loves.

The important thing in all of this, as we will see below, is to continue to fix one's heart totally—in all of one's faculties—upon God as he is in his transcendent mystery, and to avoid the temptation to "catch" him and try to hold onto him, thus reducing him to one's size. His communication dilates the heart, giving it a taste of a form of knowing and loving that transcends mere natural human capacity—based as it is in faith, hope, and love—and so the heart should respond to him precisely in faith, hope, and love: by trusting him, desiring him, and surrendering to him, reaching out to belong to him who is ever close while also being infinitely transcendent. In other words, I should simply and humbly accept this gift of God, and respond to it with gratitude and with a spirit of poverty: with open hands and open heart to receive his love and to let myself flow back, unreservedly, in response.

DAY 20
FAITH, HOPE, AND LOVE:
THE LIVED TANGIBILITY OF LOVE

One of the reasons it is so helpful and important to contemplate the rich variety and depth of these experiences of God is precisely because they reveal *the nature of God himself* and also *the nature of his union with us through grace* in a particularly vivid way. Those persons in the Church who are granted extraordinary mystical graces are in fact only experiencing, in a way more explicitly "unfolded," what occurs for *all of us* under the veil of faith, hope, and love. Mystical experience in its purest, in other words, is just faith, hope, and love transmuted into experience; it is the life of God in us making itself felt, tangible, audible in the reservoir of our human faculties, even in our bodily senses. But as these faculties of themselves cannot contain the fullness of God, cannot yet "feel" or "grasp" God as he is in himself—as his Triune mystery as Father, Son, and Holy Spirit—it is harmful to cling to these experiences as if they were God. Rather, we can truly "possess" God, truly enter into union with him, not through possession but through *poverty*. We are united to him not by the degree or depth of what we experience but by *the degree and depth of our faith, hope, and love, by the depth to which we surrender ourselves to him in trusting desire and in the openness to receive.**

Yes, we can learn so much about God through reflecting on the vivid experiences of those who have come to know him most deeply. And through this we can come to recognize and discern his own activity in our lives more deeply as well. Even if we do not experience all of the forms of experience, of infused contemplation, described in the previous reflection, the inner *essence* of this union with God is true for all of us. For God is *always* pressing in to communicate himself to us, to permeate our whole be-

---

*This also helps to clarify the proper place of "charismatic" experiences and gifts. The depth of union with God cannot be gauged by the presence or absence of particular charismatic gifts. The primary work of the Holy Spirit is not to give specific manifestations—visions, locutions, tongues, prophecy, etc.—but rather to *increase faith, hope, and love in the heart*, and to draw the heart into deeper communion with God and others. His presence is gauged by the objective fruits of love, of fidelity to the Gospel, and by the serenity and peace that always characterize his guiding hand leading persons along the path God marks out for them in love. Indeed, these charismatic experiences, as well as certain extraordinary traits of the mystical life (such as visions, hearing voices), are treated very cautiously by John of the Cross; he encourages us to perpetually "pass beyond, pass beyond," into the nakedness of love sustained by faith and hope. For only faith can unite us to God, not these experiences. There are certain profound mystical experiences, however, which are so pure, so interior, that they are not capable of holding us back, occurring as they do in the inmost interior of the soul through faith and purity: they are "divine touches" of God's substance in the substance of our soul, unmediated by any form or image. These are a taste of eternal life, and cannot be doubted or confused. Clearly, the point here as everywhere is not to reject experience, but to keep our gaze upon the essence of reality, the essence of the union wrought between God and ourselves through love, so that the heart is always free to fly to the Beloved and to be all his alone, in everything and beyond everything.

ing and our entire life with his loving presence. And thus any openness on our part to welcome him is *always* and *immediately* filled by him, even if this grace filling us only over time transforms us, renews us, and becomes in some way (and in whatever way God wishes) tangible and experiential. Plus, the essence of this union of love is never reducible to experience. For God, even in his union with us, always surpasses what we can experience or understand of him, surpasses the innate capacity of our mind, will, and affectivity, of our imagination and emotions, of our bodily sensation.

This much is clear. But I would like to focus now, in a prolonged gaze, on the reality that *does* touch God in himself, and makes us capable of receiving and being united to him in all the fullness of his mystery. I already referred to it above, and, even earlier (on day 12), expounded its meaning. Faith, hope, and love—as God's own gift of his life poured into us—alone make us *capax Dei*, capable of sharing directly and fully in the life of God, "as it is in itself," in the fullness of the Trinity's unmediated mystery. These three dispositions and acts of the person are grafted into our natural faculties and elevate them above themselves, expanding them wide open to God's own Trinitarian presence and gift. Or perhaps more accurately: from the very first moment of our existence, even on the natural level, the human person is *capax Dei,* a capacity for God; and yet this openness to receive and enter into communion with God is an openness to *grace,* an openness to a fulfillment that cannot come about on the basis of nature or natural experience alone, but only on the basis of an elevation and transfiguration of our nature that comes about by God's own gift in us, manifest as faith, hope, and love.

Thus we can see why, at the end of these reflections on the experience of God, it is important—and actually profoundly liberating and life-giving—to return to the simple truth of love and intimacy. The depth of my intimacy with God does not depend on the depth of my experience of him, but on the depth of my fidelity to his grace transfiguring me, even in darkness, even in suffering, even in obscurity. It is something personal, not merely experiential. It is something lived in the vibrant space of mutual self-communication between him and me, something far surpassing any attempts to classify, grasp, control, or drag down into the realm of my ordinary experience—even as it gradually seeks to pervade and transfigure precisely this experience. In other words, surpassing all experience, it nonetheless draws me to live more and more "in the realm of God," bathed in the light of his own vision upon me and upon the world. Thus, even if I can't grasp the "feeling" of God, or pin him down in intellectual concepts, or lay hold of him with my will, I can stand in the light of his gaze and gaze upon him in faith, hope, and love, a gaze that also allows me to see all things in the perspective of his own radiance.

Yes, even as union with God surpasses experience—like the light of the sun itself which we cannot directly see, but in which we see all things—it nonetheless illuminates all experience, our relation with ourselves, with others, and with the whole of reality, springing from our primal relation with God himself. This is the "light in which we see light," (cf. Ps 36:9), the light that cannot be directly seen or felt in this life but which, transfiguring us in itself, enables us to see all things anew. This, as I said on day 12, is the "light of glory" that will fill us in heaven, in face-to-face vision of God, made already present within the shadows of our fallen world under the form of faith, of hope, and of love. And in this way union with God, even in experiences of darkness, pain, and loss, is *real*. It is real union because it is real mutual belonging. It is real union because it is shared vision born of trusting faith, desiring hope, and surrendering love. It is the poverty of acceptance, the nakedness of vulnerability, and the unity born of total gift.

+ + +

In the light of what I said above, we come right to the true *essence* of union with God: it lies in the personal contact of faith, hope, and love (of trust, desire, and surrender come to full flower). Thus the depth of union with God, and therefore the maturity of Christian life, lies in *the maturity of the theological virtues of faith, hope, and love*, and, through them, in the wholeness of the entire person, who is healed and transformed by grace. Faith. Hope. Love. This, as I said, is the single-yet-threefold reality of God's own life present and active within us, grafting itself into our faculties of intellect, affectivity, and will, and illumining also all of our other faculties. Everything in the life of relationship with God is suspended upon these dispositions, on this reality; everything occurs within it and on the basis of it. Indeed, even the experience of God of which I have spoken—infused contemplation, mystical experience—is ultimately nothing but the *making-tangible* of what always occurs in the sanctuary of human heart and life as *faith, hope, and love*. And so too, in ordinary Christian experience, union with God in his ineffable and intangible mystery (through faith, hope, and love) transforms *all* experience, such that my every thought, feeling, choice, and emotion is pervaded by the mysterious and intangible light of God's love and his presence.

But what does this mean concretely? Focusing so much on the so-called "virtues" seems to be a large and painful step backwards from contemplative wonder at the awesome initiative of the God who seeks us out, ever pressing upon us to communicate himself and his love, and to transform us in this love. But in fact I do not intend to turn away from God to look again at ourselves. Rather, the point is the exact opposite. Faith, hope, and love—as the gift of God's own life elevating us to become "partakers of the divine nature" (2 Pet 1:4)—are the only proximate and proportionate means to union with God, a union not merely of feeling but of the very *substance of our being* and of the very *existential truth of our life*.

Re-read that sentence and let it sink in. God wants to be united to us to the very innermost core of our being, our inmost heart, the sanctuary of our spirit. He wants to be that close, that totally given, that intimately united: to the deepest depth of the innermost interior. And he wants us, in turn, to let ourselves be drawn into his own deepest depth and innermost interior, which is the very heart of the reciprocal relationship of the Father, Son, and Holy Spirit, the very space where the Father and the Son breathe forth to one another the single Spirit whom they share, in an ecstasy of eternal delight!

So too he wants to totally penetrate and pervade every moment of our life, the whole of our existence, such that it becomes *a ceaseless act of intimacy with the Trinity*. And this occurs not by us perpetually experiencing

God in some tangible or mystical way. Rather, it occurs through the *ceaseless exercise of faith, hope, and love*, of reciprocal presence to God in responsiveness to his abiding presence to us, and in the manifestation of this in every thought, feeling, desire, choice, and act. This union is truly *total*, total in the only way that, within the limits of this fallen world, it can be total. The experience of God in this life cannot be kept at a permanent level of clarity and intensity. But faith, hope, and love can always abide, undimmed and unobstructed, in every moment and circumstance.

And this vibrant living of relationship with God in this life—even amid all the obscurity and shadows inherent in creation's limitations—prepares us for the eternal destiny that awaits us, when the experience of God *shall* be both *permanent* and *complete*, the complete permeation of our whole consciousness and experience by the radiant beauty and tangible embrace of the Father, Son, and Holy Spirit!

DAY 21
SHARING IN THE LIFE OF GOD:
THE CONVERGENCE OF ALL IN HIM

The title to the previous reflection was perhaps a little puzzling. What do I mean by that unusual phrase: "the lived tangibility of love"? If it is true that no extraordinary or mystical experiences constitute substantial union with God (though they can be part of our transformation and profound influences in our life), does this mean there is *no* experiential element of our relationship with God? As I have made clear, this is not the case at all. That would in fact be the opposite of the truth. It is not that God asks us to renounce all experience in order to enter into an "annihilation of experience," such that we enter into nothingness.* Nothingness in itself is nothingness; it does not bring us closer to God. It is more akin to hell, or to non-existence, than it is to union with God. What God asks is that we allow all experience to be purified, healed, and renewed by him, such that our whole existence becomes *radical openness to his presence and his gift*. He desires us to open wide our hands and hearts to welcome him as he comes to us, in all his ever-surpassing mystery. And in this way, too, we are gradually enabled to *discern his presence through all experience and beyond all experience*.

And in order for this to happen, a deep purification of my being is called for, one that reaches to the very roots of my human capacities and desires, and transfigures them from within. Eased off from its clinging to created realities or particular experiences (from "pet ideas," from bitter regrets, from anxiety about the future, from self-watching, from manipulation of circumstances, etc.), my heart gradually opens wide, "in poverty and nakedness of spirit," to receive the gift of God himself.

This is very significant, and I don't want it to be passed over. The call of love is not inviting us to embrace a life of superhuman negation of every desire or experience; rather the call is for us to let go of every fear-induced, possessive, or obsessive tendency that keeps us bound and shackled from experiencing the "abundance of life" to the full, in the poverty, purity, and vulnerability with which God desires. Thus every disordered clinging is like a cord that keeps a bird from taking flight into the embrace of the "Divine Eagle" (a phrase of little Thérèse), and numbs the heart from receiving and responding to his gift in the vibrant fullness and intimate depth for which it was made. It doesn't matter if the cord is a giant chain of metal or a thin thread of string; whenever a heart willingly clings to it against God's intentions, it is enough to hinder flight. For poverty is complete or it is not

---

*Certain phrases in John of the Cross's "vocabulary" incline in this direction, and while it is admittedly *not* what he means, it makes authentically understanding and applying his teaching rather difficult. I am trying in these reflections, therefore, to understand the purification of the human person through the theological virtues in a more *holistic* and therefore *incarnate* and *sacramental* way, one more appropriate to the full richness of humanity that God has given us, without thereby lessening the radicality and depth of purification and its subsequent union, to which John so ardently desired to lead us.

poverty. Openness is unconditional or it is not openness. Vulnerability is total or it is not vulnerability. God does not condition his gifts to us, the outpouring of his very self, and so our response cannot be conditioned either, but rather total and unreserved, in the radicality of love.

Let us take some time, therefore, to ask the important question: what is the particular thing that I am clinging to as my source of security, my "crutch," which is keeping my heart from flying freely in the liberty of love? God is not asking me to renounce so many other things which it would not be difficult to renounce, and which would only make me feel better about myself. Rather, where is the place where God's call is actually seeking to free my heart from its shackles, to liberate me from my compulsions, fears, and possessiveness. It is here that he wants to love me; it is here that he is already looking upon me with love. And it is here that he wants to free me into the joy of total surrender and the security of pure intimacy with him—naked heart joined to naked heart in the vulnerability of gift.

In all of this, in other words, what God desires is the freedom of love. All the words of invitation to detachment, purity, and poverty in the Bible are ordered towards this one thing: the freedom to love. Yes, the freedom to be loved and to love, and to live the full richness of relationship without the narrowness of sin or blindness of wounds that threaten to obstruct it. What is called for, therefore, is a pure heart, a poor heart—a "Beatitudes heart"—that receives God and gives itself to him without clinging or possessing. In love, not in use. In reciprocal belonging, not in "having." In the nakedness of vulnerability, not in a power struggle. In true intimacy born of mutual seeing, a seeing of utter exposure and total surrender, and not in the analyzing and controlling gaze.

This gift of God that comes to me in my poverty and vulnerability can never be comprehended within my limitations, pinned down by me, but it can and does *fill me* to overflowing, bathing me in light and peace that remain not in being possessed, but in possessing us in poverty, with open hands and heart. For it is in fact by a Person, by three Persons eternally united in love, that I am possessed; and faith, hope, and love consists precisely in giving over possession of myself to him, a surrender which is first born and sustained by my prior acceptance of the marvelous gift of his very self to me.

+ + +

The great call for us, then, is simply to *live the truth in love,* and to let experience take its rightful place as the echo of truth, of life, in our consciousness. And at the heart of this experience, at the core of the life of union with God, is *living in the very manner in which God himself eternally lives,* and in which Jesus Christ lived on this earth. This is how faith, hope, and love are the very *pathway* back into the purity of intimacy, into that beautiful reality that we lost in original and personal sin, but which God desires to restore. And not only are they the pathway, but they are also the *dispositions* and *acts* that make up the very stuff of a healthy relationship with God, with oneself, with others, and with the whole of creation.

Here, indeed, we can recognize a beautiful truth. In his Theology of the Body, John Paul II speaks about three "original experiences" that characterize the existence of the human person as the "image of God." These experiences, transparently and purely lived before sin, nonetheless also persist after sin, even if they are now fractured and wounded. They are: 1) original solitude, 2) original nakedness, and 3) original unity. Let me share some words here from another book, *At the Heart of the Gospel: The Love in Whom All Lines Converge*, in order to allow us a deep and intimate "feel" of these experiences and their significance.

These three experiences together, John Paul II says, remain at the root of every human experience: "Indeed, they are so interwoven with the ordinary things of life that we generally do not realize their extraordinary character" (TOB 11:1). Yes, solitude, nakedness, and communion (he ordinarily uses the phrase unity)—or, phrased differently, interiority, vulnerability, and intimacy—are the threefold expression of what is deepest about humanity, and indeed about God himself in the innermost depths of his Trinitarian life.*

Solitude expresses the incomparability of the person, willed for his or her own sake and uniquely beautiful and valuable like no other person that has ever been or ever will be. It expresses their interior mystery of subjective consciousness, in which the person is not a mere "something," but a "someone." It expresses that they are an "I" who is called to enter into loving relationship, into the joy of encounter with another "I," with a "you," and above all with the eternal "Thou" and "We" of the Trinity. In this intimate relationship the person, already given to themselves by God's gratuitous gift—a gift of their very personal identity already given and never revoked—experiences the full flowering of their identity precisely in the joy of communion.

And this communion, this blossoming of identity within the embrace of intimacy, passes by way of vulnerability. It is expressed and communicated through *nakedness*. Nakedness is precisely the gift of the person in their pristine and unchanged truth, in the simple and unaltered state of their original being as created by God—wounded by sin, yes, but also touched and permeated by the ever-present grace of Redemption. Bodily nakedness expresses this beautifully, in that, unclothed, the person is no longer hidden or "protected" by exterior clothing, and has nothing, absolutely nothing, to veil themselves from the gaze of another. And this is precisely why nakedness is vulnerable, because it is to lay oneself open to the alternative of being either loved or unloved, reverenced or abused, cherished or hurt. And shame is our response to such an uncertainty, and, insofar as this shame is not absorbed within the security of love, it is a healthy experience that expresses our desire to reverence and protect our-

---

*These three experiences emerge before us out of the Biblical text itself, in the richly significant words of the first three chapters of Genesis. What appears on the surface to be a simple text reveals profound depths of meaning, both for our objective understanding of God's creative plan as well as of the nuances and meanings inherent in human subjectivity as it stands before God and before the whole of creation. "It is not good that the man should be alone..." (Gen 2:18). "The man and his wife were both naked, and were not ashamed..." (Gen 2:25). "Therefore a man leaves his father and mother and clings to [unites with] his wife, and they become one flesh..."(Gen 2:24). These three experience permeate every human experience in such depth and richness that we will never cease plumbing their profundity and the way in which they image the very beauty of the life of God himself.

selves from the eyes or touch of another who does not have the capacity to reciprocate the gift of our own vulnerability with the gift of their vulnerability. Nonetheless, when nakedness (whether literal physical nakedness or the nakedness of the person in other ways) is seen and reverenced in authentic love, a profound communication is established, a profound encounter that brings about a deep communion. (See TOB 62:3.)

When the vulnerable gift of my being encounters the reciprocal gift of another person, communion is born. And this is true whether it occurs in the encounter of bodily nakedness or in the multiform other expressions of "nakedness" that reveal the person in and through the body; for even a simple glance of the eyes, or a word, or a gesture, can communicate the deep mystery of the heart to another person and unveil the vulnerability of my own person before them. Here we see precisely how the body retains its spousal/unitive meaning in all circumstances, retains its nature as a gift-oriented-towards-communion.

Here solitude is expressed and given through nakedness, interiority is made visible and given through vulnerability; and whenever two solitudes encounter and reverence one another in their nakedness, this brings about the deepest joy and the true fulfillment of human existence: unity, communion, intimacy. It brings about the *communio personarum*. Here the solitude of each person is not dissolved, harmed, or constricted, or even threatened, but rather enriched and deepened, expanded, as it enters into a profound union with the solitude of the other person . Here "I" and "you" are joined and come to *live with and in one another*, retaining our distinctness and yet also becoming one, becoming "we" in the communion of shared vulnerability. And here is the highest expression of the "image of God" (Gen 1:27) within humanity, in the union of human persons in the likeness of the Persons of the Trinity.*

I would like to note, in addition to the above words on the original experiences, how it is not often recognized that John Paul received this profound insight into our primordial experience, not merely from a deep analysis of the first three chapters of Genesis, but also through the mediation of John of the Cross. John is, in a way, the primal exponent of a spirituality of *restoring* the "original experiences," of returning anew to God's original gift of solitude, nakedness, and unity.

For he defines the path to union with God precisely as the 1) *return to our inmost solitude*, to the inner heart of the inmost spirit, and 2) the *opening out of this heart in vulnerability before God*, so as to receive and reciprocate his gift totally, and thus 3) to *experience the unity of complete mutual belonging, an intimacy with God that is both fully filial and totally nuptial*. Thus when John of the Cross talks about a mature love for God being manifest in "poverty and nakedness of spirit," as opposed to any particular experiences, insights, or possessions, he is not so much talking about austerity as he is talking about *a filial and bridal disposition*. He is talking about the vulnerability of love, the nakedness to welcome the other as he comes to me, and to surrender myself unreservedly to him in return.

Indeed, we can go one step further. This intimacy with God, while fulfilling the filial and nuptial meanings inscribed in our humanity, also bursts

---

*Here ends the excerpt.

beyond the limits of these images, these archetypes. For God, while being the origin of parenthood and filiation, while being the origin of the nuptial or spousal relation, also transcends these in his infinite mystery. They stretch out to him; they impel our hearts towards him; they truly reveal dimensions of our relationship with him, and his with us. But at the heart of the heart, at the inmost core of communion with God, we realize that our communion with God is simply a participation in his own *Trinitarian intimacy*. In other words, it is a direct sharing in the way of living and loving proper to God himself. This is the super-eminent fullness towards which all relationships point, yet which surpasses them all in depth, totality, and closeness of belonging. Our union with God, thus, is a sharing in the ever circulating love, in the affirming gaze and cherishing tenderness, between the Father, Son, and Holy Spirit, from which we were created in the beginning, which we are granted to live even now in this life, and which shall be our abiding destiny and everlasting happiness for all eternity.

WEEK IV

The Night:
Bathed in His Healing Light

DAY 22
A LOOK AT SPIRITUAL DARKNESS

I would like to begin a series of reflections, now, on the reality of spiritual darkness or night, which I hope will prove illuminating and fruitful for all of us. Darkness is a reality that many of us struggle to understand, and certainly do not desire, and yet it also seems to be a trait that doggedly marks our experience of life and prayer. Indeed, all persons feel it in innumerable ways, even those who do not pray, even those who do not acknowledge God. In this reflection, I want to give a kind of "experiential" reflection on spiritual darkness, to bring out into the open what we are dealing with. In the following reflections I am going to go back to the "beginning," in order to unfold this reality in a more holistic manner, hopefully to dispel our fear and to give confidence and security in God's tender love, in the outpouring of his light, in all that this life bears for us, even in the darkest places.

There are two different kinds of darkness, distinct, even though in experience they flow into one another. (In following reflections I try to make this clear by distinguishing *seven* different causes or forms of darkness.) There is 1) the darkness of the human heart, making itself felt in the vulnerable space of prayer and the pursuit of God; this is the darkness of our own wounds, our own "lies," and all the burden of guilt and shame that we carry within us, drawn out into the open by the illumining and atoning fire of divine love. This only needs to be felt, acknowledged, and surrendered to the loving gaze of God, who will take it to himself and heal and purify it by his own tender touch, even if such a process occurs gradually, and indeed imperceptibly, over time. On the other hand, 2) there is the divine darkness, which is really no darkness at all but the brilliant light of the Trinity too radiant for us to comprehend. It is the darkness of the ineffable mystery that communicates itself to us in a way that our minds and hearts are not accustomed to experiencing, and thus is experienced as darkness. It is, as John of the Cross says, a "mystical inflow of God into the soul." It is dark because it is intangible, spiritual, not reducible to reason, feeling, or will. But it is real, and becomes ever more real as it grows within us.

How can we tell the difference between one and another? How can we tell a darkness which arises from our own wounds, lukewarmness, or struggle to approach God in prayer, from a darkness which is induced by his proximity, by the blinding closeness of his light? It is not all-important, nor always possible, to classify our experience in this way. For the two are actually joined together, except in certain forms of experience in which the theme of darkness is not the purification of the praying heart, but rather solidarity with the darkness of the world—mystical co-experience in the Body of Christ—and thus is not connected with particular wounds or places of growth in this heart, but in a joint prayer-experience with others, and with Christ himself who bore the darkness of the world on the Cross, in order to bathe it in divine light in the undying glory of the Resurrection.

But there *is* a question that a person finds important in the experience of darkness. What is important is the question of *fidelity*. Am I being faithful to God in this experience? This is the really important question. And one of the most painful things—and for those who really thirst for God, the undoubtedly most painful thing—is precisely that persons in the divine darkness fear precisely their own infidelity, and, aware as they are of the depths of their sinfulness and their human frailty, cannot simply rest with the consolation given to them by others. They need a direct word of God; nothing else can be enough for them. For they see and experience the desperate poverty that is human existence without God; they feel the depths of the human need for God's presence, guidance, and grace. They are like a gaping hole that only God can fill.

Here we can come to offer some answer to the difference between a darkness born of human infidelity and that born of divine love. The first closes the heart in upon itself, and begins to dull the conscience and the heart, to cause a person to ease up in their thirst for God; the second is a denuding—a stripping naked—of the desire for God, and thus its purification, giving birth to desire more deeply than before, even as more humbly. And yet even this is not adequate, for in the moment when a person is in the transition from one mode of prayer to another—turning the page to deeper intimacy with God by means of purifying darkness—one may well feel numb, unable to desire, to think, or to turn to God in any way. But deep down the desire for God is burning strongly, indeed even more strongly than it has before. And as long as one clings to God in faith, hope, and love—in trust, desire, and surrender—however frail these may seem, and however one's prayer may seem to be destroyed, eventually the divine darkness will become more and more apparent, and the numbness of human incapacity will lessen and give way.

Thus the darkness becomes something rich and full, and yet in a fullness that is the very opposite of possession, of security born of control, or even of normal human comprehension. It is rather the unspoken and unspeakable awareness of *presence*, a presence that is intimately personal, so very close, and yet infinitely mysterious, the most breathtaking grandeur and beauty. And as we know, in a truly intimate encounter with another person, the only adequate response is *open-handed poverty that simply reverences without grasping, receiving the gift and letting oneself flow back in the response of surrender*. This darkness of encounter is true encounter, even in all its unexpected mysteriousness. And even if it appears first as dryness, as aching emptiness, it gradually unveils itself as the closeness of the One so deeply desired. This presence is *felt* in the darkness, somewhat like one feels a beloved person's presence in a pitch-black room. It is not just like hearing their breathing, or them shifting in their seat; no, it is like feeling their very *being*, the radiance of their personhood, in proximity to one's own.

It is a great paradox that God brings us to life by means of death. It is part of the unspeakable wisdom of divine love, active within the world, that the loss of all possession leads to the possession of all things, and the experience of being hemmed in by limitation opens the way to expansive freedom, and the apparent frustration of the aspirations of our hearts for nearness to the Beloved opens the way precisely to closer union with him.

There is an interior law of poverty that marks out the way to union with God.

This is not to give an absolute value to negation—for every "no" finds its meaning only for the sake of a deeper "yes"—but it is to recognize that the path to God is not bound to the limits of our earthly comprehension, control, or experience. Rather, God in his infinite majesty surpasses all of these things, even while being made present to us at the heart of our humanity; and by being present to us he draws us on, ever deeper into his ineffable mystery. Here we possess him in non-possession, in being possessed by him in poverty; here we find freedom in the powerlessness of total surrender; here we experience him, tangibly and truly, in the intangible overflow of mystical contemplation that touches us in the heart-of-hearts, in the inner sanctuary of the soul.

DAY 23
THE RESONANCE OF THE NIGHT

In his book *The Impact of God: Soundings from St John of the Cross*, Father Iain Matthew beautifully presents the teaching of the mystical doctor in a way that is both affirmative and applicable to all of us, taking John's more esoteric and one-sided language and unfolding it within the sphere of holistic human experience and the wider teaching of the Church. It is not my intention in this book to explain the teaching of John of the Cross; rather, I am seeking to stand before the "great mystery" of God's love for the Church, for all of humanity, and for each human person—and to try to unfold something of the rich nature of nuptial intimacy that he desires to have with each one of us. Seeking to contemplate this breathtakingly beautiful reality as directly and as deeply as I can, from here I hope to express for you a "word" that will prove fruitful in your own relationship with God, helping you to be touched by his thirst for you, ravished by his beauty, and stirred to ardent thirst for him in return (wherever you may be along the trajectory of the life of faith).

But the "night," of which John of the Cross spoke so eloquently, and whose insight is one of the specific graces given by God to the Church through him, is a reality in the life of *each one of us*, even if its specific contours are always unique. Let us therefore seek to understand what is meant by this reality, how it appears *in the eyes of God*, and in a *gaze of nuptial love from a bridal heart*. Often the "dark night" of which John spoke has become a dry theological category that refers to a "stage" of the prayer experience, one marked by aridity, dryness, interior suffering, a sense of the loss of the presence of God, and a profound feeling of guilt, and yet also of a deep-seated longing for the One who feels so far away. This, of course, is also true, indeed deeply and profoundly true. But we must understand of what we are speaking, so that the full richness of the symbolism and meaning of the night may be grasped, felt, and lived. I don't know if I could do much better than Iain Matthew here, so let me simply quote him:

> John had a fascination for night-time which seems to have run in the family. His brother Francisco would sometimes be found outside in the fields late at night, lying beneath the starlit Castilian sky, arms outstretched in the form of a cross. So, long after dark, the friars would come across John outside near the trees praying, or he would be leaning at his window looking into the dark. It seems that he and his own were close enough to nature to let the natural world speak.
> This is the first aspect of John's discovery: the symbolic quality of 'night,' a symbol which speaks before we ever try to decode it. If John's primary word is his poetry [as opposed to his prose], and his poems revolve around symbols, it is appropriate to soak in the symbol in its own right. ... Our first step is, then, to let 'night' speak. Abstracting from any knowledge we may have of John's teaching, it is worth letting the resonances which night-time has

for us surface.

Some words may come to mind: darkness, solitude, fear, the unknown, immobility, stillness, rest, peace, silence, sleep, dreams, moonlight, adventure, owls, stars, refreshment, friendship, romance, perception.

If these are the resonances, then such is the journey of faith. The 'night' symbol suggests, not organized gloom ('I think it's the dark night' [i.e. the "prayer stage of dryness"]), but that which comes upon us and is mystery, beauty, terror and new birth.[23]

It is indeed profoundly helpful to dig deep into our hearts to find the resonances that the reality of night has to offer to us—not only our own personal memories or preferences, but the inner "word" that night speaks to us as a reality designed and willed by God as a part of his creation. To use the terminology of Gerard Manley Hopkins, what is the "inscape" of night? What is the bounded infinity contained within it by which it points our contemplative gaze straight to the heart of God?

John had a profound experience of the convergence of the spiritual night and the visible night, as they came together for him in his escape from prison in Toledo (he was held captive by his old religious brothers for spurious reasons, as they resisted the new reform movement he had helped to begin). During his captivity he had undergone a profound spiritual experience of inner purification, birthing an experience of resurrection and intimacy that was then paralleled in his escape and his return to the communion of his own religious family. For John, therefore, from the heart of his own experience, the symbol of the "night" "is able to carry humanity's pain," but it is also able

> to hold the 'spiritual resurrection' which Toledo had brought him, the 'night that has unified...' The poem echoes closely the 'Exsultet' song which the Church sings on Easter night, where the paschal candle pierces the darkness as a sign of the rising Christ. The Exsultet heralds Easter night as the union of heaven and earth, the night of escape from Egypt, the 'most blessed of all nights,' chosen by God 'to see Christ rising from the dead!' Night carries all the weight of the Lord's passover.

This is the resonance of the symbol for John. Night signifies that which comes upon us and takes us out of our own control; it announces that as the place of resurrection. A God who heals in darkness—this is John's word of hope in a destabilized world.

It is important not to let the vitality of the symbol die as...we enter into this healing darkness.

After John escaped from prison, he reached the sisters in Beas. It is said that, seeing him still fragile and subdued, they tried to raise his spirits with a song. They chose a predictable little piece about love and suffering. John motioned to them to stop. He was trembling, weeping. He stayed there, clinging to a support, silent, for an hour. They allow him to do that, even though no one understood it—how could they?

John's works rest on that silence. His symbols suffer if we try too hard to decode them. 'Mysteries' then become mere 'things'—

if too specific, then exclusive, and thus irrelevant to the many. This can happen with two phrases characteristic of John: 'contemplation' and 'dark night.' Both speak of development in a person's relationship with God, particularly in prayer. They can sound abstruse. But in fact they convey mystery. They are really names for letting God be who he is.

Contemplation: prayer where I am no longer a tourist, where sense has shifted to spirit—where plenty of insights and aspirations have given way to a less picturesque, more total form of togetherness with God.

'Contemplation is nothing but a hidden, peaceful, loving inflow of God. If it is given room, it will inflame the spirit with love.' (*Night* 1.10.6)

If God *is* a self-bestowing God, then his gift is liable to engage us. If he is active, then, in prayer, provided we stay around, he is liable to act.

Night: if God is beyond us, his approach is also liable to leave us feeling out of our depth. When the divine engages us more deeply, our minds and feelings will have less to take hold of, accustomed as they are to controlling the agenda, to meeting God on their terms and in portions they can handle. A deeper gift will *feel* like no gift at all. His 'loving inflow' is 'hidden;' it is night.

If anything is felt it will probably be our own selfishness and narrowness (wood crackling and twisting as the fire makes progress). When God approaches as who he is, I am liable to feel myself for what I am. As a physical sign of growth is growing pains, so a sign of God's gift is the pain of being widened. This is the blessedness of night, that God, who wants to give, undertakes to make space in us for his gift.[24]

There are only two things that I would presently like to add to this. The first is that John's descriptions of prayer-experience, while admittedly needing to be expanded in their import to include the innumerable different ways in which human hearts progress to intimacy with the Trinity—since there are as many experiences of God as there are persons!—nonetheless reveal a trend underneath *all* experience of God. They reveal an authentic reality that, regardless of the differences in the subjective resonance of each person, is truly *objective*, a solid fact of substantial being and of subjective experience. Thus "contemplation," as the inflow of God into the soul in a particularly vivid way, is a true *act* of God, a real initiative of his that occurs within human hearts on the path of prayer. And the subjective experience of this act, therefore, despite all of its variety, is gauged against this objective action.

Even, therefore, if it is experienced as darkness or absence or deep awareness of my sinfulness, it is objectively the illumining light of God pouring into my soul to *efficaciously* heal and transform it. And so too, this light will gradually lead to a *subjective* resurrection as well, as the purification of my heart leads me to experience this inflow of God, this ray of divine light, more and more as it truly is: as pure joy of mutual presence and the bliss of intimacy.*

The second thing I would like to add is that this reality of purifying night, while most properly referring to an inner experience of God's inflow into our being, healing us from within by his own direct, unmediated touch, also encompasses all the circumstances and experiences of life—daily struggles, loss, illness, and any number of other things—which God's loving providence also uses to renew us deep within, and to complement and deepen his interior and unmediated work in prayer. The two ways of God's work—interior and exterior—are never in fact wholly divorced, but flow into one another in a single dance, a single movement arranged by him "to work all things for good" for us and for all of his children. God truly desires us so much, desires our wholeness, happiness, and intimacy with him so deeply, that he never ceases to work in all things to bring his loving dream for us to fruition.

---

*This is not to exclude the possibility of the "night" returning as a painful state, as spiritual darkness and a resonance of inner suffering—not now so much as a personal purification but as a form of compassionate solidarity with humanity and with the Heart of Christ himself, who bore the darkness of the world on the Cross in order to illumine it with the undimmed light of the Trinity, present already in the Passion and manifest fully in the Resurrection. We can see this "night of compassion," indeed in the vocation and experience of both Thérèse of Lisieux and of Teresa of Calcutta.

DAY 24
THE REDEEMING NIGHT OF LOVE: DARKNESS TRANSFORMED INTO LIGHT

As I tried to show in the Introduction, my early experience of God was an in-breaking of divine light and love, the revelation of the Trinity's intimacy, which both ravished me with its beauty and wounded me with longing for the fullness. And yet it would be wrong to imagine that this was some spectacular or mystical experience (God has lovingly chosen to refrain from giving me any explicit, extraordinary mystical graces throughout my life, and for good reason). It was rather a humble burning in the heart, an ever clearer and deeper illumination of mind and will, of affectivity and emotions, spreading out to irradiate my whole existence.

And this mystery was to grow in me throughout the years, to the point that I found living in this world very difficult, since I felt that, before the God whom I knew, the whole universe was as nothing. As John of the Cross says, "Outside of God, all things are narrow." (Though *in* him, of course, all things can be discovered as bearers of his own immense mystery.) This mystery, over the years, was also to grow in other ways as well, ways different but also essential to my living according to the truth of my being before God: in humility and the acceptance of the concrete beauty of bodiliness, in the cherishing of our whole lived humanity in this world, and in the acceptance of limitation and "ordinariness" in the life of holiness. It was to lead, indeed, to the desire to live in the most hidden and humble way that I could, in the littleness that is the locus of God's activity in human hearts in this world. For God is able to give his grace not to the great but to the little, and plants his Cross in the humble soil of humanity in order to sanctify and make new.

From the beginning, I also experienced that aspect of the life of faith of which I have been speaking, that is, the reality of spiritual *darkness,* what John of the Cross calls "night." I do believe that many hearts in our contemporary world often bear, for shorter or longer periods of time, an inner darkness in prayer and their relationship with God—as well as in the circumstances of life which seem to be crumbling apart rather than coming together in harmony, or opening up to a mystery of poverty rather than offering immediate security. And they often do not know how to make sense of this, to come to grips with what it means and how to live in the midst of it and through it. Have I done something wrong? Is this a sign of my infidelity? Why does God treat me like this if he loves me? But the truth is often the very opposite: the darkness is a sign of truth, of a heart that is authentically seeking God. For to journey out of the security of one's self-made "home," and to step forth into the night-time and to look up upon the stars, blazing with glory from God and "shining with joy for him who made them" (cf. Bar 3:34-35), how can this be anything but also an experience of darkness, even as it is a mystery of light?

In truth, darkness is a richly multifaceted reality, the facets of which I hope to elucidate a little below. We will then be able to see and cherish God's intimate activity even where at first he may appear absent. Is this not a desperate need of our contemporary world? Scarred as we are by atheistic humanism and the trauma of totalitarian oppression, of diabolical genocide, and now by materialistic secularism which grips our culture—by a hedonism that squeezes out the divine darkness and imposes a dull darkness of narrow self-absorption—we need to learn anew to listen to God's silence, to see the light of God's darkness, to long for him who surpasses all human control and comprehension, and yet ardently desires to communicate himself in the fullness of his ineffable mystery, person to person, heart to heart.

+ + +

I have already tried to convey the resonance—with the aid of Iain Matthew—of the reality of *night*. What, however, is the resonance of *darkness*. Is it different? Darkness, clearly, is an aspect of the night, the dimension which is perhaps central, since darkness is what distinguishes night from day and is the cause of all the other differences, such as the cessation of the day's activity, restfulness, stillness, the gentle song of owl or dove, the visibility of the stars and moon. "Darkness" is a scriptural term, taken from the rich symbolic and incarnate language of the Bible. As the Evangelist John writes at the beginning of his Gospel: "The light shines in the darkness, and the darkness has not overcome it" (Jn 1:5). In this he expresses the dichotomy between light and darkness, portraying darkness as something evil that stands over and against the light. It can neither comprehend nor overcome the light. Here we reach back to the beginning of the Bible when God "separated light from darkness" (Gen 1:4), and thus day and night. Here darkness represents the absence of God's creative activity, on the one hand, the void or emptiness awaiting the outpouring of his gift—as in the darkness that precedes creation. And yet darkness also has a positive trait as well: it is a complement to the light, in fact an aspect of the light insofar as it is manifest in an imperfect creation yet on its way to definitive consummation.

Thus our eyes are directed forward to the conclusion and fulfillment of history of which Revelation speaks, in which "the city has no need of sun or moon to shine upon it, for the glory of God is its light, and its lamp is the Lamb" (Rev 21:23). Here the darkness shall be no more, and all will be undimmed light. This signifies first the dispelling of all the forces in this world which resist the light, all the negative effects of sin, all the slightest traces of lingering evil, of lies, of distortion. But is also signifies, not the dispelling of mystery—like the mystery of the night sky dancing with trillions of stars precisely because of its darkness—but precisely the *making radiant of mystery*, an abundance of light that fulfills the very essence of darkness as super-abundance, as face-to-face vision of God and the joy of his unmediated embrace. This, after all, is what the positive dimension of darkness longs for throughout this life, what it draws our hearts to seek and desire: the fullness of light.

Yes, and, finally, we can contemplate this shining of light in the darkness, this darkness impelling towards the light, at the heart of history. We can come to understand the interplay of light and darkness, and the victory of light over darkness, from the vantage point of Redemption: in the Incarnation, Passion, and Resurrection of the God-Man, the Incarnate Son of God. The birth of Jesus took place at night, in the stillness of a sacred darkness in which the true Light was born into this world. The Last Supper, the gift of the Eucharist, occurred on a sacred night in a holy meal, and Christ's agony in the garden occurred at night, under the stars, and illumined by a full moon. So too, even in the middle of the day, as he hung upon the Cross bearing the spiritual darkness of all of us in order to illumine it with the full noonday light of God's redeeming love, the sky was darkened. The darkest night invaded day as all the forces of evil came forth, all the recesses of darkness buried in this world and in human hearts, in order to converge upon the compassionate Heart of Jesus Christ. And yet precisely here Jesus opened himself wide to accept them, to suffer through them, not in order to be overcome, to let the light be eclipsed by darkness, but the very opposite. The Light shined in the darkness, and the darkness could not overcome it. Rather, the Sun of Justice rose right at the heart of the Passion of Christ, right at the heart of our history converging in this moment which gathers all moments together and redeems them. So too, what occurred already in the Passion was revealed fully in the Resurrection, with the Father raising Christ from the dead—in the silence of the Easter night and the dawning of the definitive Day. Here all of time and space, from beginning to end, from height to depth, intersects in the Heart of Jesus Christ, who has come as Light into the world and made all things new.

DAY 25
THE DARKNESS CRYING OUT FOR THE LIGHT

Any reflection on darkness must be, in truth, a reflection on the light that conquers darkness. Indeed, in the Catholic spiritual tradition (as we saw with John of the Cross) the experience and concept of darkness is not purely negative, but bears a certain richness of meaning in itself. What, then, are some different sources of darkness in human experience? By trying to understand the rich "panorama" of darkness, we can begin to discern the lines of God's loving providence at work in us and for us at every moment. I will share seven sources or expressions of darkness here (some of which, obviously, are mutually exclusive), and try to give some understanding into them in hopes of offering a lantern in the night.

The first four, which I will cover rather quickly, are *negative* forms of darkness in the sense of the darkness that resists the light, that cannot comprehend the light, or that is the absence of the light. The fifth is the transition from darkness to light, or darkness shown, by the light, to be what it is. The sixth refers to the darkness in the more positive sense, as a movement into mystery and as a form of surpassing presence, the brilliant light of the Trinity poured out in love. The seventh is darkness as a particular manifestation of the light of compassion, by which a heart possessed by the light carries, with Christ and in Christ, the first of the four forms of darkness through compassion solidarity, and in the perspective of redemptive love and the joy of resurrection.

1. The first and most obvious form of darkness, to which John the Evangelist refers in his Gospel, is the darkness of sin and its accompanying wounding effects on our humanity and our experience. Sin is darkness in the most vivid sense: as resistance of the light, turning away from the light, rejection of the light. As John Paul II himself said, "original sin" seeks "the abolishment of fatherhood," the fatherhood of the heavenly Father whose primordial light has birthed the whole universe and bestowed all good things upon his children as pure gift. Sin is thus a deception—as we saw, a "missing of the mark"—in that it turns from the radiant beauty in which the heart finds rest, and instead clings to darkness, deceived into thinking that it is light, or indeed preferring it to light for its apparent desirability.

And all sin, as a choice and an act of darkness, also begets darkness within the human consciousness: dulling the mind, weakening the will, numbing and distorting the affectivity, and leading the conscience away from the light of truth. Thus the sinner bears darkness within himself, hidden away in his broken nature, a darkness that Christ has come precisely to bathe in the light, to reveal, and thus to dispel, replacing it with the light of goodness, beauty, and truth. As John the Evangelist wrote: "For every one who does evil hates the light, and does not come to the light, lest his deeds should be exposed. But he who does what is true comes to the light, that it may be clearly seen that his deeds have been wrought in God" (Jn 3:20-21). And Saint Paul explains:

> Once you were darkness, but now you are light in the Lord;

walk as children of light (for the fruit of light is found in all that is good and right and true), and try to learn what is pleasing to the Lord. Take no part in the unfruitful works of darkness, but instead expose them. For it is a shame even to speak of the things that they do in secret; but when anything is exposed by the light it becomes visible, for anything that becomes visible is light. Therefore it is said, "Awake, O sleeper, and arise from the dead, and Christ shall give you light." (Eph 5:8-14)

2. The second darkness I want to recognize is that of personal wounds (as opposed to disordered tendencies springing directly from sinful choices and dispositions). From the traumas and misconceptions of life, a lack of love, a lack of true education, an experience misunderstood or falsely interiorized, we begin to believe lies or falsehoods about ourselves, about God, and about the universe. And these lies keep us bound to darkness, and hinder our openness and responsiveness to the light, to what is true, good, and beautiful. Obviously, this form of darkness, while not identical with that of sin and the guilt of sin, is nonetheless related to it: a result of the fragmentation, obscurity, and brokenness that are present in this world due to original and personal sin, both ours and that of others. And here too Christ has come to meet us, as redeeming Compassion, to bring forth our darkness of fear, shame, anxiety, or confusion into the open and to show us the radiant truth that replaces it, that indeed heals our hearts to the deepest wellsprings of mind, will, and affectivity, illumining our conscience and our inmost subjectivity with the light of grace and truth. But we are getting a bit ahead of ourselves.

3. Next is the darkness of human suffering, whether physical, moral, or emotional, born of the experience of a fractured world or, most gravely of all, of the *mysterium iniquitatis*, the mystery of evil, present in this world. This is a darkness, somewhat like the previous one, that is not necessarily tied up in any way with personal responsibility on the part of the one who suffers—as the sufferer may be entirely innocent—but nonetheless also calls forth a deeper faith and surrender in the darkness, and a more radical openness to the light. Here we begin to shade over also into what was referred to previously as the "night" in its more positive meaning. Not all suffering, of course, is night in the positive, healing sense, but it *can* be, it is invited to be so. Or rather, whatever suffering we may be confronted with, whether our own inner woundedness surging to the surface, or circumstances and events that cause us pain, or physical illness or loss of persons whom we love, we are invited to discern within it the loving and provident presence of the Trinity, who is working for good and who is calling us closer to himself through the night.

Suffering as an experience has come into this world due to sin, and thus afflicts all who live in this world, even those who are not directly responsible for a given evil. We are all inheritors of original sin and the blindness that it has effected in our human nature, and we have all sinned personally as well, at least in some way making this inheritance our own (as I said in point 1); we also bear various wounds because of our nurturing and experiences in such a world (point 2); and we all suffer, too, even through external circumstances, even if they are not due in any way to either our personal sin or to the wounds that we bear (this point). This suffering, a cosmic suffering, a communal suffering, a simple human suffering, is in fact one of the mysterious remedies for the first two forms of darkness. Of course, suffering in itself is an evil, or the "voice" of an evil: the cry of the heart that something is missing, that the light of God is missing, or that this universe and our own hearts are not as they are meant to be, not yet whole and entire. And yet in this way the experience of suffering also becomes a path, a path of redemption, a path towards wholeness. Christ has come to meet us precisely here, in our suffering, and, by suffering with us he enables us to suffer with him—to suffer with him along the path of maturation in love, in which pain is transfused into gift and surrender, and thus gradually gives way to the joy of communion, intimacy, and mutual belonging.

4. In the face of the beautiful redemptive work of Christ in suffering of which I have just spoken, the spirits of evil—the fallen angels that rebelled against God in the beginning and who tempted Adam and Eve to sin at the beginning of world history—are envious. They want to obstruct the path to God, and to do all that they can to keep us from experiencing and resting in God's love, and of loving God as he deserves. They seek to hinder love, to obscure clarity born of the light, and to fracture intimacy, both the intimacy of human hearts with God and the intimacy of human hearts among themselves. This fourth form of darkness, thus is caused by the presence and activity of the evil spirits, the demons. Indeed, the direct oppression or proximate presence of the evil spirits begets darkness and affliction in the human heart and faculties. Even before they are acknowledged, they are *felt*.* Our hearts, created good by God and always remaining good in our inmost essence, interiorly recoil from the presence of sheer evil that the demons have become. Thus the evil spirits come with an obscuring cloud of darkness, with a narrowing affliction, with an off-putting oppression, which we should learn to recognize, to resist, and to transcend by immediate flight into the sheltering light of God's embrace and the vision of his love.

Indeed, even if the evil spirits are capable of causing a particularly agonizing form of spiritual pain, an anguish of spirit, they also hold *no power* over the human spirit. As Teresa of Avila said, she feared a lukewarm nun more than she did the entire legions of evil spirits. This is because they cannot harm us directly against our will; they can only seek to influence, to obscure, and to taunt. Yes, and this affliction can be a terrible trial. But it is a

---

*For a more thorough treatment of the traits of the presence of the evil spirits, I would recommend Saint Ignatius of Loyola's Rules for the Discernment of Spirits. A good treatment of them can be found in the two books by Fr. Timothy Gallagher. Let me simply say here that their goal is always to *blind*, to obscure and fragment and distract from the essential, from the heart of God's relationship with us and his will for us. This is true even when they come disguised as "an angel of light," in false consolation; they cannot give *real* consolation, the consolation God gives, the consolation born of truth. Rather, if one discerns deeply enough, one can discover that what on the surface appears as consolation is but another form of desolation, of darkness: it creates a fog, a fracturing away from the heart of life into an obscure and unrealistic ideal built on false reasonings, a mere parody of consolation by flattering our pride or tempting us to grasp for a false security. True consolation always leads into deeper poverty and vulnerability, the deception of the evil spirits always leads into greater possession and control.

trial held by God's love, and one allowed by God in his all-surpassing and ever-present wisdom, in which he never departs from us but is continually at work overcoming all the darkness present in us and in the world, so as to bring to fulfillment his plan of perfect intimacy between himself and us.

In all of these forms of darkness, whatever they may be, the essential response is one and the same: *to flee into the embrace of God and surrender totally to his embrace.* The best response, whether confronted with my own disordered tendencies or the shame of my sins, whether encountering suffering or trial, or the *mysterium iniquitatis*, is to simply turn to God: to *make an act of faith, hope, and love,* of trust, desire, and surrender, by which I place myself anew in the embrace and gaze of the One who loves me, and open my being to his healing and consoling light. In this way, indeed, all darkness can already become a space of redeeming grace, since through it God becomes particularly present, as healer and redeemer, to us where we need him the most.[*]

I would just encourage you, before we begin to focus more on the redeeming light pouring out into and through the night, to discern the presence of God's light in your own darkness as manifested in these four forms I have just examined. For his light, in the end, is everything. Let us surrender to it without reserve, with a childlike "yes" of total trust and surrender, and a spousal receptivity, virginal and whole, to welcome his touch and his activity, which makes all things new and carries them to their consummation in perfect intimacy.

---

[*]In this respect, I love the expression of Fr. Francis Mary, CFR: to be a "childlike warrior." It is to wage all of our battles like a child, not by relying on our own supposed strength or expertise, but to follow the two most fundamental pieces of advice given to children: 1) "Don't talk to strangers;" and 2) "Whenever you are in trouble, run to your parents." In a real way, this summarizes the whole spiritual battle, does it not? To learn to ignore the voices of strangers, the voices of the evil spirits—of the world, the flesh, and the devil—not even to dialogue with them...and to run and jump into the arms of our Father with carefree abandonment and trust. In fact, Jesus gives us the same advice: "He who enters by the door is the shepherd of the sheep. To him the gatekeeper opens; the sheep hear his voice, and he calls his own sheep by name and leads them out. When he has brought out all his own, he goes before them, and the sheep follow him, for they know his voice. A stranger they will not follow, but they will flee from him, for they do not know the voice of strangers" (Jn 10:2-5).

DAY 26
THE RADIANCE OF THE DIVINE OUTPOURING

Upon a night, in darkness,
with ardent longing, in love itself inflamed,
—ah, most blessed adventure!—
I departed unnoticed,
my house now having come completely to rest.

In the darkness, and secure,
by the secret ladder, in disguise concealéd
—ah, most blessed adventure!—
in the darkness and the concealment,
my house now having come completely to rest.

On that most blessed night,
in secret, for here no one saw or beheld me,
nor did I something behold,
without other light or guide
except that which, within my heart, burned so brightly.

It is this that guided me
more certainly than the light of midday itself,
to the place where awaited me
the One whom I knew so well,
the place where no one else, no one but he, appeared.

Oh, night that has guided me!
Oh, night more kindly than the moment of sunrise!
Oh, night that has united
the Lover with beloved,
beloved in her Lover totally transformed!

Upon my flowering breast,
which I guarded, in its entirety, for him alone,
he reclined, gently sleeping,
and I, giving all to him,
as the breeze, through the cedars, was also giving.

The breeze blowing from the turret,
while the hair of his head I softly parted,
with its serene hand touching
on my neck, it wounded me,
and all of my senses, it then suspended.

Myself, surrendered, forgotten,
I then reclined my face upon my Beloved,
all things ceasing, myself leaving,
in leaving all of my cares
forgotten, lost among the fields of lilies.

 (*The Dark Night,* John of the Cross,

translated directly from the Spanish)

Let us pick up where we left off in our examination of the different causes of the experience of darkness, as the reality that stands over and against the light, either as resisting it or, when positive, as complementing and enhancing it.

5. We have come to the transition point from the negative forms of darkness to the positive darkness, in other words, darkness not as a mere lack or even a rejection of the light, but darkness as a stretching out for the light, or even as an abundance of light too brilliant for us to take in within the limitations of this life. Thus we come, also, to the more specific and spiritual meaning of "night" in the mystical tradition of the Church. The first one to note here, therefore, is the darkness felt when our own wounds and sins are bathed in the light of God's infinite mystery. In such a light, even the smallest and most hidden forms of darkness and resistance are brought into the open and seen for what they are. In a word, when God's redeeming light pours out into us in ever increasing measure, the first four forms of darkness already mentioned are revealed for what they are. They come out into the open, as dust particles in a room, at first invisible, become visible when light shines in through an open window.

Indeed, this experience of darkness is a direct result, necessary in this life but eventually to pass away as our being is transformed by grace, of the brilliance of the divine light that pours into us from God. Here is fulfilled in our own personal experience what occurred in the redeeming Passion and Resurrection of Christ: "The light shines in the darkness, and the darkness has not overcome it;" yes, in fact, the darkness itself is illumined, healed, and gives way to light, until no darkness remains and all is transfigured in light. This is the specific meaning of the "dark nights" of which John of the Cross writes, this transfiguration that occurs through God's light shining into our darkness, unto the fullness of the light of spiritual marriage, of union with God in complete personal transformation. He refers, indeed, to particular experiences in prayer that come about through God's own initiative, in which he "takes in hand" our own process of healing and transformation. By his own divine inflow into our soul he begins to purify us, to heal us, and to renew us—in a majestically direct way, in which his substantial being touches our substantial being with nothing between them (and thus also beyond our direct conscious experience, even if we feel the "overflow" of this activity in our faculties).

John likens this to the process by which a log of wood is "transformed into flame." At first the fire, applied directly to the wood, dries it out, brings out all its imperfections, and blackens it, but this is only so that the wood may at last be completely united with, joined to, the radiance, warmth, and beauty of the fire. Of course the image isn't perfect, since God's love, as divine fire, does not destroy anything good, true, or beautiful—anything authentic—about the humanity that he has given us. Rather, his divine fire joins together with us in making us most fully human even as it makes us most fully participators in his own divine life. Here wood and fire are joined together in a single song and dance, flesh and spirit are united in a single gift of love and communion of breathtaking intimacy.

6. Most importantly, we come now to the "divine darkness" of God's presence and mystery, which is in fact pure and radiant Light. It is in the perspective of God's mystery—his all-surpassing Beauty that attracts and draws the human heart—that darkness is a trait of the life of prayer for every person, regardless of the unique contours of our particular experience of prayer. Just as the rich and radiant beauty of the earth is surrounded by galaxies of darkness (a darkness, however, pervaded by celestial light), so too the visible beauty of our daily lives, and the incarnate radiance of the essence of each created reality that we encounter, is held within the atmosphere of the divine. This divine presence at the ground of all created things, being spiritual, is intangible for us, ungraspable by any possessive hand; but this does not mean that it is far away. Indeed it is more intimately close than anything else can be, since all being exists only because is participates in his Being, and all is beautiful only because is partakes of his Beauty.

This presence of God, the immortal and holy One-in-Three and Three-in-One, the Trinity, is pure light, sheer and undimmed goodness. "God is light, and in him is no darkness at all" (1 Jn 1:5). The term darkness here, therefore, is used analogously, and not in a literal sense. God is pure Light, but this light appears to us as darkness because it exceeds our capacity for comprehension, and thus invites to be received and experienced in a way that is so far beyond our normal mode of experiencing. In order that the light may be experienced as light, therefore, and not as darkness, a process of transformation must occur within us, such that we are conformed to the light that communicates itself to us. Then are the words of the Psalmist proved true: "In your light we see light" (cf. Ps 36:9). Yes, by entering into God's Light, we see his Light; we see all things, too, in their authentic radiance bathed within this original light in which all things "live, move, and have their being" (cf. Acts 17:28).

This divine light, manifest as darkness, gradually, through the mystery in which we participate in faith, hope, and love, manifests itself as it is, and is experienced as it is: as light. Thus we come to the specific experience of contemplation, of infused prayer as God's direct self-communication of himself to us: the divine inflow into our being. God alone can make his love directly felt. No other creature can do this. We experience the love of other persons, even those closest to us, through their words, gestures, and actions. It is mediated through the incarnate relation of persons in our bodiliness, such that we access the spirit through the flesh, the heart through the sacramentality of the body and of life. This too is also (and even more) true in our relationship with God, who communicates himself through everything visible, audible, and tangible—through all of our senses—and bestows grace upon us through incarnate means, whether our own bodies or through the Sacraments of the Church, particularly the Eucharist. We experience his love through these means, in a real and authentic way, touching him under the veil, or through the medium, of created reality. And this contact is real, not fake, not inauthentic, not imaginary.

And yet in and through these means, we are in contact with God precisely through the mystery of faith, hope, and love, which, as I said, is God's own life present within us. By this disposition and act of trust, desire, and surrender we receive God through all things, and all things in God, such that a ceaseless communication of life and love is established between God and ourselves. This is the living heartbeat of the entire Christian life, the heartbeat of prayer, in the mutual self-giving of persons and their deepening intimacy. But it is also true that, in the midst of this richness of sacramental and incarnate relationship—and without in any way neglecting it or lessening its importance—God also communicates himself to us *beyond any incarnate mediation, in the inmost sanctuary of our spirit.* This is the meaning of infused contemplation, of the divine light that is experienced as darkness (since it has no created form or image or sensation). It is the direct touch of God's spirit upon our spirit, of his heart against our heart, in a substance-to-substance union of love. This is the deepest meaning of the reality of nakedness, with nothing mediating between Lover and beloved. It is God's kiss upon our inmost being.

But at the same time this kiss, welling up from within, also seeks to be impressed upon our whole bodily existence, every atom of our body, and all of our faculties and experiences. Here is a rich interrelationship of love between God and myself, in my inner spirit as well as in my whole incarnate being. Here is a rich interplay of light and darkness, of the darkness of the spiritual mystery impressing itself upon the created light of the body, and of the light of the spirit radiating forth through the capacity of the body. Both flow into one another and enrich one another, the intangible and the tangible, the spiritual and the bodily, the sacramental and the mystical, the light of insight and the darkness of reaching out beyond into the ever-deeper Beauty of the Three who surpass us even while being intimately close. Thus it is not helpful to distinguish these dimensions of the life of faith and love too much from one another; they live together, and they are meant to become ever more intimately united. After all, at the end of time, when we participate eternally in the Resurrection of Christ, our very bodies will experience the outpouring love of the Trinity, joined to our spirit which is united to him, such that our whole being, inseparably body-and-spirit, is nuptially joined to him who has joined himself to us. Here all will be contemplation, all will be fully bodily even as it is fully spirit, permeated through and through with the spiritual light of God that dispels all darkness and transfigures all things in itself that, in him, they too are pure light.

DAY 27
LEARNING TO PRAY ANEW

For I know well the spring that flows and runs,
although it is night.
That eternal spring is hidden,
for I know well where it has its rise,
although it is night.
I do not know its origin, nor has it one,
but I know that every origin has come from it,
although it is night.
I know that nothing else is so beautiful,
and that the heavens and the earth drink there,
although it is night.
I know well that it is bottomless
and no one is able to cross it,
although it is night.
Its clarity is never darkened,
and I know that every light has come from it,
although it is night.
I know that its streams are so brimming
they water the lands of hell, the heavens, and earth,
although it is night.
I know well the stream that flows from this spring
is mighty in compass and power,
although it is night.
I know the stream proceeding from these two,
that neither of them in fact precedes it,
although it is night.
This eternal spring is hidden
in this living bread for our life's sake,
although it is night.
It is here calling out to creatures;
and they satisfy their thirst, although in darkness,
because it is night.
This living spring that I long for,
I see in this bread of life,
although it is night.
(Poem of Saint John of the Cross, "Song of the Soul that Rejoices in Knowing God through Faith")

Before moving to the seventh form or cause of darkness, let us pause to reflect more on the so-called "dark night" as a transition to a deeper form of prayer and relationship with God...as the ever deeper entrance into the radiant darkness of his divine mystery, which is pure light. In the movement through this dark night, it may feel like I am re-learning anew, for the first time, how to pray. Such an experience, especially for someone who has devoted his or her life to prayer and has prayed for many years, is a deeply confusing and indeed disturbing one. But it is a fruitful transition, one in which the words of Saint Paul become felt in a deeper and more vivid way:

"Likewise the Spirit helps us in our weakness; for we do not know how to pray as we ought, but the Spirit himself intercedes for us with sighs too deep for words. And he who searches the hearts of men knows what is the mind of the Spirit, because the Spirit intercedes for the saints according to the will of God" (Rom 8:26-27).

Yes, for here, in someone with a desperate desire for prayer, prayer seems impossible. How can I even begin to open myself to the gaze of God anew, since for so long I have felt nothing but his absence, and even now cannot even begin to raise my mind or heart to him? How can I speak with him and listen to his voice, when the whole universe seems mute, and I cannot rest in the savor of his love, in the light of his truth, in the sweetness of his presence, for even a moment? In circumstances like this, sometimes prayer looks very much like non-prayer; and sometimes prayer in the formal sense is not even possible. One can only desire and stumble forward along the path, trying door after door, hoping that eventually one will open.

But God is at work in all of this. The Holy Spirit himself is praying in the deepest recesses of the anguished heart, sending forth an inaudible cry not only on behalf of this one individual, but on behalf of all humanity. And one will gradually learn, if faithful to the flame of desire for prayer that God has placed in the heart, to pray anew in a different way, on another level: in the inner sanctuary of the heart, where God dwells.

Allow me to use an example to illustrate this process. There is an anime series entitled *Your Lie in April*, which I desire to use as an example of this process. It is about a young man named Kousei Arima, a piano prodigy who was described as the "human metronome" due to the incredible mastery with which he performed on the piano, following exactly, to the letter, perfectly on beat, the composer's instructions. Because of this he won every competition, and was on his way to fame before even entering his teenage years. However, his mother, who was his primary piano teacher and herself had been a pianist earlier in life, contracted a terminal illness. And as her days dwindled she began to treat Kousei with harshness and abuse, both emotional and physical, afraid as she was that he would not live up to her expectations. After her death, and understandably so, Kousei ceased to play the piano. This is because he *lost the ability to hear his own music*. No matter how hard he tried, he simply could not hear the keys that he himself was hitting. This plunged him into years of darkness, a kind of musical "dark night." The piano prodigy disappeared from the scene, and his ascetically-trained success fell into nothingness.

He has resolved to never play the piano again—because of the deep trauma buried in his heart, his intermingled, confused love and hatred for his mother, his desire to both please her and reject her expectations. And yet it is precisely in this "dead" place that he meets another woman, a young woman whose beauty immediately strikes his heart more than anything else ever has. Through love, it is like a new world dawns upon him, a world of life, and playfulness, and joy. This young woman, Kaori, is like a whirlwind of energy and passion that sweeps Kousei up into its movement. And she is also passionate about classical music, and plays the violin. Eventually, she convinces him to accompany her in a contest—an experience that unseals deep things buried within him, and teaches him a profound lesson about the nature of reality itself. He discovers another face behind music, another heart beating within it: it is a face of love and tenderness, and a heart of vigorous trust, desire, and surrender.

After this, Kousei eventually regains the courage to begin playing piano again. But he can only do so because he learns a *new*, a *different* way of playing than he had ever experienced before. Previously, he understood playing as a *strict obedience* to the notes and markings on the page, a kind of legalistic portrayal of the letter of the music. He learned this because this was the best way to win competitions, to be accepted; it was a way of playing that was not vulnerable, but "successful." It was all skill without heart. But when he encounters Kaori, he cannot restrain his admiration, his love for her and what he encounters in her: true beauty and true freedom. She plays with the heart, and from the very heart of the music. She reaches out to touch the spirit of the composer, to touch the very meaning of the music in its inner essence, and through this also to speak the deep song of her own heart.

I will not spoil the way the story progresses and ends. However, let me just emphasize that Kousei's path of piano playing is conditioned wholly upon his ability *to let go of his own control*, to cease to try to play the way he used to hear (since he can no longer hear, and never regains this); rather, he must learn *to play directly from the heart without listening to his own playing.*

In this way, his music becomes tremendously moving, so heartfelt that it reverberates throughout the auditorium, to embed itself deeply in the hearts of his listeners. For music is a language, a language beyond words. It is akin to a prayer. And Kousei must learn to pray, to pray in self-forgetfulness and total surrender, in order, paradoxically, to express his true and authentic self, to speak the "word" of his inmost heart. And even more, through this deepest word of his heart, he is able to express the word of God himself, the beauty, goodness, and truth that God has implanted in music, and in his own being, to be spoken to the world.

This is deeply illuminating for our topic now, is it not? To lose my ability to pray may well be the most important thing that can happen to me. For by this path alone can I learn to pray anew, in a way beyond my own innate capacity, by the gift of God himself. By losing the word of my heart, and even the word of God, I am hollowed out, emptied, and stirred anew to desire, so that I may receive it anew from his hands. And in receiving it, I cannot, nor desire, to "lay hold of it" as if it were my possession, for fear of losing it again. Rather, I can live and experience prayer to the degree that I let go of myself, surrendering myself to it, letting go of everything I am, my own foresight and control and even my own "righteousness based on the law" (cf. Rom 3:21-22; 10:1-9). In this way I can let the Spirit of Love breathe forth within me, and, in his breath to sing his song through me, thus, also, harmonizing the song of my own heart with his, in the praise of God and for the salvation of all.

DAY 28
THE NIGHT OF COMPASSION

7. Finally, I want to speak of the "darkness of solidarity," the "night of compassion," which is the pain of co-suffering with our brothers and sisters in the family of a single humanity, in the Body of a single, world-cradling Church. This is an experience that is very mysterious, as it is born from light and held by light, as it is, in fact, a particularly intimate experience of *intimacy with Christ*. Rather than a purifying darkness (the "excess" light of God pouring into the darkness of our heart) or a darkness rooted in human woundedness, it is a darkness that is only the flip-side of light, *an expression of mature human and Christian closeness to the darkness and suffering of this world*. And in this respect, too, it is a simple dimension of human compassion—a feeling-with others their own pain, even if this pain is not my own—and thus should never allow pain to engulf joy, or darkness to overcome light. Precisely because the light is stronger, because the joy is truer, because the intimacy is unbreakable, it can "carry" darkness, too, in atoning love and abiding tenderness...like going to find a lost soul in the darkness, and taking them on one's shoulders, into one's heart, to carry them home to the realm of undimmed Light.

I think here particularly of the two Teresas, Thérèse of Lisieux and Teresa of Calcutta, who both experienced this darkness of compassion, not merely as a form of empathy or compassionate presence to another (which is accessible to all of us), but as a unique *vocation of solidarity*, a kind of extension of a mystical, spiritual night.* For them, the night became not a stage of the journey of purification, but rather an excessive overflow of paschal love, an abundance of the expression of the gift of themselves. It was a particularly intimate manifestation of their union with Jesus Christ in his own atoning love: a kiss of nuptial love in which they felt *with* Jesus his own interior resonance at the brokenness, darkness, and sin of the world. And thus even if painful, this night, this darkness became a source of deep joy, of abiding peace, of breathtaking intimacy with God through faith, hope, and love.

Yes, and the most important thing here is not darkness, but light, not to focus on the suffering, but looking through the suffering, with eyes of

---

*Another example, also a woman responding to the ardent thirst of Jesus, is Saint Faustina. Here are two passages: "During Holy Mass, I saw the Lord Jesus nailed upon the cross amidst great torments. A soft moan issued from His Heart. After some time, He said: I thirst. I thirst for the salvation of souls. Join your sufferings to My Passion and offer them to the heavenly Father for sinners." "Today, in the course of a long conversation, the Lord said to me: How very much I desire the salvation of souls! My dearest secretary, write that I want to pour out My divine life into human souls and sanctify them, if only they were willing to accept My grace. The greatest sinners would achieve great sanctity, if only they would trust in My mercy. The very inner depths of My being are filled to overflowing with mercy, and it is being poured out upon all that I have created. My delight is to act in a human soul and to fill it with My mercy and to justify it. My kingdom on earth is My life in the human soul." (*Diary*, 1032, 1784)

love, to discern the presence of God even in the most anguished and unexpected place (like looking through the darkness of the nocturnal sky to discern the ravishing beauty of the stars and moon). For here God has made himself present in Christ, and here he is at work healing, renewing, and making all things new, carrying them into the radiant light of the Trinity. As John Paul II wrote at the dawn of the new millennium:

> Not even the drama of his Passion and Death will be able to shake his serene certainty of being the Son of the heavenly Father. ... Jesus' cry on the Cross, dear Brothers and Sisters, is not the cry of anguish of a man without hope, but the prayer of the Son who offers his life to the Father in love, for the salvation of all. At the very moment when he identifies with our sin, "abandoned" by the Father, he "abandons" himself into the hands of the Father. His eyes remain fixed on the Father. Precisely because of the knowledge and experience of the Father which he alone has, even at this moment of darkness he sees clearly the gravity of sin and suffers because of it. He alone, who sees the Father and rejoices fully in him, can understand completely what it means to resist the Father's love by sin. More than an experience of physical pain, his Passion is an agonizing suffering of the soul. Theological tradition has not failed to ask how Jesus could possibly experience at one and the same time his profound unity with the Father, by its very nature a source of joy and happiness, and an agony that goes all the way to his final cry of abandonment. The simultaneous presence of these two seemingly irreconcilable aspects is rooted in the fathomless depths of the hypostatic union.

Faced with this mystery, we are greatly helped not only by theological investigation but also by that great heritage which is *the "lived theology" of the saints*. The saints offer us precious insights which enable us to understand more easily the intuition of faith, thanks to the special enlightenment which some of them have received from the Holy Spirit, or even through their personal experience of those terrible states of trial which the mystical tradition describes as the "dark night." Not infrequently the saints have undergone *something akin to Jesus' experience on the Cross* in the paradoxical blending of bliss and pain. In the *Dialogue of Divine Providence*, God the Father shows *Catherine of Siena* how joy and suffering can be present together in holy souls: "Thus the soul is blissful and afflicted: afflicted on account of the sins of its neighbor, blissful on account of the union and the affection of charity which it has inwardly received. These souls imitate the spotless Lamb, my Only-begotten Son, who on the Cross was both blissful and afflicted." In the same way, *Thérèse of Lisieux* lived her agony in communion with the agony of Jesus, "experiencing" in herself the very paradox of Jesus's own bliss and anguish: "In the Garden of Olives our Lord was blessed with all the joys of the Trinity, yet his dying was no less harsh. It is a mystery, but I assure you that, on the basis of what I myself am feeling, I can understand something of it." What an illuminating testimony!

Moreover, the accounts given by the Evangelists themselves provide a basis for this intuition on the part of the Church of Christ's consciousness when they record that, even in the depths of his pain, he died imploring forgiveness for his executioners (cf. *Lk* 23:34) and expressing to the Father his ultimate filial abandonment: "Father, into your hands I commend my spirit" (*Lk* 23:46). (*Novo Millennio Ineunte*, n. 24-27)[*]

These words of the pope seek to stir in us *a deep confidence in the love of God* who will never forsake or abandon us, and who will remain with us always, even in moments of greatest darkness and pain. Yes, the Son of God, as he passed through the suffering of his Passion, bearing the weight of our sin in order to shatter it by the power of love, was not in any way abandoned by his Father. Rather, in this space of Christ's deep solidarity with the waywardness of sinful humanity, *the intimacy of the Trinity's life was made most radiantly manifest* in the midst of history, in the midst of time and space—a revelation that in its depth and transparency was only to be surpassed by the glory of the Resurrection itself.

And Christ *knew* that this is what was occurring, abiding in radical trust and filial self-surrender within the embrace of his loving Father, and breathing forth with the Father the single Spirit of their love in the very midst of the darkest place of our fallen creation. He knew, and reposed with unbreakable serenity, in the joy of the Father's creative and redemptive love—reposed, indeed, in the very eternal, all-surpassing, and uncreated bliss of the Trinity's divine life—even as he also bore within himself, and suffered, all the anguish, darkness, pain, and sense of loss that sin has ever incurred in the history of humanity, past, present or future. What a paradox indeed!

On the basis of the "lived theology" of the saints—indeed, the lived experience of intimate prayer granted to all believers who cling to God in the midst of the trials and sufferings of life—we can take a step towards this mystery. We can begin to understand, in the light of God filtering into our own lives, that this mixture of joy and sorrow in the human consciousness of Christ was but the reverberation within him of his profound soli-

---

[*]Another beautiful example of this lived theology of the saints is Blessed Julian of Norwich, also bringing to the fore the central theme of *the thirst of Jesus*: "For this is Christ's spiritual thirst, his longing in love, which persists and always will...to gather us all into him, to our endless joy. With all the power of his divinity, he suffered pains and passion and died for love, to bring us to bliss. He says: it is a joy, a bliss, an endless delight that ever I suffered my Passion for you. We are his bliss, we are his reward, we are his honor, we are his crown.

"For he still has that same thirst and longing which he had upon the cross, which desire, longing and thirst, as I see it, were in him from the beginning... For as truly as there is in God a quality of mercy and compassion, so truly is there in God a quality of thirst and longing; and the power of this longing in Christ empowers us to respond to his longing, and without this no soul comes to heaven.

"And this quality of longing and thirst comes from God's everlasting goodness. And though he may have both longing and mercy, they are different qualities, as I see them; and this is the characteristic of spiritual thirst, which will persist in him so long as we are in need, and will draw us up into his bliss." (*Showings*, 31; in Langford, 294)

For a more thorough exposition of these realities, see the reflection "Through the Heart of the Paschal Mystery to the Heart of the Trinity" below.

darity with us. He knew—how could he not?—that he was inseparably united to the Father, that he and the Father were one, and that nothing could tear them asunder. As he said to his apostles shortly before his arrest: "The hour is coming, indeed it has come, when you will be scattered, every man to his home, and will leave me alone; yet I am not alone, for the Father is with me. I have said this to you, that in me you may have peace. In the world you have tribulation; but be of good cheer, I have overcome the world" (Jn 16:32-33). Yes, he received from us all the pain that we bear, uniting himself to us in the deepest of solidarity, such that he bore our sins in his own flesh and suffered for them on our behalf—suffered to cross over the distance of estrangement that these very sins had caused. And yet this was precisely the point: he crossed over the distance, crossed over the distance created by sin, in order to "thread" back together within his own embrace once again the torn fabric of intimacy between God and humanity, and between human persons and one another.

Thus, in this very place, Jesus became the Meeting-Place, he became the Convergence Point where all the torn strands of human life were gathered back together, and united, within the forgiving and reconciling embrace of God. And he could not do this unless he truly crossed the distance, truly took up our pain while also truly reposing in God. Yes, all of his darkness was our darkness, and not his own, even as he gave voice to it in a movement of profound intercession, speaking to the Father on our behalf. He cried out *our* lament, and precisely in this way he opened up the path for us to experience the answer: the answer of the Father's redeeming love given in the Resurrection. Whatever the "emotional resonance" this solidarity caused in the inner consciousness of Christ during the darkest moments of his Passion, whatever the experiential pain of sin and waywardness he bore for our sake, *it did not, it could not, in any way eclipse his serene certainty in being the beloved Son of the Father, nor his gratitude for being allowed to redeem humanity through the gift of his life, nor his security and joy in the unbreakable bond of intimacy uniting the two in the Holy Spirit.*

We take this step nearer to the inner sanctuary of Christ's own experience in his Passion, not to reduce the ineffable to our limited words, nor to try to grasp this profound mystery of being into the realm of our own clinging need to "have," but rather in order *to enter deeper into the ineffable depths of God's love revealed in Christ, that we may taste in ourselves, more profoundly, the victory of his light.* For Christ is a living Person, the eternal Son of God who lives a ceaseless life of intimacy with the Father and the Holy Spirit, and who has come into our world to espouse our humanity to himself, that we, in him and through him, may share in the very inner life of God. And if this is the case, why would we not desire to get to know him, to draw near to him in order to feel, in ourselves, the resonance of his own most intimate personal experience, his own subjectivity as both God and man (as surpassing our capacities as it may be). For this is the desire of love, of all authentic love—being the ecstasy out of the isolated and enclosed self and into the depth of the mystery of the Beloved. Christ, drawn by the divine *eros*, which is one with the divine *agape*, first drew near to us in this way, entering into our own subjective experience in order to be close to us. And in doing so, he also opened up the path for us, in turn, to draw near to him and to enter into his experience. Yes, he wants to draw us so near to him that we already begin to taste—imperfectly in this life and perfectly in undimmed fullness in the next life—his own inner subjective life as the beloved Son, and to share with him in the gladness of intimate love that he shares eternally with the Father in the kiss of the Holy Spirit.

WEEK V

RADIANT NUPTIAL CONSUMMATION

DAY 29
BORN ANEW INTO PRAYER:
HE ALWAYS FULFILLS EXPECTANT FAITH

Prayer is the only ultimate source of joy that there is in the entire universe. Without prayer, nothing has meaning or substance, nothing has lasting value; it cannot unveil its true depth and beauty, its true radiance and purpose, unless it occurs within prayer and leads to prayer, unless prayer blossoms within it. And yet in prayer, all things have meaning—all things that are true, good, and beautiful, all things that exist. Prayer unseals the mystery in everything, and, conversely, everything can unseal prayer in the human heart. For prayer, while surpassing all created mediation in the aspiration of the heart for the unmediated sight, voice, and embrace of God—for the intimacy of the Trinity in beatific fullness—also springs forth in the heart of the human person's contact with each and every thing that God has made, and with all the richness of life and experience, choice, feeling, and action, within this world.

Thus prayer has many faces, often very different from what we may expect or idealize to ourselves. But in essence it is, as Saint Augustine said, nothing but the "voice" of our desire for God. A heart that truly desires God thus prays at every moment, since it desires at every moment. Even if it is fully occupied with other things, it remains vigilant in longing for the one Beloved; even, indeed, if a person is incapable of raising thought, mind, or affection to him—insofar as this is consciously experienced—the heart prays at every moment, pervading all things with that one mystery of love that harmonizes all things in a single movement towards the One who is ceaselessly in movement towards us.

Even in the very darkest of experiences, even if in certain moments or periods everything seems to go black and I cannot even call to mind God or the mysteries of the faith, if I cannot even read a single verse of Scripture or sit still for five minutes, as long as my heart continues to desire, it continues to pray. Of course, such experiences of seemingly all-pervading darkness are exceptional—and they are never *all* pervading, as the light of belovedness and intimacy always shines, as the embrace of God always holds the human heart and experience, even if it is like the light of the sun which itself cannot be seen, even though all things are seen in its light. Whether in a path of deep inner purification, or in a profound solidarity with the darkness of our sinful world, a human person who walks a path of darkness walks, mysteriously, in the light.

As we have seen, this is what Christ experienced and lived in his Paschal Mystery, in which he experientially took upon himself, into himself, all the darkness, shame, suffering, and isolation that we experience because of sin and its effect, estrangement from God. This is what it means that he "became sin who did not know sin" (cf. 2 Cor 5:21), and suffered in our place and on our behalf. As the *Catechism* affirms, "Jesus did not experience reprobation as if he himself had sinned. But in the redeeming love that always united him to the Father, he assumed us in the state of our waywardness of sin" (par. 603); even in his deepest suffering, he remained always pure in undying intimacy with his Father. Nonetheless, he felt in himself the thorns of suffering, isolation, and spiritual darkness that pierce our own hearts and lives. And he did so because he held us so close as to take us into the living space of his own compassionate Heart—and thus to welcome us anew into the living space of his own unbreakable intimacy with the Father, in this way restoring, in the very darkness of suffering solidarity, the communion that sin had torn asunder.

This is the true and deepest meaning of "atonement," the making-one, through compassionate love, of what selfishness and hate have torn apart. And only love can do this; only intimacy can do this; even as it is a love and intimacy that, in this fallen world, passes also through suffering and pain, born of compassion and "identification" with the sinful beloved who sits in darkness and the shadow of death.

Christ, in union with his Father and the Spirit, came to us in a movement of divine compassion, of infinite mercy, and took to himself all that is ours, that we may receive all that is his. "The Son of God became a Son of man, that the sons of men might become sons of God." Indeed, he experienced all that we experience, all that the most lost and miserable hearts experience in this world—and yet in this very experience, he never ceased to love and long for his Father, indeed, to repose in filial trust and total surrender in the intimacy and security of his Father's embrace.

How the agony of solidarity with our waywardness and sin could coexist in the consciousness of the incarnate Son with the undying joy of the intimacy of the Trinity is a mystery that will forever surpass our comprehension. But that Christ experienced and lived both of these realities simultaneously, that he bore both mysteries in the very heart of his Passion, is a truth of the faith. Or better: the light held the darkness, and pervaded it, even as the darkness remained a real and true experience—for only in being truly assumed, truly suffered-through, could it be illumined by light, and by this light, dispelled.

What does this mean for our own experience and living of prayer? It means that when God leads us through experiences of prayer that are quite different from what we expect, clinging narrowly to our own categories or expectations will only cause undue confusion, rigidity, and suffering. Of course, even this process of having our expectations—or even our healthy desires—frustrated is a redeeming experience, as it effects a deep purification and healing in the wellsprings of the heart, deeper than our conscious mind can ordinarily reach. It prunes away the excess branches, the brambles and thorns of control and possessiveness and self-watching, so that the deep voice of the heart—the inner aspiration of love's desire—may blossom and express itself freely.

But it is also true that God desires prayer to permeate our entire consciousness, to flower in our experience, such that we can taste, even if imperfectly, the true beauty of relationship with the Trinity, the true beauty of the vulnerability of intimate dialogue with God, and of reciprocal self-giving with the Father, Son, and Holy Spirit. For this is the ultimate origin and final goal of every human desire, and of the whole universe itself; indeed, it is the inner form and essence of all things, born of Love, held by

Love, and carried towards Love again.

Though one may walk a path of darkness in this life, or for a period of one's time in this life, one walks in the light, for one is held, carried, and protected by Love. Even if one's desire for God seems to have been extinguished, and one is at the "end of the rope," unable to even raise a single glance to heaven, to voice a single word of prayer to God (or even feels what seems to be the very opposite of prayer, in the exceptional states of deep solidarity with sinful humanity through conformity with the Paschal Christ)—even if this is the case, prayer continues to throb its living heartbeat at the core of existence, as one shares in that mysterious intermingling of joy and pain, of the light of undying intimacy and the darkness of estrangement that Jesus bore, and overcame, in his own Passion and Death.[*]

And thus the way is paved, in one's own being and existence—as well as in one's brothers and sisters to whom one is united in the mystical Body and in the common family of humanity—for the light to prove definitively victorious, for love and intimacy to dispel every last lingering cloud of darkness and to burst forth in the glory and radiance of the Resurrection. Though glimpsed in this life through faith, hope, and love, and experienced in the way that God wills, this Resurrection will find its ultimate fulfillment in the next life, when we shall see God face to face, and experience his embrace in utter fullness, as we and the whole universe are renewed and caught up into the innermost depths of his own life as Father, Son, and Holy Spirit.

+ + +

A living faith is an expectant faith. And an expectant faith is a lighthearted, joyful faith. For this kind of faith dispels the dark clouds of fear, and the grasping human heart's tendency to control for the sake of its own security. It allows my hands and heart to open, to open wide in the poverty of receptivity, in the vulnerability of love, to receive from God at each moment my true daily bread—which is always superabundant—and to let my life flow back to him in response. Yes, an expectant faith is bold, confident, and exuberant, even in its simplicity and sobriety, in its quietness, littleness, and hiddenness (all born of humility).

For faith looks to God for everything, and remains before him in trust and desire, awaiting his gifts and his care, in every moment and circumstance, and expects a good outcome from him, and, ultimately, from him alone. It does not cling to its own foresight and control, but surrenders all to God's wisdom and love, even as it receives from him ever anew his guid-

---

[*] I would also like to emphasize here that, even if one walks a path marked by darkness, prayer is still a *vibrantly living reality, an ever deepening dance of love and intimacy.* One can still hope, with all of one's heart, therefore, to rediscover prayer more intimately, more deeply, more expansively, even and precisely in and through the darkness (like our example of Kousei playing the piano earlier). We see this in the life of Mother Teresa. She came to cherish the interior darkness she carried for fifty years, and to live it as a profound form of intimacy with Christ, with the entire Trinity, and with the poor of the world. And this darkness was not, ever, merely dark, in terms of being empty. It was pervaded by ardent longing and thirst, such that she could say, "All day long I am telling Jesus how much I love him," and also could say that she felt him, very vividly, loving and giving himself through her in her daily presence to the poor. Truly, this is darkness pervaded by redeeming light!

ance and the clarity that his vision brings. In faith I am held by the truth, rather than trying to hold it; I walk in the light, rather than trying to reduce it to my own size; I know that I am seen and loved by God, and only in this way can I be sure of seeing and loving God in return.

This atmosphere of confident, expectant, and bold faith—the faith of a child—permeates the Gospels. It is their very atmosphere: the atmosphere of lightheartedness, wonder, and play. (How difficult this is for fallen human beings!) Jesus remained in this attitude at every moment, throughout his life and even in the darkest moments of his Passion. Of course, all the richness and intricacy of human life and experience has a place within this; and this playfulness is true responsibility, this lightness is also true sobriety. But how beautiful, how relieving a breath of fresh air, is this filial liberty of the Son of God, who reposes always in the love of his Father and expects all things from him! And he wants us to share in, to live, and to experience this same mystery in our own lives.

This attitude contrasts so much with the rigidity, harshness, and, ultimately, the fear-based approach to prayer, life, and religion that is represented by the Pharisees—in Christ's own time—and which, sadly, permeates a great deal of the life of the Church today. This approach, focused more on obligations than on the living relationship of love, and on "accumulating" righteousness rather than on the vulnerability of gift, the poverty of intimacy, which is the true blessedness, hurts so many hearts, even within the Church. And this is understandable, since the Church "clasps sinners to her bosom," and carries fallen human hearts through the journey of life to the home of their Father.

We can all struggle with faith, struggle to have a truly confident and expectant faith—whose security is founded not in our own oversight, control, or perfect performance—but in the goodness and love of our heavenly Father. But the joy that this faith brings, the never-failing newness in each moment and circumstance of life, is God's great desire for us. "Your faith has saved you," he wants us to hear from his own lips, echoing in the silence of our heart. "Go in peace." This faith unseals in us the wellsprings of wonder, awe, and gratitude for all that God gives, and also carries us through the darkest times when wonder is subdued, gratitude clings in trust, and desire can only hope in the darkness. It carries us close to the Heart of Christ, who in love has made himself forever close to us. It carries us—or rather allows him to carry us—through everything that this life brings, and to the home of our Father, where we will be with him forever, in the intimacy of the Trinity, in which faith gives way to sight, and hope is eternally fulfilled in the full consummation of love.

DAY 30
THE PANORAMA OF PRAYER:
HEART SPEAKS TO HEART (1)

Allow me to try to draw together, in summary form, some of the themes of which I have spoken in the last couple weeks. There are obviously too many, and there is no need to revisit them all even in reference form. Rather, what is important is to "pull out the thread" joining them together. And that is precisely *the dance of ever-deepening intimacy*. The traits of this intimacy are constant and true, being irradiations of the very inner life of the Trinity into our hearts and our lives, filtering even into our experience. And yet as constant as these traits are, it almost cannot be over emphasized how important it is to recognize that *the path of prayer for each one of us is unique, and its manifestations are unique.*

We could say* that prayer matures and deepens through an ever more vulnerable and honest surrender of our hearts to God, who sees and loves us in all of our brokenness and sin, as well as in our innate beauty which he has created and redeemed, and in which he delights. Gradually this process, by God's ever-present grace, draws us from a perpetual fear of our weaknesses and failures and rather into the disposition of acceptance, which allows us no longer to flee and turn our gaze from them, but rather to open them to God with childlike simplicity and matter-of-factness, since we trust that, in every new revelation of our woundedness, the gift of the Father is secretly present. Indeed, this progressions leads even to a vivid awareness of the profound depth of our sins and the harm that they cause to ourselves and to others, and the pain that resounds in the heart of God himself. This is the place of the "dark night" spoken of by John of the Cross and other mystics, which we have touched upon. Here the radiant light of God shines so powerfully into our hearts that it shows up all the disorder within us, such that we can no longer ignore it, but must either be overcome by it in self-relying despondency, or surrender it at last, in the powerlessness of vulnerable love and unconditional trust, into the welcoming embrace of our merciful God. Yes, and the paradoxical and beautiful thing about this is precisely that this deepening awareness of our poverty and brokenness, of our desperate need for God, grows hand in hand with a deepened certainty and security in the all-sustaining and all-pervading love of the One who will not forsake or abandon us.

Thus, in the midst of this encounter of our misery and sin with the redeeming gaze of eternal Love, gradually the deep "voice of the heart" surges to the surface and finds expression. And this voice comes forth, not as something we can limit and control, something we can categorize or harness, as if we could turn back on it and watch ourselves praying, listening to the very cry of our heart even as we speak it. Rather, the Spirit carries us

---
*The following two reflections (slightly edited and expanded) come, again, from *At the Heart of the Gospel: The Love in Whom All Lines Converge*. The preceding reflection there (not included here), goes more deeply into the themes to which I refer, and complement the specific focus offered in this book.

ardently beyond our own control in the security that is the letting go of all control into the embrace of the One who holds the universe. Here the words of Jesus prove true: "As the wind blows where it wills, and you do not know where it comes from or where it is going, so it is of those who are born of the Spirit" (Jn 3:8). And again, as Saint Paul writes, "We do not know how to pray as we ought, but the Spirit himself intercedes within us with sighs too deep for words" (Rom 8:26). Yes, for "who knows what is innermost within a man except the man's spirit within him? So also no one comprehends what is within God except the Spirit of God. Now we have received, not the spirit of the world, but the Spirit who is from God, that we might understand the gifts given to us by God" (1 Cor 2:11-12). Thus the Spirit alive within us, joining himself to our own spirit in a synergy of love and prayer, harmonizes with the Spirit in God, such that we are certain of having our prayers answered: for it is but one Spirit, the Holy Spirit, who speaks into us from God and who responds to God within us! Here the Spirit, whose great work is unity, brings us into intimacy with God through an ineffable dialogue of love that surpasses words or concepts, while also filling them with an unheard-of depth of meaning.

He takes up our weak and faltering human activity, and purifies and elevates it by joining it to his own divine and supernatural activity. This is the experience of what is termed "infused contemplation," a ray of divine light, a touch or kiss or embrace of God himself who is present to us and is active within us. Contemplation in these terms can be compared to a human encounter of touch, in which two persons, who have been speaking to one another in words, draw closer in the contact that surpasses words, and speak a language that words can never adequately capture. Or it can be likened to the natural experience of intuition, in which a reality I have encountered so many times before suddenly "unveils" itself before me, and grips my heart in a new way, in a depth of beauty and closeness that I did not know before. But all created analogies, while helpful, fall short of the full richness of contemplative prayer, for here it is the uncreated God himself who is directly operative within our humanity and our experience, making himself known to us, tangible to us, in a real way, even if this knowledge and this contact cannot yet attain the fullness which is proper only to eternity and the new creation.

At first we may feel very far from any living contact with this "prayer of God within us," this infused activity of contemplation, which is the rich savor present in all words and experiences while also surpassing them. But this does not mean that God is not present or active. Rather this crying of the Spirit within us is not some "stage" of the spiritual journey, reserved for those who have achieved a certain level of development, or for those who have surpassed the stage of meditation or vocal prayer. Rather, it is the living heartbeat of prayer from the very beginning to the very end, the very means of our incorporation into the eternal life of God, into the dialogue of love between the Father and the Son in their one Spirit. But the human person becomes susceptible to this reality only over time, as the mind, affectivity, and will are purified and joined more and more—through faith, hope, and love—to the manner of living and loving proper to God; as the imagination, emotions, and sensation become joined to the human spirit, which in turn is surrendered to the divine Spirit. And yet God is present from the beginning, imbuing all of our frail and faltering efforts, and present even in our failures and struggles and infidelities, seeking to draw us closer to him and to harmonize our own heart with the throbbing of his heart, until they beat together in unison as one.

And over time, as the human person continues to speak a "yes" of heart and life to the invitation of God, it becomes capable of hearing, surrendering to, and speaking in the Spirit who speaks within us, letting its own prayer of love flow back to God from whom love has first come. Thus we can say that, in the progress of maturation in prayer—just as in other areas of maturation—our prayer is at first more superficial, more reliant on external means such as meditation on a text of Scripture or another book, or pre-formulated vocal prayers, etc.; but gradually, as our mind, affectivity, and will are enriched by the truth of God given to us in divine revelation, as we become acquainted with the richness of reality bathed in the light of God's love, and with God himself in his mysterious beauty, all of our faculties come to be gathered together more and more spontaneously and habitually in the simple center-point of the heart.

This does not necessarily mean that we lose the capacity or desire to read, to reflect, to voice our prayer to God in tangible and intelligible words and images—though this too may happen, as we are caught up in the mystery that surpasses words and thought and brings us to a place of stillness; though this path may also, on the contrary, fill and simplify words and thought and speech itself with the simple fullness of presence, more or less tangible, or even more or less "absent" (as a form of mysterious presence-in-absence, close precisely in its hiddenness, like the light of the sun which itself cannot be seen, or the darkness that enfolds and stills all without being recognized). God's activity in prayer may, indeed, do both, at different times and in different ways—draw beyond natural meditation or discursive reason, or leave us in the midst of it—according to the intentions of God and the capacities and needs of the human heart. But it may be accurate to say that all prayer, as it grows, is marked by an ever deepening profundity of gaze and surrender, and thus by a deeper spontaneity, arising from a more interior place in the wellspring of the heart, responding in a more mature contact with the fullness of the real and with the all-surpassing mystery of God himself.* But this path of simplification into the mystery of interior silence and unmediated heart-contact in prayer (which surpasses the direct activity of the mind and will and even affectivity in faith, hope, and love) definitely *does not* mean some kind of quietism, becoming an empty slate or entering a kind of eastern "nirvana." It does not mean that we lose a conscious contact with and orientation to the Trinity to whom our prayer is directed, and who prays within us, as well as with

---

*As I hope will become clear through the long quote below, this progress in depth and spontaneity in prayer—in heartfelt intimacy of contact and docility of surrender—may go totally unnoticed by the person praying. They may, to their own eyes, be more or less praying as they always have, or even praying "worse," if they gauge themselves from the outside or according to certain desires or expectations. What is determinative is always the *objective mystery* unfolding in human heart and life; and this cannot be reduced to the subjective element, even as it sanctifies and matures our living of the Gospel, even in the very fabric of our subjective being.

the fullness of natural and supernatural reality. Rather, our prayer is *always* a prayer to our Father, our loving Abba, in the beloved Son, to whom we are conformed in adoption and who is also our divine Bridegroom, in the breath and the magnetism of the Holy Spirit.

+ + +

Before proceeding to the next reflection, focusing more explicitly on the Trinitarian nature of all prayer, a characteristic that deepens and expands as the heart comes to know and love the Trinity more profoundly, I would like to share a quote from a wise Carthusian monk, whose conferences were quite influential (and providential!) in my own life over a number of years. Speaking about the passage into deeper prayer, he shows the way quite vividly for *each one of us to follow the lead of the Spirit in his unique plans for us, and not to gauge ourselves against our own ideals, desires, or expectations.* His words merit deep pondering:

> The will and spirit, the heart...must be firmly focused on God himself, the absolute Being who is Goodness and Truth, on whom everything depends. The ascetical effort to create an emptiness, a listening ear, a heart that is attentive must be simply a response to the divine activity; it must be God who begins to silence the heart by infusing a hidden taste for an immediate presence, and gives it a glimpse of obscure light quite different from that brought by concepts and words, and enables it to divine the presence of a Person, who beholds, who communicates.
>
> Sometimes certain beginners, having read a number of spiritual books and absorbed philosophical teaching on God's transcendence of all discursive knowledge, quickly come to the simplistic conclusion that we can know nothing of God and that we ought to remain before him with a mind that is devoid of images and ideas. They are then able deliberately to impose on themselves a complete vacuum that resembles certain aspects of mystical emptiness but is not the same. It is only an *absence*, a silence effected by the will in consequence of reason (and therefore by reason), and it does not admit the subtle intuition of the intellect, informed by faith, nor the impetus of authentic love that transcends all mediation to touch the beloved Person, that ensures the quality of *presence* essential to true 'emptiness'.
>
> This is one of those situations where conceptual knowledge of the spiritual life far exceeds the person's development of the spiritual life itself, and the genuine abilities of faith and above all, love. We must have the humility to follow the activity of the Spirit and not wish to look for shortcuts.
>
> This false emptiness is bitter and its fruits are impatience with oneself (and with God!), self-centeredness, a critical spirit, and judgment of others. Thus the energy is brutally repressed without being assimilated, and looks for an outlet for its aggressive self-affirmation in outbursts of anger, excessive activity, miscellaneous compensations, etc. This is not the only cause of the impression of repressed and frustrated energy given by certain religious; it is only one application of the principle of repression, the refusal to

incorporate the full human reality in the spiritual ascent. There are others.

All the great teachers agree: one must not depart from meditation, the ordinary way, for as long as it is fruitful and helps us to focus on God, to know him and love him. It is only when the soul finds it impossible to profit from these means that it leaves them. The fundamental principle is always to follow grace to let the Spirit lead us, instead of wishing to impose our own way of seeing, which is fatally deficient and selfish. Many saints have never left a more or less discursive way, but that has not lessened their sanctity in the slightest.

For all, outside of prayer-time, a discursive element in the sense of *lectio divina* is always part of the spiritual life.

Each person has a name known only to God, each has this way to follow. For any particular person (and only particular persons exist) there is no higher or lower way. There is only the way traced by God for this particular person, and personal perfection consists in following this way with the greatest fidelity and docility possible.

The spiritual life and the life of prayer always grow into greater simplicity, and it is important that each person should consciously encourage this tendency by seeking simplicity and purity in life as in prayer. It is always appropriate to yield to moments of silence in prayer, to be silent in order to let God speak if he will. But when God acts more directly on the soul and ushers it into another form of knowledge and an experience whose nature is more passive (which is only the secret activity of 'ordinary' grace become conscious to a certain extent), that depends only on God and his plans for the particular person. Let each hear the voice of the Spirit within.

In this matter too we must be poor, we must be humble and trusting. Most of us are not strong enough for God to inundate us with manifest grace. We would become proud and claim it as our own; we would grasp the gifts instead of yielding to the Giver; we would lose the invaluable means of pure faith.

And who knows? The light of grace is so translucent and delicate that its presence in all its purity remains hidden, often unperceived. It is only when it passes through our sensibility that it becomes visible. The mystics consider ecstasy as a weakness of the body that is not yet completely in harmony with the Spirit. There are those in whose life everything is 'ordinary', simple, humble. But they radiate a certain peace, a certain joy. In such a person we can perceive a soul whose heart is so given to God that this condition is their deepest reality, but so 'natural' that it is not possible to pin it down in discrete acts. It is scarcely conscious of itself.[25]

DAY 31
THE PANORAMA OF PRAYER:
HEART SPEAKS TO HEART (2)

While emphasizing anew the profound *ordinariness* that so often marks the path of prayer, as well as the unique nature of the experience of each person, which is repeated by no other, we can nonetheless try to point to a central thread in the growth of prayer. I have already emphasized the foundational role of faith, hope, and love, not merely as human acts of trust, desire, and surrender, but, through this, as a literal, if unfelt and ungraspable, contact with God as he is in himself. Everything I say in the coming reflections should be understood in this light. Even when I speak of the explicit mystical experience of nuptial intimacy with God, I am not implying that God intends for each of us to experience him as vividly in this life. He has his reasons for leading each of us as he does. But underneath the surface, as a common thread, we are all called to a profound and total union with the Trinity, the nature of which certain mystics have experienced in an extraordinary way. This experience is a gift for us, as it helps to make more apparent to all of us what occurs under the veil of hiddenness during this life, and, just as much, the radiant beauty of the consummation that awaits us in eternity, where every veil shall be removed.

If we try to look at prayer, in all of its ordinariness, in all of its simplicity, in an *objective* light, as the growing relationship of love between my heart and the Persons of the Trinity, we can see something beautiful. Regardless of the particular path I walk, or the subjective resonances that unfold for me over time, objectively, prayer grows in a deepening knowledge and love of the three divine Persons, who want to reveal themselves ever more intimately to me. It is also, conversely, an ever deeper knowledge of my own authentic self in the light of God's gaze, a knowledge of my brokenness, sin, and disorder, as well as of my beauty, a beauty given me by God and becoming more and more alive as he heals and sanctifies me.

In sum, I want to emphasize here simply that *the Trinitarian nature* of prayer deepens and becomes more explicit as prayer matures. Here we are far from an oriental form of meditation, whether Hindu or Buddhist or any of the New Age forms propagated so widely today; we are very far from any quietism or striving for emptiness or nirvana. But we are also equally far from merely playing around with ideas in our heads. What we are talking about here, as humble as it may appear on the surface, is a love-dialogue between the human person and the Persons of the Father, Son, and Holy Spirit. And through this dialogue, each of the divine Persons unveils for us ever more deeply and explicitly not only their singular beauty in the heart of the life of God—their incomparable Personhood in relation with the other Persons of the Trinity—but also the depth and expansiveness of their relation with humanity and with creation, and especially their intimate activity within the receptive human heart. Thus the praying person comes to *know* the Father, the Son, and the Holy Spirit ever more intimately in the "heart of the heart," with that deep, implicit, and even unconscious knowledge born of love. The heart comes to know each of them uniquely in the beauty that is their own, but also in their unity in the single mystery of the Godhead, in the divinity that they share as one in an indivisible "We" of Love. Caught up, through sheer grace, into the living heart of this mystery of God, into the very throbbing heartbeat of their love and intimacy, into the dialogue of love that occurs between Father, Son, and Holy Spirit, the human person feels and knows from within the very atmosphere of the life of God, the very joy of his ineffable being, the very communication and communion of the Trinity's ever-consummated encounter of mutual belonging and total intimacy.

+ + +

Let us return to our overview of the "panorama" of prayer.* This participation in the life of God, since it occurs not in direct and unmediated vision (which is proper only to the next life) but rather in faith, hope, and love, always remains to some degree veiled and hidden from our eyes and our experience. It is lived, in other words, in the form of trust, desire, and surrender, in the living dispositions of the heart that reflect and share in the heart of God: and thus it occurs in the "night." And yet this night is not sheer blackness, pure darkness, but a darkness filled with mysterious rays of light, with glimpses of intuition, insight, and love-filled contemplation, with the impulse of the heart in longing and aspiration, and in the echoing silence of stillness that vibrates with the eternal movement of God's own all-pervading activity. Yes, how paradoxical is the mystery of the night, which is bathed with sweet light, and yet which also cradles the anguish of sorrow for one's own sin and the sinful state of the entire world! How paradoxical is this night, in which the human spirit reaches out to touch the face of God beyond the veil of mortality, and yet also feels the pain of unfulfilled desire in the very expansion of desire, longing for the consummation that has not yet come! How paradoxical, in which the love-wounded heart is impelled beyond the limitations of all created things towards the unlimited and boundless beauty of God, towards the everlasting and infinite Communion of the Trinity, and yet also comes to see and embrace this very infinite beauty as it is present, mysteriously, precisely in the sacrament of littleness and limitation! Here the ordinariness and humility of daily life is not rejected as unworthy of God, unworthy of the heart that loves him; rather, it is filled and permeated with a newfound meaning and beauty, even as it is also shot through with a new pain: a pain that is fruitful and salvific, a healing pain which shares in the redeeming pain of Christ on the Cross, birthing the newness of the Resurrection.

The particular nuances of the subjective experience of prayer, from its incipient beginning to its full blossoming, are highly individualized, expressing the unique contours of the singular person's heart and of God's unique relationship of love with them. Nonetheless, the essence of intimacy, the true nature of love and communion, is the same for all persons, since it is nothing but a living share in the very life of the Trinity. Each of us, incomparably unique, is nonetheless sharing in a single mystery, in the one and indivisible life of our awesome God, Father, Son, and Holy Spirit.

---

*Here we return directly to the text from *At the Heart of the Gospel*, after expanding more on the Trinitarian communion than is done there.

And to let him draw near to us and to communicate himself to us—to welcome his gift in faith, to allow it to expand us in hope, and to let it harness us in a total reciprocal gift in love—is not only to enter into union with him (though it is certainly and primarily this!), but also to enter into union with all of our brothers and sisters and with the whole created universe. This is because by our union with God, we are truly in union with the heart of all reality, for he is the white-hot light from which all the rays of created reality flow, and to which they return, in which, indeed, they unceasingly inhere. To be in him, therefore, is to be in touch with the center and deepest meaning of all things; to be loved by him is also to learn to hear the word of love spoken in and through all things; and to love him is also to dilate in the capacity to love each person and all things in their true and innate value and dignity. In the very living heartbeat of prayer, therefore—even if it occurs in the hiddenness of my own room and in the most secret recesses of my heart—the convergence of incomparable singularity and universal communion is also manifest.

And all prayer, taking fully into account the uniqueness of each person —or rather being realized precisely in the uniqueness of the person—does progress in similar ways. In particular, it progresses from more superficial to more profound, from the surface to the depth, and from complex to simple. Isn't this the nature of love in all forms of relationship? How much more true it is in our relationship with God, who is utter Profundity, utter Depth, and the Simplicity of utter fullness in whom all the diverse lines converge on a single point in the Trinitarian embrace! All that was before approached from the "outside," with a piecemeal searching for the partial glimmers of God hidden within it, is now approached with a deeper intuition that, so to speak, penetrates more quickly to its very heart and its deepest significance. Living more and more in the center-point, one approaches all things from this place. Scripture becomes more and more simple, and indeed it comes to live inside oneself, and thus the need to read it perhaps becomes less, even as it speaks more fully in every word and verse. Nature itself becomes more radiant and full, more transparent to the beauty of God of whom it speaks; indeed, the praying heart becomes capable of hearing and co-speaking with God his own word of affirmation towards created reality, and to find deep delight in this. But in all things as well as beyond all things, what occupies the heart so much, what harnesses every movement, thought, and desire of the heart is precisely to make ever deeper contact with God himself in his direct and unmediated fullness.

Of course, this kind of encounter and intimacy is not possible in its consummate fullness until the veil of this mortal life is torn and the person enters into eternity. But it can be glimpsed, tasted, in the mysterious realm of the heart, in which the naked God is present to the naked human person in the self-communication of love, awakening reciprocal loving gift, and thus sealing a breathtakingly profound and true intimacy, even if such intimacy remains hidden in this life. And this communication of God and his child, of Christ and the bridal heart, of the Spirit and the human person— spiritualized by grace—constitutes the living heartbeat of prayer, which gives meaning to everything else and fills it with fullness. Yes, this communication surpasses everything else in its depth and profundity, but it does not therefore drain anything else of meaning. Rather, it casts forth light, from this center place, into everything else, illumining it and revealing its true beauty and significance. And thus everything becomes both a vessel of gift which the human heart receives with gratitude and a spirit of humble and lighthearted responsibility, as well as an arrow of beauty from God's heart which wounds the human heart with even more ardent longing for intimacy with God himself beyond his imperfect manifestations in created reality.

Thus, through the love that is the perfect union of eros and agape, that is the harmony of receptivity and gift, the voice of the heart emerges in unison with the voice of the Spirit, and reposes in the heart of the Trinity himself. And God's word and gift, too, reposes in the heart of man or woman, such that the words of Christ are fulfilled: "Whoever loves me will be loved by my Father, and I will love him, and manifest myself to him...and we will come to him and make our home within him" (Jn 14:21, 23). And again, "If you abide in me and my words abide in you, ask for whatever you will, and it shall be done for you" (Jn 15:7), and again, "Even as you, Father, are in me, and I am in you, may they also be in us" (Jn 17:21). A silent glance of the eyes, or a few words or syllables in the ears, or the sense of touch, and the heart vibrates with longing for God, and cries out to him in ineffable love and surrender. Or the heart sits in silence in prayer, eyes closed and in solitude, and in this darkness, in which all created things have become hushed—waiting in expectation with the longing heart for the manifestation of God—the ray of divine light pours forth, not directly visible, but felt mysteriously welling up from the deepest and most hidden place of the heart. Here peace flows forth, and longing, and gratitude—and, beyond all feeling while also giving rise to feeling, the living activity of God within the human person in faith, hope, and love. Yes, and it is in faith, hope, and love—these dispositions that, as they mature, harness all the rest of our humanity in every moment—that we are united to God as he really is, in the fullness of his mystery, as well as in his mediated gift of self through created reality. In all things and beyond all things we come to welcome him, and to give ourselves back to him, letting each moment thus be a sacrament of encounter, a sacrament in which, through which, and beyond which the very invisible, infinite, eternal, and uncreated Reality kisses us, and espouses us to himself.

DAY 32
THE SPIRITUAL MARRIAGE:
NAKED SOLITUDE FULFILLED IN INTIMACY

After these reflections on the "night" and on the "panorama of prayer" as it grows and develops between the human heart and God, let us turn our gaze back to the theme that immediately preceded. I spoke of the path of healing and transformation as the journey back to the truth of the "original experiences" of solitude, nakedness, and unity. We are coming now to be able to speak of the highest manifestation of the life of intimacy possible in this life, in the transfiguration of the human person through grace. It is traditionally called the "spiritual marriage" or the "transforming union," a true and reciprocal surrender of persons between God and the human heart, sealed in mutual belonging. It is the essence of sanctity in the permeation of our whole humanity by the divine light in faith, hope, and love, in the total "yes" of all that we are to God, and his "yes" to us. The path to this state is a restoration of the truth of our humanity which God fashioned in the beginning, but, even more, a living participation in the manner of living and loving proper to God as Trinity. For the three divine Persons abide eternally in a ceaseless act of love, an act which is the simultaneous fullness of solitude, nakedness, and unity: of presence-to-oneself, presence-to-the-other, and intimacy-in-mutual-indwelling.

Through original and personal sin, I have been fractured away from my own inner self, the truth of my being. My energies and capacities are dissipated, taken up with so many superficial and fading things, caught up in clinging to false securities, and lost among shadows and lies. What is true of humanity as a whole, in the estrangement of hearts from one another ("scattered like sheep on the hillsides"), is also true within me, in the estrangement of my own self from itself, in my exile from the sanctuary of my own heart and spirit, and even from being at home in my own body. In my conscious life I am "exiled;" I no longer abide fully within myself, as Saint Benedict said: "*habitare secum.*" Because of the fracture of my consciousness and my factulries from unity in the core of my being, I am incapable of acting from within that deep place of my innermost freedom, my "I," my heart.

But God has come, in Christ, to gather me together again, to take up his abode in my innermost spirit through grace, in the core of my very incarnate flesh, and to be here like a divine magnet drawing me back together into harmony within myself through harmony with him.

He has infused into me the precious gift of his own life, which is active within me as faith, hope, and love, "the love of God poured into our hearts through the Holy Spirit who has been given to us" (cf. Rom 5:5). This presence of God's own life within me has a healing, liberating, and unifying effect on my whole being, to the degree that I accept it, acquiesce to it, and cooperate with it.

Yes, and this "return to self" is much more than a mere return to self. For what good is returning to my own self if I am alone and isolated, an island amid an ocean of anonymity? No, my inner self is not myself alone: my innermost self is God. As John of the Cross says: "The center of the soul is God, and to return to God is to return to the innermost center of the soul." This is because, at the core of my solitude, I am not alone and enclosed in self-sufficiency; rather, I am radical openness, radical self-transcendence to Another. I am relationality, relationship, capacity for communion. I am *gazed* into existence by love, and thus in the core of my being, in my true self, I am *beloved*.

But insofar as I live on the surface levels of my being, far from sinking into that truth at my core, that "still-point" at the center of my consciousness, I do not know who I am. I live according to lies and self-definitions embraced either out of my own self-defense or out of the projections of others. As I walk this path back into my innate *solitude*, therefore, I realize that solitude is in essence *openness to communion, capacity to be loved and to love*. In my inmost being, my solitude is crying out for *nakedness* and *unity*.

Thus my gradual return to solitude becomes, and must become ever more, a homecoming to the attitude of true vulnerability, the nakedness of my whole being before the gaze of the One who ever looks upon me with love. Only his gaze, indeed, can unify me in myself. Only moving beyond myself towards him can grant me access to my innermost core. I cannot find myself unless I lose myself in order to find him, as he himself said: "Whoever would save his life will lose it, but whoever loses it for my sake will find it" (cf. Mt 16:25).

All that I am, all that I have ever felt, known, had, or desired—all shame and fear, all desire and effort, all failure and guilt, all capacities and incapacities, all experience and expectation—everything, absolutely everything, is to be *laid before him in trusting nakedness*, and to be opened wide, in unconditional poverty, to receive his gift as he wishes to give it. And this gift is ultimately his very Self, which brings with it all healing, transformation, and renewal. It is the gift of God the Father, communicated in the gaze, the surrender, and the very flesh of his eternal Son made man, Jesus Christ, poured out in and through the Spirit of Love whom they share.

Thus my return to solitude and nakedness—two movements inseparably one and sustained always by trust and desire, by faith and hope—brings forth in me the capacity and experience of *unity with God*, of intimacy with the Three who are the very Origin of my being and the ground of my consciousness. I leave behind the realm of shadows and projections, of clinging for security which is actually slavery, of power and possession and pleasure-seeking, and step into the light that bathes my naked solitude in the peaceful glow of love.

Yes, by accepting all that I am as seen, known, and loved by God, and willingly opening and vulnerably surrendering all that I am to him, unity is born. By letting him look upon me, and looking upon him, too, a dance of reciprocal presence is born—a dance in which I realize that, however much I have desired and sought him, my Lover has been seeking and desiring me infinitely more. His love, his gaze, has gone before and led me every step of the way, such that even in my place of greatest exile he has been present in mercy, unto my innermost reconciliation with him in the meeting of gazes. Here is the true homecoming to the heart of God, my only true place of rest. And here gaze becomes gift, reciprocity of surrender; look becomes touch, self-communication. Nakedness flows into consummation of union, nuptial intimacy: bridal union with Christ the Bridegroom, totally given, and filial intimacy with the Father, in his love's womb, all pervaded by the Spirit who is the kiss, embrace, and vibrancy of love.

DAY 33
THE SPIRITUAL MARRIAGE:
THE "YES" OF TOTAL SURRENDER

The perfection of the Christian life consists in love buoyed by faith and hope, in love come to full blossom. This is what makes the path that I have tried to illustrate in these reflections possible, and it, that is, love, is indeed the very path that we walk. The journey of love is the path to the restoration of authentic solitude, nakedness, and unity, my path back into intimacy with God, and thus also into harmony with myself, communion with and charity for my brothers and sisters, and true stewardship over and delight in the whole creation. By my re-centering in God—by my ecstasy of love into the gaze and embrace of God, who is always in an attitude of ecstasy towards me—fulfillment is found, and all things are made new. The order of my life is restored, that order lost in the Garden of Eden in sin, and perpetuated in every personal sin that I choose throughout my life. And in me and through me, God's order—the order of love and communion—reaches out to spread itself into other hearts, to take root in the very cosmos, healing, renewing, and transfiguring.

Let us look at the core of this union more deeply. John of the Cross illustrates it quite beautifully in his description of the distinction between the state of spiritual "betrothal" and that of spiritual "marriage." The betrothal is that state before definitive marriage, a state of preparation and of imperfect if nonetheless deeply real intimacy; marriage is the state of total gift and the highest possible intimacy. He writes, first speaking of natural human relationships, and then leading into the divine:

> In betrothal there is only a mutual agreement and willingness between the two, and the bridegroom graciously gives jewels and ornaments to his betrothed. But in marriage there is also a communication and union between the persons. Although the bridegroom sometimes visits the bride in the betrothal and brings her presents, as we said, there is no union of persons, nor does this fall within the scope of betrothal.
>
> Likewise, when the soul has reached such purity in itself and its faculties that the will is very pure and purged of other alien satisfactions and appetites in the inferior and superior parts, and has rendered its "yes" to God concerning all of this, since now God's will and the soul's are one through their own free consent, then the soul has attained possession of God insofar as this is possible by way of the will and grace. And this means that in the "yes" of the soul, God has given the true and complete "yes" of his grace.
>
> This is a high state of spiritual betrothal between the soul and the Word, in which the Bridegroom favors it and frequently pays it loving visits wherein it receives wonderful delight. Yet these delights are not comparable to those of marriage, for these are preparations for the union of marriage. Although it is true that this betrothal occurs in the soul that is greatly purified of every [disor-

dered] affection for creatures—for the spiritual betrothal is not wrought until this comes to pass—the soul still needs other positive preparations from God. It needs his visits and gifts by which he purifies, beautifies, and refines it further so it might be suitably prepared for so lofty a union. (*The Living Flame of Love,* 3.24-25)

Here we see how the stage of betrothal—nowadays it would be called "engagement"—is an increasing familiarity between bride and bridegroom, in which they come to know each other and to solidify their "mutual agreement" to be wed through the gifts they give to one another. These, of course, are much more than jewels and ornaments (John's description is more symbolic than literal here), but rather the gift of presence, of time spent together, of care, of ever deepening mutual knowledge through reciprocal openness and communication. But in the state of betrothal, the "gift of persons" has not yet been totally given, as this is proper only to marriage. To use John's terms, the "union between persons" is precisely the gift of marriage, which refers precisely to the *total gift of self and joining together of life* that marriage effects between bridegroom and bride. This is manifest in the mutual "yes" by which they hand themselves over to one another without reserve, and forever, a "yes" sealed and communicated in the joining together of their lives and persons even in the body.

The point John is making is that it is the same, though on an infinitely higher level, with the divine Bridegroom. He too promises himself to us, and prepares us for the gift of marriage; for he ardently desires, not merely to communicate things *about* himself, or to give us any number of gifts or insights into himself and his love. Rather, he wants to *give his very self.* And yet in our sinful state, so wounded by disordered desires, and so narrowed by our brokenness, we are not yet capable of receiving and containing this gift of God himself, nor of reciprocating it with the gift of ourselves. But *this* is precisely what God wants, and he is satisfied with nothing less! He wants *total* union with us in the full surrender of persons, a union so complete, so intimate, that the most profound spiritual and physical unity of man and woman pales in comparison with it. John goes on to write, concerning the experience of God in spiritual marriage:

> This feeling, then, of the soul that was once obscure, without this divine light and blind through its [unhealthy] appetites and affections, has now together with the deep caverns of its faculties become not only bright and clear, but like a resplendent light.
>
> Now give forth, so rarely, so exquisitely,
> both warmth and light to their Beloved.

When these caverns of the faculties are so wonderfully and marvelously pervaded with the admirable splendors of those lamps that are burning within, they give forth to God in God with loving glory, besides their surrender to him, these very splendors they have received. Inclined in God toward God, having become enkindled lamps within the splendors of the divine lamps, they render the Beloved the same light and heat they receive. In the very manner they receive it, they return it to the one who gave it, and with the same exquisite beauty; just as the window when the sun shines on it, for it then too reflects the splendors. Yet the soul reflects the divine light in a more excellent way because of the active intervention of its will.

... And according to the exquisite quality of the divine attributes (fortitude, beauty, justice, and so on) that the Beloved communicates, is the quality with which the soul's feeling gives joyfully to him the very light and heat it receives from him. Having been made one with God, the soul is somehow God through participation. Although it is not God as perfectly as it will be in the next life, it is like the shadow of God.

Being the shadow of God through this substantial transformation, it performs in this measure in God and through God what he through himself does in it. For the will of the two is one will, and thus God's operation and the soul's are one. Since God gives himself with a free and gracious will, so too the soul (possessing a will more generous and free the more it is united with God) gives to God, God himself in God; and this is a true and complete gift of the soul to God.

It is conscious there that God is indeed its own and that it possesses him by inheritance, with the right of ownership, as his adopted child through the grace of his gift of himself. Having him for its own, it can give him and communicate him to whomever it wishes. Thus it gives him to its Beloved, who is the very God who gave himself to it. By this donation it repays God for all it owes him, since it willingly gives as much as it receives from him.

... A reciprocal love is thus actually formed between God and the soul, like the marriage union and surrender, in which the goods of both (the divine essence that each possesses freely by reason of the voluntary surrender between them) are possessed by both together. They say to each other what the Son of God spoke to the Father through St. John: ... All my goods are yours and yours are mine, and I am glorified in them ... [Jn. 17:10]. In the next life this will continue uninterrupted in perfect fruition, but in this state of union it occurs, although not as perfectly as in the next, when God produces in the soul this act of transformation. (*The Living Flame of Love*, 3.76-79)

Here we see the full flowering of the gift of *divinization* that we receive in seed at baptism: the gift of participation in the very life of God himself. As John says, through the union of persons effected through grace and free reciprocal surrender, we become *God through participation*, not in an essential way as is the Son of God—who is eternally God, by nature, with the Father and the Holy Spirit—but rather by way of *relationship* and of the *substantial union* of our being with the Being of God through love. And our being and faculties here become so limpid, so pure, that they are like caverns of pure receptivity for the burning lamps of God's attributes to shine forth. Indeed, they begin to shine with the very gift of God that they have first received—even the very essence of God becomes the soul's through grace come to full flower in this marriage-surrender—such that they shine forth to God in God the gift they have first received from God.

Here all the natural meaning and symbolism of conjugal union and parenthood in the created order is both surpassed and super-fulfilled. In this total gift of God's very essence to me, transforming me into himself, I am enabled to give back to God my own self, and the very gift of himself that he first gave me, in an act of perfect reciprocal love. Here the union of persons, insofar as possible in this life, is consummated, in both of us becoming a single gift within the one gift of the divine essence and life. And here the radiance of transparent fruitfulness is also achieved, in which I can give back to God the very gift of God that I have received, just as a wife can give to her husband a child that comes first as his gift to her in conception (and yet more deeply).

And here Lover and beloved are so totally united—not just substantially through grace, nor just in the inner "yes" of the will or heart, but in *all* of the faculties of the human person joined to the divine activity—that they co-operated together as with a single will. As John said: the soul "performs in this measure in God and through God what he through himself does in it. For the will of the two is one will, and thus God's operation and the soul's are one. Since God gives himself with a free and gracious will, so too the soul (possessing a will more generous and free the more it is united with God) gives to God, God himself in God; and this is a true and complete gift of the soul to God." The person's own gift, in other words—her own unique and unrepeatable "yes" of love to God—is fulfilled in union with the divine will which communicates God to the person and enables the person to communicate God back to God along with the voluntary gift and surrender of herself.

Here we see the highest fulfillment of the *thirst* of God, of his ardent desire *to love and to be loved*. This, precisely, is what is fulfilled here, in the total transformation of the human being by grace, in the marriage surrender and union of the divine Persons and the human person. For here God can *love*, can give himself the way that he has always desired, since the human heart is finally capable of receiving him as he communicates himself; and here he can also *be loved*, can receive the gift of his beloved, given with a love that is deep and adequate, since in giving herself she also gives him the fullness of divine love itself that she has first received and that has permeated and taken possession of her being.

DAY 34
SPIRITUAL MARRIAGE:
TOTALLY PERMEATED BY LOVE

I would like to try and unfold more deeply the profound beauty of the transformation of the human person in God, to which I have referred so often throughout these reflections. As we have seen, the term "spiritual marriage" refers precisely, in the mystical tradition of the Church, to that highest state of transformation attainable in this life, in which the individual is utterly possessed by the ardor of divine Love, flooded with rivers of glory, and permeated by the presence and activity of the three Persons of the Trinity. They are, as it were, pressing against the veil separating this life from the next, so intimately united to and transformed within the Father, Son, and Holy Spirit that the veil is at the point of tearing.

In such a state of union, this person's every act becomes one of love in the likeness of the Trinity, love, indeed, springing forth from the Trinity whose presence within the sanctuary of the heart pours forth to inundate, without the obscurity of disordered inclinations or any possessiveness, the activity of all the person's faculties, from the most interior spiritual movements to the very emotions and sensations of the body.

In describing this state, I cannot come close to the depth of the words of John of the Cross, so allow me to simply let him speak. I will only try to clarify and unfold some of his words, so that they may more intimately touch and inflame our own hearts.

> The soul now feels that it is all inflamed in the divine union, its palate is all bathed in glory and love, that in the intimate part of its substance it is flooded with no less than rivers of glory, abounding in delights, and from its depths flow rivers of living water [Jn. 7:38], which the Son of God declared will rise up in such souls. It seems, because it is so forcefully transformed in God, so sublimely possessed by him, and arrayed with such rich gifts and virtues, that it is singularly close to beatitude—so close that only a thin veil separates it.
>
> And the soul sees that every time the delicate flame of love, burning within, assails it, it does so as though glorifying it with gentle and powerful glory. Such is the glory this flame of love imparts that each time it absorbs and attacks, it seems that it is about to give eternal life and tear the veil of mortal life, that very little is lacking, and that because of this lack the soul does not receive eternal glory completely. With ardent desire the soul tells the flame, the Holy Spirit, to tear the veil of mortal life now by that sweet encounter in which he truly communicates entirely what he is seemingly about to give each time he encounters it, that is, complete and perfect glory. (*The Living Flame of Love*, 1.1)

These words are on fire. And rightly so, for they express the mystical experience of a soul on the very brink of eternity, stretching thin the veil through love, desirous of passing over into the endless consummation of heaven. Touched, ravished, and transformed by the love of the Trinity, the heart is aflame with the very love of the Trinity, and desires nothing else than to be with the Trinity forever in full and unmediated intimacy.

Let us, however, take a step back and look at some traits of this union with the Trinity as it grows to maturity in this life. Through this, too, we will come to glimpse, and hopefully to thirst more ardently for, the destiny that awaits us in heaven, and in the complete and perfect glory of the new creation. John of the Cross writes:

> [T]here he taught me a sweet and living knowledge;

The sweet and living knowledge that she says he taught her is mystical theology, the secret knowledge of God that spiritual persons call contemplation. This knowledge is very delightful because it is a knowledge through love. Love is the master of this knowledge and what makes it wholly agreeable. Since God communicates himself to the soul, it is very delightful to the intellect since it is a knowledge belonging to the intellect, and it is delightful to the will since it is communicated in love, which pertains to the will. Then she says:

> and I gave myself to him,
> keeping nothing back;

In that sweet drink of God, in which the soul is imbibed in him, she most willingly and with intense delight surrenders herself wholly to him in the desire to be totally his and never to possess in herself anything other than him. God causes in this union the purity and perfection necessary for such a surrender. And since he transforms her in himself, he makes her entirely his own and empties her of all she possesses other than him.

Hence, not only in her will but also in her works she is really and totally given to God without keeping anything back, just as God has freely given himself entirely to her. This union is so effected that the two wills are mutually paid, surrendered, and satisfied (so that neither fails the other in anything) with the fidelity and stability of an espousal. She therefore adds:

> there I promised to be his bride.

Just as one who is espoused does not love, care or work for any other than her bridegroom, so the soul in this state has no affections of the will or knowledge of the intellect or care or work or appetite that is not entirely inclined toward God. She is as it were divine and deified, in such a way that in regard to all she can understand she does not even suffer the first movements contrary to God's will.

... Obviously, then, the soul that has reached this state of spiritual espousal knows how to do nothing else than love and walk always with its Bridegroom in the delights of love. Since in this state she has reached perfection, the form and nature of which, as St. Paul says, is love [Col. 3:14], and since the more a soul loves the more completely it loves, this soul that is now perfect is all love, if one may express it so, and all her actions love. She employs all her faculties and possession in loving, in giving up everything like the wise merchant [Mt 13:44], for this treasure of love has been found by her, hidden in God. She is conscious that love is so valuable in her Beloved's sight that he neither esteems nor makes use of anything else but love, and so she employs all her strength in the pure love of God, desiring to serve him perfectly.

She does this not merely because he desires it, but also because the love by which she is united to him moves her to the love of God in and through all things. Like the bee that sucks honey from all the wildflowers and will not use them for anything else, the soul easily extracts the sweetness of love from all things that happen to her; that is, she loves God in them. Thus everything leads her to love. (*The Spiritual Canticle,* 27.4-8)

How beautiful a description this is of the rediscovery of the innocence lost in the Garden of Eden, an innocence restored through grace operating in the human person through the heart of Redemption! This is what the appropriation of the mystery of Redemption, what the path of sanctification, leads to. It is also, therefore, a foretaste of our eternal destiny in heaven, and in the new creation, when the whole universe will be taken up into this ceaseless act of perfect love between the Trinity and all those whom he has redeemed. While such a total possession by love fluctuates in intensity in this life, as John of the Cross himself acknowledges, we should not doubt that such a radical transformation and union of the human person with God is truly possible.* After all, this is the very reason for which he created us! This is the very reason for which he came into this world in Christ, born as a child in Bethlehem, living among us for thirty-three years, humbly working, teaching, healing, and loving, and ultimately suffering and dying with us and for us, so that he may rise from the dead, carrying us all back out of the fragmentation and lostness of sin and into the joy of the Trinity's embrace!

I would encourage you to read that final paragraph from John of the Cross again, and to think of how truly it expresses the joy of freedom. This is the freedom for which every human heart longs, found not merely in obedience to God externally, but in being *moved* by his love in everything, joyfully and spontaneously, to love with the love that is living in us and loving through us. In *all things,* in whatever happens to us, it is truly possible to discover God's love communicating itself to us, and to be drawn to love God himself in and through all things. Thus a ceaseless communication of love, an abiding reciprocal gift, is established between us, and through this a true and unbroken intimacy of heart and life.

---

*Elsewhere John distinguishes between the "habitual" state of union, of spiritual marriage, and the "acts" stirred up by God in this union, or unique moments of greater intensity. He compares it to the difference between a log being habitually enfolded in flame, and the flames leaping up: "The interior acts [the Holy Spirit] produces shoot up flames, for they are acts of inflamed love, in which the will of the soul united with that flame, made one with it, loves most sublimely. Thus these acts of love are most precious; one of them is more meritorious and valuable than all the deeds a person may have performed in the whole of life without this transformation, however great they may have been. The same difference lying between a habit and an act lies between the transformation in love and the flame of love. It is like the difference between the wood on fire and the flame leaping up from it, for the flame is the effect of the fire present there." (*The Living Flame of Love,* 1.3)

DAY 35
CARRIED IN PERFECT LOVE, FROM THE BEGINNING TO THE END

> *The most important thing for us to remember is that Christ called each of us by name and that He said, "You are precious to Me, I love you." If you remember that, it makes all the difference.* (Mother Teresa)

Beyond the human comfort this brings, the experience of being loved and cherished by God is important at a yet deeper, spiritual level. Knowing that we are freely and immensely loved becomes *the* foundational Christian experience. If this is true for us, it is because it was true for Jesus—of whom the Father proclaimed at the Jordan, "*You are my beloved Son*" (Mk 1:11). This cherishing love, which Mother Teresa spoke of and modeled, is the ground on which our entire relationship with God is built.

The gospels hint at this *awareness of being beloved* as the daily bread that sustained Jesus throughout his life, and particularly during his passion. This was his baseline, the fabric of all his days, and of every night spent in the divine embrace, alone in the hills of Galilee. These are the deep gospel roots that underlie Mother Teresa's own awareness of being loved, an awareness she held to, "solid in her faith" (cf. 1 Pt 5:9), throughout her dark night.

Here we return anew to the wellspring of our life, the foundation that sustains us at every moment, from beginning to end. Even the highest reaches of the life of mystical transformation that I have been speaking of are nothing but another expression, a fulfillment, of this simple fact of being loved, cherished, and desired by God. It is really just allowing all the implications of God's amazing love, awakening my love in response, to unfold themselves through my very being and existence, in my relation to my divine Beloved and to all of those whom he also loves. As Langford continues:

> It is not enough, however, simply to know that we are loved, and to receive God's love in prayer, nor simply to turn our desire from worldly appetites and begin to thirst for God. This is essential, and the first step—but only the first step. We are called to return and spread about the love we have received—to love God with more and more of our being, in good times and bad. All that takes place in our life, in God's plan, is for the sake of love, a school of love. ...

The cycle of grace Mother Teresa invites us to is not complete until our desire for the God of love becomes love for the God we desire—until we *love the Lord our God with all our heart, and with all our soul, and with all our strength* (cf. Dt 6:5).

This is the final goal of our conversion and our transformation, this alone is the full flowering of our longing for God. In this lies our highest dignity—in loving as God loves, for "love is of God, and he who loves is born of God..." (1 Jn 4:7). Remember that God not only thirsts to love us, but that he thirsts as well to *be loved by us*—as Mother Teresa reminds us, God's desire is "to love *and to be loved."*

Loving the God who is love unifies and elevates all the operations of the soul, and every aspect of our lives. As St. John of the Cross explains in his *Spiritual Canticle:*

> All my occupation now is the practice of the love of God, all the powers of soul and body, memory, understanding, and will, interior and exterior senses, the desires of spirit and of sense, all work in and by love. All I do is done in love; all I suffer, I suffer in the sweetness of love. (28.8)

Love is not only the end and goal of our process of transformation; it is our path and door of access. Love *is itself* the process —for the path to the God of love is only love. Love is an enterprise always at hand, always but a choice away. As Mother Teresa assures us, love's fruit is always in season, always awaiting and inviting us—calling out from the depths of our soul where his glory dwells, and from the wounds and needs of our neighbor, where his crucified thirst for love is most touching and urgent. ...

What this means is that there is no need to wait, no need to better ourselves before making some return of the immense love we have received—and continue receiving in prayer. Nothing stands in the way of our experiencing the full "*joy of loving,"* and completing the circle of divine love received and given. As an anonymous author unknowingly echoed Mother Teresa's message, giving voice to the Almighty's thirst for our love no matter our condition:

> Love Me as you are. I know your misery, the inner struggle of your heart and the tribulations of your soul, the weakness and infirmities of your body. I know your sins, your failings; and I tell you just the same, give Me your heart. Love Me AS YOU ARE.
>
> If you wait to become an angel to deliver yourself to Love, you will never love Me. Even if you fail often in those sins that you would rather never know, even if you are lazy in the practice of virtue, I do not permit you to not love Me. Love Me as you are, whether you be in fervor, in dryness, or in tepidity; whether you be in fidelity or infidelity, love Me just AS YOU ARE.
>
> I want the love of your poor heart, your indigent heart. If you decide to wait until you are perfect to love Me, you will never love Me. ... I definitely intend to form you, but in the meantime, I love you as YOU are. You...love Me as YOU are. I desire to see this love that you have rise and increase from the bottom of your misery. I love you even in your weakness, I love the love of the poor.[26]

Wherever I may be on my journey into the burning furnace of God's love, however pliable and transparent my being and faculties have become to his divine touch and to the radiance of his light, I can *always love*, here and now. For the infinite beauty and ardor of divine love is already enfolding me, already pressing upon me, in each moment of my life—in this moment of my life—and always will. God therefore does not desire me to become restless and agitated by the awareness of my frailty or limitation, to cease to live in the present moment due to my pressing forward to the future. He does not wish for me to stand before him under a cloud of shame-filled inadequacy and the perpetual preoccupation of "not doing enough." A true self-awareness, born of recognition of my sinfulness, of the many mistakes that I have made, and of my desperate need for God, gives birth rather to a *lightness*, a gradual forgetfulness of self or unselfconsciousness, in which I cease to try to "measure up" and instead simply try to *love without measure*. Yes, and this is what God wishes: for me to simply live each moment to the full, letting go of all self-directed calculations and fears; to simply be loved and to love, to play, to wonder, to work, to rest, with total abandonment into the hands of his paternal tenderness and his spousal cherishing.

My own growth and transformation is, after all, *his business*; he alone can bring it to full flourishing. It is grace that will lead me to sanctity and to the full flowering of nuptial intimacy; and even my own daily "yes" is awakened and sustained by grace, grace that operates most fully and freely in a heart that is relaxed, malleable, and at peace. Yes, grace comes to teach my heart to consent to be little, and to find God's immense and immeasurable love precisely in littleness: like finding the infant God asleep in a manger, or finding the eternal Son sweating in his father's workshop, or walking the road to Calvary, or suffering in the hearts of the poor, the sick, the suffering, my brothers and sisters, or like finding the beauty of the love of Christ in the tiny Eucharistic Host!

Yes, love transfigures us in littleness, through the humility of a God who has made himself thirst for love of us, whose eternal torrent of love, the everlasting wellspring of all things, thirsts to be thirsted for by us! He is, truly, the Thirsty Fountain, who yearns to love us in each moment, however mundane and insignificant it may seem, and to sanctify the whole of our existence with his presence and the very vibrant activity of his own love alive and at work within us and through us. And in loving me, he finds joy. Let me not rob him of this joy! And in receiving my reciprocal love—for he so desires it!—his heart is consoled, and mine, too, finding in him all that I desire. This is possible in each moment, truly possible, as thirst meets thirst, until the day when thirst shall be no more, or rather shall be fulfilled and satiated in the everlasting consummation of intimacy that awaits us in heaven. For my part, therefore, all he wishes is for me to receive his love each day anew, with deep desire and with childlike lightness born of trust, and to let my gift flow back to him—however frail it may at present be—letting it continue to grow in intensity and totality until coming to full consummation in the intimacy for which he created me, and which, by his grace, he will bring to full flower.

WEEK VI

COMING FULL CIRCLE

DAY 36
A SINGLE ACT OF PURE LOVE

I have spoken of the transformation of the human person in God that culminates in her "every action becoming love," because "the love by which she is united to him moves her to the love of God in and through all things. Like the bee that sucks honey from all the wildflowers and will not use them for anything else, the soul easily extracts the sweetness of love from all things that happen to her; that is, she loves God in them. Thus everything leads her to love." And indeed, one comes to realize, in this intimate space, that "God makes use of nothing else than love." All the fruitfulness of missionary activity, of pastoral ministry, of writing, culture, and work, of personal presence, comes from the hidden wellspring of love...love as a participation in the essence of the divinity, in the life of the Trinity.

These words on love inflamed the heart of little Thérèse, and led her (along with 1 Corinthians 13 and the words of John of the Cross I am about to quote) to the joyful cry: "I have at last found my place. My vocation is to be love in the heart of the Church!"* Yes, and this recognition of the primacy of love—indeed the all-sufficiency of love—stands at the origin and the heart of *every* vocation within the Church. Even as I speak about the "contemplative" vocation below, I do so not only to affirm its beauty but

---

*"My eyes fell on the 12th and 13th chapters of the First Epistle to the Corinthians. I read that all cannot become Apostles, Prophets, and Doctors; that the Church is composed of different members; that the eye cannot also be the hand. The answer was clear, but it did not fulfill my desires, or give to me the peace I sought. "Then descending into the depths of my nothingness, I was so lifted up that I reached my aim." Without being discouraged I read on, and found comfort in this counsel: "Be zealous for the better gifts. And I show unto you a yet more excellent way." The Apostle then explains how all perfect gifts are nothing without Love, that Charity is the most excellent way of going surely to God. At last I had found rest. Meditating on the mystical Body of Holy Church, I could not recognize myself among any of its members as described by St. Paul, or was it not rather that I wished to recognize myself in all? Charity provided me with the key to my vocation. I understood that since the Church is a body composed of different members, the noblest and most important of all the organs would not be wanting. I knew that the Church has a heart, that this heart burns with love, and that it is love alone which gives life to its members. I knew that if this love were extinguished, the Apostles would no longer preach the Gospel, and the Martyrs would refuse to shed their blood. I understood that love embraces all vocations, that it is all things, and that it reaches out through all the ages, and to the uttermost limits of the earth, because it is eternal.

'Then, beside myself with joy, I cried out: "O Jesus, my Love, at last I have found my vocation. My vocation is love! Yes, I have found my place in the bosom of the Church, and this place, O my God, Thou hast Thyself given to me: in the heart of the Church, my Mother, I will be LOVE! . . . Thus I shall be all things: thus will my dream be realized. . . ."

'Why do I say I am beside myself with joy? This does not convey my thought. Rather is it peace which has become my portion—the calm peace of the sailor when he catches sight of the beacon which lights him to port. O luminous Beacon of Love! I know how to come even unto Thee, I have found the means of borrowing Thy Fires. I am but a weak and helpless child, yet it is my very weakness which makes me dare to offer myself, O Jesus, as victim to Thy Love.' (*Story of a Soul*, ch. 11)

also to come around again, "full circle," to affirm *that love which surpasses the distinctions of all vocations and thus unites them all together at the center.* Here what matters is love. In love, we are all made one.

Let us pick up where we left off with John of the Cross two days ago:

> Because we said that God makes use of nothing other than love, it may prove beneficial to explain the reason for this before commenting on the stanza. The reason is that all our works and all our trials, even though they be the greatest possible, are nothing in the sight of God. For through them we cannot give him anything or fulfill his only desire, which is the exaltation of the soul. Of these other things he desires nothing for himself, since he has no need of them. If anything pleases him, it is the exaltation of the soul. Since there is no way by which he can exalt her more than by making her equal to himself, he is pleased only with her love. For the property of love is to make the lover equal to the object loved. Since the soul in this state possesses perfect love, she is called the bride of the Son of God, which signifies equality with him. In this equality of friendship the possessions of both are held in common, as the Bridegroom himself said to his disciples: *I have now called you my friends, because all that I have heard from my Father I have manifested to you* [Jn. 15:15]. ...
>
> I no longer tend the herd, ...
> nor have I any other work
>
> Before reaching this gift and surrender of herself and her energy to the Beloved, the soul usually has many unprofitable occupations by which she endeavors to serve her own [disordered] appetite and that of others. For we can say she had as much work as she had many habitual imperfections. These habitual imperfections can be, for example, the trait or "work" of speaking about useless things, thinking about them, and also carrying them out, not making use of such actions in accord with the demands of perfection. She usually has desires to serve the appetites of others, which she does through ostentation, compliments, flattery, human respect, the effort to impress and please people by her actions, and many other useless things. In this fashion she strives to please people, employing for them all her care, desires, work, and finally energy.
>
> She says she no longer has all this "work" because all her words, thoughts, and works are of God and are directed toward him without any of the former imperfections. Thus the verse means: I no longer go about satisfying my appetite or that of others, nor am I occupied or detained with other useless pastimes or things of the world.
>
> Now that my every act is love.
>
> This is like saying that now all this work is directed to the practice of love of God, that is: All the ability of my soul and body (memory, intellect, and will, interior and exterior senses, appetites of the sensory and spiritual parts) move in love and be-

cause of love. Everything I do I do with love, and everything I suffer I suffer with the delight of love. David meant this when he said: *I shall keep my strength for you* [Ps. 59:10]. ...

The soul, indeed, lost to all things and won over to love, no longer occupies her spirit in anything else. She even withdraws in matters pertinent to the active life and other exterior exercises for the sake of fulfilling the one thing the Bridegroom said was necessary [Lk. 10:42], and this: attentiveness to God and the continual exercise of love in him. This the Lord values and esteems so highly that he reproved Martha when she tried to call Mary away from her place at his feet in order to busy her with other active things in his service; and Martha thought that she herself was doing all the work and Mary, because she was enjoying the Lord's presence, was doing nothing [Lk 10:39-41]. Yet, since there is no greater and more necessary work than love, the contrary is true. The Lord also defends the bride in the Song of Songs, conjuring all creatures of the world, referred to by the daughters of Jerusalem, not to hinder the the bride's spiritual sleep of love or cause her to awaken or open her eyes to anything else until she desire [Sg. 3:5].

... She should not become involved in other works and exterior exercises that might be of the slightest hindrance to the attentiveness of love toward God, even though the work be of great service to God. For a little of this pure love is more precious to God and the soul and more beneficial to the Church, even though it seems one is doing nothing, than all these other works put together. ...

Great wrong would be done to a soul who possesses some degree of this solitary love, as well as to the Church, if we were to urge her to become occupied in exterior or active things, even if the works were very important and required only a short time. Since God has solemnly entreated that no one awaken a soul from his love [Sg. 3:5], who will dare do so and remain without reproof?* After all, this love is the end for which we were created.

Let those, then, who are singularly active, who think they can win the world with their preaching and exterior works, observe here that they would profit the Church and please God much more, not to mention the good example they would give, were they to spend at least half of this time with God in prayer... They would then certainly accomplish more, and with less labor, by one work than they otherwise would by a thousand. For through their

---

*Here is a prime example of how taking John literally can lead to imbalance or narrowness in the spiritual life. While his advice here springs from his own experience and unique vocation—and in this sense is valid—it cannot by any means be applied literally to every one of us. Here, as elsewhere in his writings, it is important to extract the "essence" while letting go of the narrow shell: to understand the primal importance of ceaseless attentiveness to God beyond all that distracts us from him, while recognizing that this is manifested uniquely in the life of every person, and that we each have our particular path to walk. What is important is that the particular contours of each life, from the purely contemplative to that which blends contemplation and action, is safeguarded with great reverence and gratitude.

prayer they would merit this result, and themselves be spiritually strengthened. Without prayer they would do a great deal of hammering but accomplish little, and sometimes nothing, and even at times cause harm. God forbid that the salt should begin to lose its savor [Mt. 5:13]. However much they may appear to achieve externally, they will in substance be accomplishing nothing; it is beyond doubt that good works can be performed only by the power of God. (*The Spiritual Canticle,* 28:1, 6-8; 29:1-3)

The encounter with the thirst of Christ, with the love of God in his ardent longing for his children, naturally gives birth to a thirst to draw near to others, to share in their pain and their suffering, their hopes and their desires, and to help them draw near to the God who loves them and seeks them out. This is the course of the encounter with Christ in prayer, for all of us: we experience his love for us—his thirst for us and our thirst for him meet—and these two thirsts then join together in thirsting for the salvation of others.

This thirst blossoms in a deep desire to serve others, and, unless a specific call of God to a life of solitude and prayer (such as a cloistered monastery) intervenes, it specifically gives birth to concrete actions for the good of others. We see this illustrated profoundly in the life of Mother Teresa and her Missionaries of Charity; and all who have witnessed the works of love done by them see the Gospel enfleshed, made manifest, in the most beautiful and convincing way. Mother Teresa's spirituality, standing at the far end of the development begun in John of the Cross, indeed transcends the distinction between "contemplative" and "active," such that, through praying so intensely before the Eucharistic Jesus and also serving the same Jesus in the poorest of the poor, she and her family became "contemplatives in the heart of the world." They live to the utmost the intuition of John of the Cross that "a single act of pure love is worth more than all other works put together." And thus they strive for their every act, both in the silence of prayer and in the nitty-gritty of presence to the poorest of the poor, to be an act of pure love given to Jesus, an act of spousal tenderness and self surrender. And yet this witness tells us that *each one of us* can also live the same mystery, the same ceaseless prayer, a life of ceaseless acts of love for God born of deep union with him. It also shows that the path God marks out for us is not determined by pragmatic considerations, and depends not on organization and planning and our own ability to comprehend and control—these in fact can be temptations to become "big," whereas God wants to work precisely in our utmost littleness and poverty—but on simple and unaffected love in each moment, on responsiveness to the call of God as it comes to us in the littleness of our daily lives, pervaded by the intimate presence of God who loves us and receives our love. To be loved and to love. That is the stuff of every life, and it is what endures.

Regarding a more contemplative vocation—as per John of the Cross—this sharing in the thirst of Christ, incarnate in the life of each person, can also be manifested in a specifically mystical way, in a form of prayer that demands the *whole* of a person's existence in a specific way, to the exclusion of all else. In this case, a person's life becomes, in a special way, a ceaseless prayer for the salvation of the world.* Even as this call to ceaseless prayer and abiding intercession is meant for all of us, just as ministry to others in obedience to Christ is also meant for all of us, each of us has our unique place in the Body of Christ by the plan of God. Some of us are called, from the heart of prayer-filled union with Christ, to give ourselves in active ministry for our brothers and sisters, or to love our families and all those, from this place, whom God entrusts to us as neighbor and friend. Some of us, on the other hand, are called upon to renounce forms of active ministry and availability to others, so that, in the space opened up by this movement, we may be wholly available to God in a life of contemplation, to participate intimately and mystically in the redeeming gift of Christ on the Cross, in the secret word of atoning love that occurs in hiddenness and silence. Indeed, this hidden mystery occurring in the silent space between the thirst of God incarnate in Christ and those who welcome his approach —this nuptial intimacy wrought at the foot of the Cross—is the true wellspring of all apostolic and ministerial fruitfulness throughout the Church and the world. And thus, with unique contours, it throbs as a heartbeat in the life of each one of us.

If this "pure love" of which John speaks is indeed the origin of all fruit, born of the hidden wellspring of God's love grafted intimately into human heart and life, then it is of utmost importance that such love is made present everywhere that there is human suffering, everywhere that human hearts thirst for God (or flee his face), throughout history. But what of those events in history that bear the most terrible suffering, events in which human malice and diabolical evil seemed to win the day? If only there was some way that the balance-sheet of history could be swayed in the direction of goodness, truth, and beauty, towards nobility of spirit, devotion to God, and authentic communion. We can live integrity *now*, and seek to foster a world in which such horrible evil is never allowed to grow or express itself, or at least not to thrive. But it is also true, in a most beautiful if unexpected way, that my fidelity *now*, in all the humble details of my life, in prayer and activity, can pour forth abundant fruit, not only throughout space, but also *throughout time*.

A vivid awareness of this reality came to me just after finishing the

---

*It takes great trust for those who have devoted their lives to prayer and pursuit of the face of God—renouncing in this act external ministries and active forms of fruitfulness—to believe in the fecundity of their life and their prayer. Having nothing to "show" for themselves, they can rely only on the naked fecundity of pure love. And if this deep attunement to the primacy of love before God is lost—the fact that love, love-as-prayer, alone is the source of all true fruit—there can arise a temptation to fear that more active forms of service would be more fruitful, rather than the hidden, ordinary, and invisible fruitfulness born of simple love, prayer, and suffering born with joyful surrender. It is also simply quite painful for a loving heart to draw near to the compassionate Heart of Christ, agonizing with thirst for suffering human hearts, and to share in his thirst and his pain, and yet not to act on this in external and tangible ways. Here the words of John of the Cross can be encountered as deeply consoling. In my case, they in fact mediated and confirmed the awareness of my own unique vocation. In the face of the desire to serve the poorest of the poor in the most vivid way possible, they helped me to discern anew that God had a different place for me: he wanted me to *be* one of the poor, hidden, in complete poverty of surrender, in compassionate solidarity, and in redemptive suffering and atoning love.

novel *Auschwitz Lullaby* by Mario Escobar, which tells of a woman, Helene Hannemann, who, founding a nursery and school for children in Auschwitz during World War II, interacted closely with Josef Mengele. For those who are not acquainted with his name, he was the most terrifying incarnation of the "mad scientist," performing all kinds of horrible medical experiments on adults and children in the camps, none of which I desire to describe here. Though the narrative of the story is given from Helene's perspective, the Epilogue is given from Mengele's, as he rides in a plane years after the war has ended, reading her journal. (He was never captured and brought to justice, as he fled to Argentina with a fake identity.) The novel portrays that, in all of his inhumanity, Mengele had nonetheless felt a breath of goodness and nobility, of love, in the presence of Helene, a loving mother, devoted wife, and believer in God. This encounter and relationship was, as it were, an invitation to conversion for him, to recognize the shard of humanity and compassion buried deep within his heart, and to let the breath of God himself set it free, in repentance and surrender, to live again.

After reading this, I prayed, "May he have converted before the end of his life," seeing that he had so many years of life after the war, unlike other Nazis who were hung for war crimes as early as 1946. But then I realized that there was no need to pray in the past tense in that way. Through the world-cradling presence of God, and through the "ever-now" reality of the Paschal Mystery, my prayer in my *present* for persons in the *past* could have a true effect on their hearts as if I had prayed for them in *their present*. For by being present to Christ *now*, my prayer becomes present to them *then*, for Christ, who unites us, is present everywhere always, throughout time and space. This insight struck me in a new way, and deeply personally, in this moment. God himself is outside of time, and all of history is present to him simultaneously, in the fullness of its unfolding as if a single moment. Thus my prayer now, in the year 2022, can truly have an effect in hearts and minds in the past, in 1943 or 1967, or in 33 A.D., or in any other period.

The events themselves will not change, of course, since the history that has happened *is* the only history, the one shared by all of us, a single story in which we are all actors. But my prayers for these things in the past are perhaps part of the reason things did not become worse, or part of the reason that goodness and love burst forth victorious even in the places where it seemed most threatened with defeat. And who knows what deep interior effect my prayers and humble acts of love can have in the hearts of others, both past, present, and future, to prepare the way for God's loving advent into their lives, bringing them to conversion, repentance, and fullness of life?

God invites me to embrace my unique life within this world, with all of its limitations, even its apparent narrowness and irrelevance, and to *find in it the throbbing heartbeat of love*. Yes, as I said above, all vocations and expressions of life, whatever they may be, converge upon the single mystery of *love* springing from the heart of God into the human heart, and from the heart of man into the heart of God. Yes, they all converge into the welcoming embrace of the Trinity, into the intimacy of his divine embrace in which we are seen, known, loved, cradled, and transformed, to be all aflame with his love in our very flesh and life. And in this light, every moment of my life becomes beautiful, every aspect of creation becomes ravishingly transparent, radiant with a mysterious light, because in and through it I find God loving me, and I love him in response.

This—*this* is the fulfillment of all desire, and also the source of abounding fruit. In this perspective, no life is insignificant. Rather, the whole richness of the drama unfolding throughout the entire universe and all of history is condensed, as it were, into the intimate space of loving dialogue between God and myself. And in the same moment this intimate dialogue flows out, like ripples from the center, to spread far and wide, touching, healing, and transfiguring other hearts and the cosmos itself, until, at the consummation of all things, we are all united as one in him, in the intimate embrace of the Father, Son, and Holy Spirit.[27]*

---

*In the end notes I have included the text of a poem that tries to express the significance of the quote of John of the Cross on "a single act of pure love" in my own life, but also in the life of each one of us. May it help to bring the meaning of this meditation more deeply into our hearts and lives—for all of us, precisely in our unique vocation or the particular contours of our lives, can let God draw us to this place of pure love, of gratuitous intimacy, and thus can let abundant fruit pour forth throughout time and space for the good of the Church and the world.

DAY 37
AGAINST HIS BREAST:
THE MOST PROFOUND COMMUNION

Let us continue to unfold the beauty of intimacy that blossoms between the human person and the Persons of the Trinity through mature self-surrender. John of the Cross writes:

> In this interior union God communicates himself to the soul with such genuine love that neither the affection of a mother, with which she so tenderly caresses her child, nor a brother's love, nor any friendship is comparable to it. The tenderness and truth of love by which the immense Father favors and exalts this humble and loving soul reaches such a degree—O wonderful thing, worthy of all our awe and admiration!—that the Father himself becomes subject to her for her exaltation, as though he were her servant and she his lord. And he is as solicitous in favoring her as he would be if he were her slave and she his god. So profound is the humility and sweetness of God!
>
> In this communication of love, he exercises in some way that very service that he says in the Gospel he will render to his elect in heaven; that is, girding himself and passing from one to another, he will minister to them [Lk. 12:37]. He is occupied here in favoring and caressing the soul like a mother who ministers to her child and nurses it at her own breasts. The soul thereby comes to know the truth of Isaiah's words: *You shall be carried at the breast of God and upon his knees you will be caressed* [Is. 66:12].
>
> What then will be the soul's experience among such sovereign graces! How she will be dissolved in love! How thankful she will be to see the breasts of God given to her with such supreme and generous love! Aware that she has been set among so many delights, she makes a complete surrender of herself and gives him the breast of her will and love. She experiences this surrender to her Bridegroom in the way the Bride did in the Song of Songs when speaking to her Bridegroom: *I to my Beloved, and his turning is toward me. Come, my Beloved, let us go into the field, let us abide together on the grange; let us rise very early and go to the vineyards to see if the vine is in flower and if the flowers bear fruit, if the pomegranates flourish; there will I give you my breasts* (that is, I will employ the delights and strength of my will in your love) [Sg. 7:10-12]. Because this mutual surrender of God and the soul is made in this union, she refers to it in the following stanza:
>
>> There he gave me his breast;
>> there he taught me a sweet and living knowledge;
>> and I gave myself to him,
>> keep nothing back;
>> there I promised to be his bride.

In this stanza the bride tells of the mutual surrender made in this spiritual espousal between the soul and God, saying that in the interior wine cellar of love they were joined by the communication he made of himself to her, by freely offering her the breast of his love in which he taught her wisdom and secrets, and by the complete surrender she made of herself to him, keeping nothing back for herself or for any other, promising to be his forever. The verse follows:

>There he gave me his breast;

Giving one's breast to another signifies the giving of love and friendship to another and the revealing of secrets to him as to a friend. When the soul says there he gave her his breast, she means that he communicated his love and secrets to her there. God grants this communication to the soul in this state, and also that of which she speaks in the following verse:

>there he taught me a sweet and living knowledge;

The sweet and living knowledge that she says he taught her is mystical theology, the secret knowledge of God that spiritual persons call contemplation. This knowledge is very delightful because it is a knowledge through love. Love is the master of this knowledge and what makes it wholly agreeable. Since God communicates this knowledge and understanding in the love with which he communicates himself to the soul, it is very delightful to the intellect since it is a knowledge belonging to the intellect, and it is delightful to the will since it is communicated in love, which pertains to the will. Then she says:

>and I gave myself to him,
>keeping nothing back;

(*The Spiritual Canticle,* 27.1-5)

How deeply beautiful these words are! Here John is leading us to the very heart of the experience of intimacy, of true togetherness in mutual self-surrender. And the language he uses is indeed the most adequate he can find—not abstract philosophical language, not conceptual expositions, but the language of the body, the language of persons. He digs deep into the heart of our experience of love and relationship as human beings, fashioned in God's image and likeness. He speaks of the body and of the relationships that characterize us in the body. And yet he carries it, in all of its vividness, into the heart of spiritual marriage with Christ, of childlike communion with the Father, of participation in the life of the Trinity. And through this John stretches thin the veil of the symbolism of human flesh to its ultimate meaning as a manifestation of God, as a sacrament of God.

For our very bodies, in all of their concreteness and limitation, bear an intrinsic and divine meaning within them. Their very structure and all of their parts, their harmonious unity and transparency to the person, the very beauty of their form and order, speaks of something very specific: of our call to intimacy-through-self-giving. As John Paul II said, in words that are so deeply significant: "The body, in fact, and only the body, is capable of making visible what is invisible: the spiritual and the divine. It has been created to transfer into the visible reality of the world the mystery hidden from eternity in God, and thus to be a sign of it" (TOB 19:4). In all love and relationship, we live as incarnate, embodied persons; the body is not something accidental to who we are, but the very domain of our conscious being as persons. This is true even in our growing communion with God in prayer and in life. We always pray as enfleshed, in all that this entails in terms of human experience, of engendered masculinity and femininity (there are no non-gendered souls), of needs and desires and appetites, capacities and incapacities.

Thus the "ascent" to union with God does not consist in leaving behind the flesh, in separating ourselves from our bodiliness, but in fact in descending into it most fully, and opening it wide to the gift and presence of God. As I indicated earlier, the path of holiness and union passes by way of *solitude*—return to my own innate solitude as a person—a solitude which is thus opened wide in *nakedness* to the gaze and gift of God, and to reciprocal gift in total vulnerability. What I want to emphasize now is that this solitude is always tied in with my unrepeatable body. It is not as if my spirit is separate from my body, and uses the body as a vessel or tool, replaceable by another body as it would in "reincarnation." No, my spirit inhabits my unique body, lives within it, vivifies it, such that, in God's intentions, body and spirit together, alone, constitute the fullness of "me." In a real sense, my body truly *is* me. This is why at the end of time, at the dawn of the new creation, God will resurrect our bodies in the likeness of the Resurrection of Christ, so that we can be joined to the Trinity forever in the fullness of our humanity, spirit alive in the body, and body living in the spirit.[*]

Let us return now, however, to the words of John quoted above. The imagery that John gives is that of the breast—which symbolizes, of course, the gift of the *heart*. For the breast—in biblical terminology this includes the bosom—is that physical symbol of the innermost heart made visible, as a space both of gift and of welcome. It is, thus, tenderness, generosity, nourishment, safety and security, warmth and softness, both vulnerable ex-

---

[*] There is a fascinating thread of contemplation that opens up here, which we simply don't have time to reflect upon here. It is to recognize how deeply our bodies—and in a specific way our engendered orientation and capacity for relationship—are *essential* to our wholeness and holiness. A healthy relationship with our body and the bodies of others, a spirit of purity and chastity, indeed a mature and healthy orientation of sexual capacity and desire in accordance with the purity of the Trinity's love, is part and parcel of being "transformed into the likeness of the Lord, from glory unto glory" (cf. 2 Cor 3:18). It thus also undergirds all that has been said in this book, as a subtle but present theme: the natural capacity for and openness to, as men and women, the fulfillment of all filiation and nuptiality in communion with the Blessed Trinity.

I have contemplated these themes at great length in my book *Loving in the Light of Eternity: Love and Intimacy as the Heart of All Reality*. It also plays a large role in *At the Heart of the Gospel: The Love in Whom All Lines Converge*. I believe that these are, along with the current book you are holding in your hands, my most important works. If therefore you wish to enter more deeply into the mystery that you have encountered here, I would humbly offer the other two books to you as an avenue of continued contemplation. God has his way of teaching each one of us. May we simply allow him to lead.

posure and chaste veiling. It has so many subtle connotations, going back to the earliest days of our lives, that it is not possible to put them all into words. I would encourage you to simply let the symbol speak for itself. Then it becomes profoundly moving to see and experience the significance of what John of the Cross is saying. For he is saying that God offers us the breasts of his own love, in a way more intimate, total, and tender than a mother offers her breasts to her child to nurse. He gives, in this, his very self, his inmost heart, the living water (spiritual milk!) of his own being. And John points out that this gift is an education, an initiation into the secrets of God.

For what, after all, does one feel when resting on the bosom of another? Two things: *breath* and *heartbeat*. And this is what God unveils to us when he admits us into his embrace. He draws us so close that he allows us to hear his eternal breathing, the breathing of love that ever passes between the Father and the Son, a breath which is the Spirit himself. (More on this soon!) And he allows us to hear his heartbeat, the pulsation of his eternal love, by which the vibrancy of his divine life surges in the intimacy of the communion of the three divine Persons; and also as this pulsation sends forth the divine life and presence throughout the entire cosmos, like the heart sending blood through the veins even to the furthest limits of the body.

Joined with this divine breathing and this divine heartbeat, we become initiates in the mystery of God, participants in the inmost life of the Trinity. And thus, so too, we let God repose against our breast, offering him the bosom of our love and our total surrender. As John wrote: "How thankful she will be to see the breasts of God given to her with such supreme and generous love! Aware that she has been set among so many delights, she makes a complete surrender of herself and gives him the breast of her will and love." What a beautiful mutual gift of the heart, a radiant reciprocal surrender of tender love! To know that we have such a God, that he loves and nurses us more tenderly than a mother her child, a lover his spouse! And that this same God desires us to love him, too, with a reciprocal tenderness, wanting to be so close to us as to rest against our heart, to drink of our inmost breast in love!

Here we are at the heart of biblical revelation, at the heart of the surging current of God's love revealed to us in salvation history. Let us try to feel it vibrating forth from God's breast, through the words of Holy Scripture:

"No one has ever seen God; the only-begotten Son, in the bosom of the Father, he has made him known" (Jn 1:18).

"One of the disciples, whom Jesus loved, was reclining against the bosom of Jesus" (Jn 13:23).

"You are stately as a palm tree, and your breasts are like its clusters. I say I will climb the palm three and lay hold of its branches. Oh, may your breasts be like clusters of the vine. ... Under the apple tree I awakened you. There your mother was in travail with you, there she who bore you was in travail" (Sg 7:7-8; 8:4).

"When Israel was a child I loved him, and out of Egypt I called my son. ... It was I who taught Ephraim to walk, I took them up in my arms;

but they did not know that I healed them. I led them with cords of compassion, with the bands of love, and I became to them as one who raises an infant to his cheeks, and I bent down to them and fed them" (Hos 11:1, 3-4).

"Rejoice with Jerusalem, and be glad for her, all you who love her; rejoice with her in joy, all you who mourn over her; that you may suck and be satisfied with her consoling breasts; that you may drink deeply with delight from the abundance of her glory. For thus says the LORD: 'Behold, I will extend prosperity to her like a river, and the wealth of the nations like an overflowing stream; and you shall suck, you shall be carried upon her hip, and fondled upon her knees. As one whom his mother comforts, so I will comfort you; you shall be comforted in Jerusalem" (Is 66:10-12).

DAY 38
AT THE FOOT OF THE TREE
I AWAKENED YOU

As profoundly personal as is the intimacy of which we have been speaking, as deeply buried in the depths of the human heart in its solitude before God, it is also rooted just as deeply in the heart of God's plan of salvation playing out in history. It is simply, as it were, the mystery of redemption, salvation, and sanctification playing itself out to its furthest consequences in the individual human person. It is the fullness of righteousness "that exceeds that of the scribes and Pharisees," it is, indeed, nothing but the fullest realization of the mystery of the *Beatitudes:* here the poor inherit the kingdom of heaven and the pure of heart see God as far as it is possible to see him while the shadows of this life still remain.

The transformation of hearts through prayer, sacrament, and the spirit of the Beatitudes indeed lies at the heart of the Church's life, the summit of her being and the wellspring of her activity. For what else does God desire for us but to experience in ourselves the fullness of those words: "Blessed are you!" "Happy are you!"? And truly happy indeed is the person who has totally given himself or herself to the divine Bridegroom, awakened and sustained by his prior gift of himself to them! And where is this gift of the Bridegroom, this outpouring of himself and this laying bare of his thirst, most fully realized? In the Paschal Mystery. In all that unfolds in the life of Christ, and through him in the life of each one of us, from the evening of Holy Thursday to the dawn of Easter Sunday. Here is the nuptial intimacy first sealed; here is the act of consummation; here is the pledge of complete mutual belonging. It is given first, gratuitously, by God in Christ, to all, and impressed upon us specifically in baptism; and it is realized, over time, in the lives of each one of us by our willing assimilation into Christ through the mystery of Redemption. As John of the Cross writes, beautifully expounding upon the climactic words of the Song of Songs—"Under the apple tree I awakened you, there where your mother was in travail with you, there where she who bore you was in travail" (Sg 8:5):

> In this high state of spiritual marriage the Bridegroom reveals his wonderful secrets to the soul as to his faithful consort, with remarkable ease and frequency, for true and perfect love knows not how to keep anything hidden from the beloved. He mainly communicates to her sweet mysteries of his Incarnation and the ways of the redemption of humankind, one of the loftiest of his works and thus more delightful to the soul. Even though he communicates many other mysteries to her, the Bridegroom in the following stanza mentions only the Incarnation [including the Redemption] as the most important. In speaking to the soul he says:
>
> > Beneath the apple tree:

> there I took you for my own,
> there I offered you my hand,
> and restored you,
> where your mother was corrupted.

The Bridegroom explains to the soul in this stanza his admirable plan in redeeming and espousing her to himself through the very means by which human nature was corrupted and ruined, telling her that as human nature was ruined through Adam and corrupted by means of the forbidden tree in the Garden of Paradise, so on the tree of the cross it was redeemed and restored when he gave it there, through his passion and death, the hand of his favor and mercy, and broke down the barriers between God and humans that were built up through original sin. Thus he says:

> Beneath the apple tree:

That is: beneath the favor of the tree of the cross (referred to by the apple tree), where the Son of God redeemed human nature and consequently espoused it to himself, and then espoused each soul by giving it through the cross grace and pledges for this espousal. And thus he says:

> there I took you for my own,
> there I offered you my hand,

That is: There I offered you my kind regard and help by raising you from your low state to be my companion and spouse.

> And restored you,
> where your mother was corrupted.

For human nature, your mother, was corrupted in your first parents under the tree, and you too under the tree of the cross were restored. If your mother, therefore, brought you death under the tree, I brought you life under the tree of the cross. In such a way God manifests the decrees of his wisdom; he knows how to draw good from evil so wisely and beautifully, and to ordain to a greater good what was a cause of evil.

The Bridegroom himself literally speaks this stanza to the bride in the Song of Songs: *Sub arbore malo suscitavi te; ibi corrupta est mater tua, ibi violata est genitrix tua* (Under the apple tree I raised you up; there your mother was corrupted, there she who bore you was violated) [Sg. 8:5].

The espousal made on the cross is not the one we now speak of. For that espousal is accomplished immediately when God gives the first grace that is bestowed on each one at baptism. The espousal of which we speak bears reference to perfection and is not achieved save gradually and by stages. For though it is all one espousal, there is a difference in that one is attained at the soul's pace, and thus little by little, and the other at God's pace, and thus immediately. *(The Spiritual Canticle,* 23.1-6a)

Here we are so very close to the throbbing heartbeat of reality, unveiled to us and made accessible to us in Christ Crucified and Risen, in the

Son of God who died and rose for us and is perpetually present to us in his humble glory. Yes, and here he is present in the Eucharist most vividly, which makes present again, in every time and place, the world-transcending and time-permeating mystery of Redemption, the Paschal Mystery of his Passion and Resurrection. Yet he does not re-present the events of Holy Thursday to Easter Sunday only for us to behold them and reverence them externally. No, they are meant also to play themselves out within us, in our very hearts and lives. Our whole existence is meant to become Christic, Eucharistic, Paschal. As the *Catechism* says in two different places, quoting Saint John Eudes:

> We must continue to accomplish in ourselves the stages of Jesus' life and his mysteries and often to beg him to perfect and realize them in us and in his whole Church... For it is the plan of the Son of God to make us and the whole Church partake in his mysteries and to extend them to and continue them in us and in his whole Church. This is his plan for fulfilling his mysteries in us. ... I ask you to consider that our Lord Jesus Christ is your true head, and that you are one of his members. He belongs to you as the head belongs to its members; all that is his is yours: his spirit, his heart, his body and soul, and all his faculties. You must make use of all these as of your own, to serve, praise, love, and glorify God. You belong to him, as members belong to their head. And so he longs for you to use all that is in you, as if it were his own, for the service and glory of the Father. (par. 521 and 1698)

We see the same in a prayer of Elizabeth of the Trinity:

> O My God, Trinity whom I adore, help me to forget myself entirely so as to be established in you as still and as peaceful as if my soul were already in eternity. May nothing be able to disturb my peace, nor make me depart from you, O my Unchanging One, but may each moment carry me further into the depths of your Mystery. Pacify my soul: make it your heaven, your beloved abode, your resting place. May I never leave you there alone, but may I be entirely present, my faith completely ready, wholly adoring, fully surrendered to your creative action.
>
> O my beloved Christ, crucified by love, I would like to be a bride for your heart. I would like to cover you with glory, I would like to love you... unto death. I feel my powerlessness, however, and I ask you to clothe me with yourself, to identify my soul with all the movements of your soul, to overwhelm me, to invade me, to substitute yourself for me, that my life might be but the radiation of your Life. Come into me as Adorer, as Healer, as Savior.
>
> O Eternal Word, Word of my God, I want to spend my life listening to you. I want to be completely docile, ready to learn all from you. Then, through all nights, all voids, all weakness, I want always to fixate on you and to remain under your great light. O My beloved Star, fascinate me to the point that I could not forsake your shining light.
>
> O Consuming Flame, Spirit of love, come over me until my

soul is rendered into an incarnation of the Word; may I be for Him another humanity in which he renews His whole Mystery.

And you, O Father, bend over your little creature, cover her with your shadow, and in her only the Beloved in whom You are well-pleased.

O my Three, my All, my Beatitude, Infinite Solitude, Immensity in which I lose myself, I surrender myself as prey. Bury yourself in me in order that I might bury myself in you while waiting to contemplate in your light the immeasurable depths of your grandeur.

How can this transfiguration of human persons in the grace and love of the Trinity made manifest in Christ *not* be the heart of God's intentions for us? It is the heart of his intentions because the heart of his intentions is *intimacy*, it is *communion* with each one of us in an embrace that is more-intimate-than-spousal, more-profound-than-filial, in an embrace that can adequately be described as nothing but *trinitarian,* a living participation in his own life and love as Father, Son, and Holy Spirit!

DAY 39
THROUGH THE HEART OF THE PASCHAL MYSTERY TO THE HEART OF THE TRINITY

The reason of our existence is to quench the thirst of God. I don't say even "Jesus" or "on the cross," but "of God." Try to deepen your understanding of these two words, "Thirst of God." (Mother Teresa) [28]

These few words indicate, I believe, a deep intuition and experience of the heart of Saint Teresa of Calcutta, which, in her simplicity, she saw no need to expound upon. And indeed it is best known by walking the path ourselves, the path of love-responding-to-love, the path that leads us ever deeper into the discovery of the thirst in the heart of God. We should indeed pray and contemplate deeply on these words: the thirst of God.

This is not merely the thirst of the man Jesus; it is the thirst of the entire Trinity, the fullness of the Godhead: Father, Son, and Holy Spirit. And it is not merely a momentary thirst either—"on the Cross"—but rather an eternal trait of the divinity itself, one of the attributes of the interpersonal relations of the Father, Son, and Spirit. It is, in fact, simply a God-given icon, an image, of the very nature of God's own love, both in the ardor of its eternal movement—the never-ceasing dance of mutual delight and reciprocal self-giving between the three divine Persons—as well as in its condescending, compassionate, and pained longing for the redemption and salvation of each one of God's children.

Is not God's desire for us to know the nature of his thirst an expression of the ardor, purity, and intimacy of his love? In other words, he wants us to experience his love so deeply that we know not only what it feels like to *be loved by him* but also *what it feels like for him to love*. This is indeed a trait, perhaps the essential trait, of a mature love, even on the natural human level. Whenever my heart is expanded to the point that I am able to feel with and for another person their own experience, and not merely to be preoccupied with my experience of them or with what they think of me, the true *tenderness* of love is born. And here a thirst is awakened that far surpasses what so often parades itself as true love, as *eros,* as desire for another. For it is a thirst born not only of my innate desire and capacity for relationship, for intimacy, my own desire to be loved, but equally and inseparably of my capacity to love in the act of going out of myself, to empathize with another, to care for them and enter into their own subjectivity. Here, indeed, *eros* and *agape* are already becoming one as they are inseparably one in God.

John Paul II indeed understood sanctity and the new creation—that state of eternal consummation that awaits us and the entire cosmos at the end of time—in these terms: in terms of "intersubjectivity" through love. He writes:

> The reciprocal gift of oneself to God—a gift in which man will concentrate and express all the energies of his own personal and at the same time psychosomatic subjectivity—will be the response to

God's gift of himself to man. In this reciprocal gift of self by man, a gift that will become completely and definitively beatifying as the response worthy of a personal subject to God's gift of himself, the "virginity" or rather the virginal state of the body will manifest itself completely as the eschatological fulfillment of the "spousal" meaning of the body, as the specific sign and authentic expression of personal subjectivity as a whole. In this way, then, the eschatological situation in which "they will take neither wife nor husband" has its solid foundation in the future state of the personal subject, when, as a consequence of the vision of God "face to face," *a love of such depth and power of concentration on God himself* will be born in the person that it *completely absorbs the person's whole psychosomatic subjectivity.*

This concentration of knowledge ("vision") and love on God himself—a concentration that cannot be anything but full participation in God's inner life, that is, in trinitarian Reality itself—will at the same time be the discovery in God of the whole "world" of relations that are constitutive of the world's perennial order ("cosmos"). This concentration will above all be man's rediscovery of himself, not only in the depths of his own person, but also in that union that is proper to the world of persons in their psychosomatic constitution. Certainly this is a union of communion. The concentration of knowledge and love on God himself in the trinitarian communion of Persons can find a beatifying response in those who will become sharers in the "other world" only *through realizing reciprocal communion commensurate with created persons.* ... We should think of the reality of the "other world" in the categories of the rediscovery of a new, perfect subjectivity of each person and at the same time of the *rediscovery* of a new, *perfect intersubjectivity of all.* In this way this reality means the true and definitive fulfillment of human subjectivity and, on this basis, the definitive fulfillment of the "spousal" meaning of the body. The total concentration of created, redeemed, and glorified subjectivity on God himself will not take man away from this fulfillment, but —on the contrary—will introduce him into it and consolidate him in it. One can say, finally, that in this way the eschatological reality will become the source of the perfect realization of the "trinitarian order" in the created world of persons. (TOB 68.3-4, 395-396)

We see the radiant fruit of the total mutual surrender of love: permeating our consciousness completely with participation in the life of God, and indeed making the entire cosmos radiant with the light of the Trinity. In the new creation, all things, all relationships, will be perfectly fulfilled precisely through returning fully into God, not there to be submerged, lost, or made anonymous, but rather to be affirmed and consummated in their true meaning and beauty in the light of the love of the Trinity.

To return now to the theme of this reflection. We see unfolded before us a central dimension of the Catholic faith and of true spirituality: it passes by way of Christ, in the Spirit, to the Father. It passes through the heart of the Paschal Mystery into the heart of the Blessed Trinity. For the Paschal Mystery is not defined merely on the basis of death and resurrection, of suffering and solidarity—being the passage of Christ's loving gift of self from the Eucharist on Holy Thursday, through the Passion on Good Friday and the silence of Holy Saturday, to the glorious Resurrection on Easter Sunday. It also marks out our own path of healing and transformation, our own passage into the fullness of love: assimilating into ourselves the very life of Jesus, passing with him from death into life, from loneliness into communion, from the narrowness of sin into the expansiveness of love, in which, in fact, we are assimilated into him. Through this assimilation, we are made partakers of the divine nature, made capable of sharing, with Christ and in Christ, in the very eternal life of the Trinity.

Yes, for in fact the Paschal Mystery seen in its deepest meaning is a window onto the heart of God. This is the impact of Mother Teresa's words quoted at the beginning of this reflection. The thirst revealed to her through the Crucified Jesus, the thirst with which the Son of God cried out as he hung upon the Cross, was not a merely passing thirst, a desperate cry of pain or loneliness or suffering. No, it was a manifestation of the eternal thirst in the heart of the Trinity to give himself to us in love, and, through this love, to awaken and receive our reciprocal gift. It was the revelation of God's infinite desire to love and to be loved. It was a marriage of God and humanity, wedded as one in the flesh of Jesus Christ, totally given and totally welcoming us. It was the exhalation of the very breath of the Holy Spirit into the suffocating lungs of humanity, and the inhalation of humanity into the heart of God himself: this is what the cry of love, and the final breath of Christ on the Cross, means! And this is the significance of his Resurrection! His Paschal Mystery, in other words, was the unveiling—and the gift!—of the essence of God as intimacy, as the perfect communion of Father, Son, and Holy Spirit, which even in the pain of the Passion was not torn asunder, not even lessened in intensity or subjective depth, but rather pervaded our entire universe, even into its darkest places, with the healing and consoling light of eternal love.

For here Christ cries out: "I still love you and long for you, however broken you find yourself to be! I have come to you, touched you, and redeemed you, espousing you in this way to myself, that I may be one with you in this life and for all eternity. Yes, I want you to be with me forever, where I myself eternally am, in the bosom of the Father, that you may behold there my glory which he has given me before the foundation of the world. Yes, in beholding my glory you are made one with my glory, taken up like the log of wood into the burning flames, pervaded, healed, transfigured, and made a participant in the very Love that first created you. And now this Love has redeemed you, granting you the capacity—by responding to my thirst, my invitation, my gift—to share in this Love forever, with me, breathing before our Father the one Holy Spirit who eternally unites us."

The Paschal Mystery in its historical dimension, therefore—as suffering, solidarity, light breaking through darkness—begins to fade, even as its eternal significance comes to the fore and proves everlastingly significant, eternally present before and within the heart of the Trinity. For it is nothing but the mutual breathing of Father and Son in the Holy Spirit, nothing but their ecstatic mutual self-giving, penetrating into the entire cosmos and every human heart, in order to sweep us all up into the innermost embrace that is theirs. Through this gift we share with them, with utmost subjective intensity and totality, the joy of their own subjective life of love: in the gaze of mutual delight, the perfect gift of reciprocal self-donation, and the utter and endless joy of complete intimacy.*[29]

---

*For further contemplation, I have provided a poem in the end notes.

DAY 40
THE DIVINE, BREATHLIKE SPIRATION

I have spoken of the spiritual marriage as the complete reciprocal "yes" of loving surrender between God and the human person, and as the intimacy born of this complete mutual gift. I have also tried to show, illustrated by the experience recounted by John of the Cross, how this union—achieved by the pure grace of God transfiguring all the faculties of the person—effects a complete permeation of the individual by divine love, such that in all things they are moved by love to love in the very likeness of God's own love, "loving God in God through God with the love of God." Here all the energies of soul and body, previously fractured, dissipated, and dulled by sin, are healed and set free by love, to flow in undimmed light and unhindered intensity back to God. And in God they flow also in response to the authentic voice of all created reality, speaking its word from God, and allowing the person to discover and love God in and through them, since now, indeed, it discovers and loves all things in God whom it loves beyond all things.

After this, I tried to illustrate how this "pure love," this gratuitous exercise of love in God, is the source of all authentic fruitfulness, healing, and transformation in the world, since, in the last analysis, "God makes use of nothing else than love." Whatever may be our vocation or the unique contours of our life, God looks and sees only love, naked before him to whose gaze all things are revealed. And so tapping into this boundless source of love, this abundant wellspring of charity, this font of intimacy, is the all-important gift and task of human life. Sanctity is the great mystery to which we are invited, sanctity as a return to the original state lost in Eden, and indeed a holiness transcending what was possible there, through the Redemption and Transfiguration wrought by Jesus Christ through his Paschal Mystery. By letting this Redemption unfold itself in our lives—through the reciprocal encounter of thirsts, through the growing movement of shared surrender, through a gaze of love that becomes love loving love, beloved loving lover and lover loving beloved, purifying the heart to its deepest wellsprings and ordering it wholly to God in God—by truly allowing Redemption to have its effect in us, we come to know, live, and experience what it means to be "partakers of the divine nature" (2 Pet 1:4).

And here we come to the most important, most central of the dimensions of sanctity, of transformation in and union with God. For as I have tried to emphasize again and again, sanctity is not merely a state of virtue or natural human wholeness, nor is it best understood as an ascetical achievement nor even, in fact, as the climax of human virtue. It is rather the manifestation and fruit of *passionate love*. Yes, in its inner core and throbbing heartbeat it is *the Trinity*. Sanctity is union with the Trinity, a living, vibrant, unreserved intimacy with the Trinity in faith, hope, and love, that permeates all of a person's life and the entirety of their being. Let us take a look now more deeply at what this intimacy looks like, as a way of glimpsing—through the lens of mystical experience—the breathtaking destiny that awaits us in heaven:

> This breathing of the air is an ability that the soul states God will give her there in the communication of the Holy Spirit. By his divine breathlike spiration, the Holy Spirit elevates the soul sublimely and informs her and makes her capable of breathing in God the same spiration of love that the Father breathes in the Son and the Son in the Father. This spiration of love is the Holy Spirit himself, who in the Father and the Son breathes out to her in this transformation in order to unite her to himself. There would not be a true and total transformation if the soul were not transformed in the three Persons of the Most Holy Trinity in an open and manifest degree.
>
> And this kind of spiration of the Holy Spirit in the soul, by which God transforms her into himself, is so sublime, delicate, and deep a delight that a mortal tongue finds it indescribable, nor can the human intellect, as such, in any way grasp it. Even what comes to pass in the communication given in this temporal transformation is unspeakable, for the soul united and transformed in God breathed out in God to God the very divine spiration that God—she being transformed in him—breathes out in himself to her.
>
> In the transformation that the soul possesses in this life, the same spiration passes from God to the soul and from the soul to God with notable frequency and blissful love, although not in the open and manifest degree proper to the next life. Such I believe was St. Paul's meaning when he said: *Since you are children of God, God sent the Spirit of his Son into your hearts, calling to the Father* [Gal. 4:6]. This is true of the Blessed in the next life and of the perfect in this life according to the ways described.
>
> One should not think it impossible that the soul be capable of so sublime an activity as this breathing in God through participation as God breathes in her. For, granted that God favors her by union with the Most Blessed Trinity, in which she becomes deiform and God through participation, how could it be incredible that she also understand, know, and love—or better that this be done in her—in the Trinity, together with it, as does the Trinity itself! Yet God accomplishes this in the soul through communication and participation. This is transformation in the three Persons in power and wisdom and love, and thus the soul is like God through this transformation. He created her in his image and likeness that she might attain such resemblance.
>
> No knowledge or power can describe how this happens, unless by explaining how the Son of God attained and merited such a high state for us, *the power to be children of God,* as St. John says [Jn. 1:12]. Thus the Son asked of the Father in St. John's Gospel: *Father, I desire that where I am those you have given me may also be with me, that they may see the glory you have given me* [Jn. 17:24], that is, that they may perform in us by participation the same work that I do by nature; that is, breathe the Holy Spirit.

And he adds: *I do not ask, Father, only for those present, but for those also who will believe in me through their doctrine; that all of them may be one as you, Father, in me and I in you, that thus they be one in us. The glory which you have given me I have given them that they may be one as we are one, I in them and you in me; that they may be perfect in one; that the world may know that you have sent me and loved them as you have loved me* [Jn. 17:20-23]. The Father loves them by communicating to them the same love he communicates to the Son, though not naturally as to the Son but, as we said, through unity and transformation of love. It should not be thought that the Son desires here to ask the Father that the saints be one with him essentially and naturally as the Son is with the Father, but that they may be so through the union of love, just as the Father and the Son are one in unity of love.

Accordingly, souls possess the same goods by participation that the Son possesses by nature. As a result they are truly gods by participation, equals and companions of God. Wherefore St. Peter said: *May grace and peace be accomplished and perfect in you in the knowledge of God and of our Lord Jesus Christ, as all things of his divine power that pertain to life and piety are given us through the knowledge of him who called us with his own glory and power, by whom he has given us very great and precious promises, that by these we may be made partakers of the divine nature* [2 Pet. 1:2-4]. These are words from St. Peter in which he clearly indicates that the soul will participate in God himself by performing in him, in company with him, the work of the Most Blessed Trinity because of the substantial union between the soul and God. Although this participation will be perfectly accomplished in the next life, still in this life when the soul has reached the state of perfection, as has the soul we are here discussing, she obtains a foretaste and noticeable trace of it in the way we are describing, although as we said it is indescribable.

(*The Spiritual Canticle,* 39.3-6)

"The soul united and transformed in God breathes out in God to God the very divine spiration that God—she being transformed in him—breathes out in himself to her." I remember quite vividly that, when I was in high school, I had printed out this sentence on a small slip of paper and put it on a poster board on the wall of my bedroom. I read it often, as the words burst with meaning, almost the like breath of God himself, the Holy Spirit shared by the Father and the Son, was reaching out to make himself known and felt. Such is God's desire for us. He uses every means possible in order to draw near to us, to open our hearts to him, to make space in us for his gift, and, finally, to transform us and elevate to make us capable of participating in the very innermost mystery of his own divine life! And as we see in these words of John of the Cross, the innermost life of God is a most blessed embrace, a sweet and everlasting kiss, the union of the Father and the Son in the shared breath of their single Spirit.

How should it be incredible, indeed, that these words deeply touch the heart, for they reach back to our most fundamental origin in God at the beginning of our lives—breathed forth through his creative Spirit—and towards our eternal destiny, in which we shall breathe with the Father and the Son the one Holy Spirit whom they share? But it is indeed incredible! Yet God wants us to believe, and not to doubt, for "how could it be incredible that she also understand, know, and love—or better that this be done in her—in the Trinity, together with it, as does the Trinity itself!" To understand, know, and love in the Trinity as the Trinity itself understands, knows, and loves. What greater union is there than this, to be so immersed in God, so permeated with God, so intimately joined to him that, as Saint Paul says, "I shall know even as I myself am known" (cf. 1 Cor 13:12). To see, know, and love all things as God himself does, since God's own mind, his own heart, his own gaze of love, his own experience, has become my own, my birthright through adoption and my very life through nuptial union! Yes, this is my destiny, to know and love all things in God, through God, to know and love myself in the gaze of his own love for me, to know and love each person in his gaze upon them; but above all, it is to know and love God himself in God, to love the Father with the love of the Son, and the Son with the love of the Father, and the Spirit with the love of both and both Father and Son with the love of the Spirit! For the love of God is one, shared indivisibly among the three divine Persons, this love that is the very substance, the very essence, of the divinity. And through grace it too becomes the very substance and essence of my own life, joined as my own human nature is to it, elevated and transfigured by the mystery of Redemption and sanctification.

What blessed beauty, what radiant joy, what perfect freedom! To be caught up by God's sheer gift into the innermost embrace of the Trinity, to be right in the midst of their ecstatic intimacy! To be so close, to be so intimately given and received, and to receive them so deeply, to be so permeated by their love, that I breathe with the Father and the Son the breath of their Spirit, poured out ceaselessly into me with all the force and intensity of their love for me; and that my whole being thrills with joy as the Spirit vibrates through me, speaking a word of pure and perfect love back to the Son, my Bridegroom, and, with the Son, to the Father, who has become my Father too, and in whose delighted gaze I eternally rejoice.

EPILOGUE

As intimate as the words of this book have become, as deep as we have let ourselves be carried into the secret space of communion between the human heart and God, we can also acknowledge that we are putting our finger on the heartbeat of the universal Church herself, the Bride of Christ and the living-space of our communion with the Trinity. This is not therefore some individualistic, isolated spirituality severed from the life of the Church, from care for one's brothers and sisters, from everything that is important to men and women, to the whole human family, on their journey through history. Rather, we are coming to the center-point towards which all is directed, and from which all flows.

For holiness, as the fullness of love born of profound intimacy with God, is the wellspring of all authentic healing and renewal in the Church and in human hearts. It is also the source of true evangelization, the impetus of the missionary efforts of believers, and the very substance of the true communion that unites those who believe in the likeness of the unity of the Father, Son, and Holy Spirit. This holiness is also the goal towards which all is directed: that they may all be one, as the Father and the Son are one. That each singular person may be child of the Father, spouse of the Son, possessed by the Spirit, breathing with God the very breath of love that is eternally his. And that, on the basis of this communion, all hearts may be united together in the most authentic mutual seeing and understanding, in true reverence and self-surrender, and in the purity of mutual belonging in the sight of God. As Christ prayed, expressing his deepest and most ardent desire:

> I do not pray for these only, but also for those who believe in me through their word, that they may all be one; even as you, Father, are in me, and I in you, that they also may be in us, so that the world may believe that you have sent me. The glory which you have given me I have given to them, that they may be one even as we are one, I in them and you in me, that they may become perfectly one, so that the world may know that you have sent me and have loved them even as you have loved me. Father, I desire that they also, whom you have given me, may be with me where I am, to behold my glory which you have given me in your love for me before the foundation of the world. O righteous Father, the world has not known you, but I have known you; and these know that you have sent me. I made known to them your name, and I will make it known, that the love with which you have loved me may be in them, and I in them. (Jn 17:20-26)

The popes at the dawn of this new millennium have called for a "new evangelization," a new ardor of missionary activity in bringing Christ to the places in the world that have either forgotten him or have never known him. And there are so many fruits hidden in this call, awaiting to be poured out upon us in our generous response to God, in letting ourselves be loved by him and then, from this experience, sharing his love with others. But at the heart of the new evangelization, as its true wellspring and ultimate goal, is another term of which the popes have spoken: *the "new springtime of holiness."* The new springtime of holiness, like flowers coming to bud and blossom after a painful winter of so much division, heresy, conflict, violent war, and aggressive rejection of God, is the path for the Church in the third millennium.

This path of holiness, of radical fidelity to the Gospel of Christ and to the immeasurable love of the Trinity revealed in him through the gift of the Spirit, is the path God marks out for our feet. And our Blessed Mother also shows us the way. God is thirsting, thirsting to love us tenderly and deeply, and thirsting also for our reciprocal love. He is thirsting that we may love one another as he loves us, manifesting in our lives and relationships the tenderness and intimacy of the inner life of the Trinity. This path can lead to the evangelization of those cultures that have still not received the light of Christ, and to the re-awakening of those cultures that have grown old and stale, too arrogant to accept the call to childhood, to the ever-renewed youthfulness of spirit born of God's love. This path can lead to the long-desired and desperately needed reunification of all who believe in Christ, and the healing of all the wounds to the unity of the Church of Christ, founded on the Paschal Mystery of Jesus ever present in the Eucharist, and safeguarded upon the rock of Peter and sharing in a single communion of faith, sacrament, life, and love. It can lead to the overcoming of the grip of the culture of death and the birth of a culture of life and love, in which every individual person is cherished and cared-for in their God-given dignity and beauty. Let us not be afraid to pray, to work, and to offer our lives boldly and confidently for these intentions, for the healing of our bleeding and suffering world. God is a God of miracles. And he wants to be generous more than we want to receive his generosity.

God is pouring out his love so vividly in our time, this time of mercy, this time of renewal, this time in which God is showing us the depths of his thirst to love and to be loved. He wants us to know and experience him as Trinity—as the intimacy of Father, Son, and Holy Spirit—to experience his cherishing gaze of love and tenderness, and to love him in response. He wants intimacy with each one of us children—with me. And, indeed, he wants the whole universe to be renewed in the likeness of the Trinity, through the "trinitarian" living of those who have accepted his love as the very essence of their own lives. Yes, in this time in history, God's love is pouring out to touch the hearts of the littlest and the least, the weakest and most frail, to beget in them a profound and abiding holiness that radiates in his sight and in the sight of all. None of us are too weak, none of us are too little. After all, it is always the littlest ones, the poorest ones, who—to the surprise of the learned and proud—are most ready and open to welcome the miracles of love that God never ceases to work in the world, making all things new.

+ + +

At the end of these reflections, we can only stand in awe, bathed in gratitude and wonder. Perhaps the light even feels too dazzling, too bright, awakening in us feelings of unworthiness, of shame, of inadequacy or fear. How are we ever going to respond adequately to such a loving God, to his gift which is so ardent and so total? How are we ever going to attain to the state of sanctity and the depth of intimacy that he desires for us? Well, the beautiful truth is that we cannot do it, not on our own; and we do not need to try. Sanctity is ultimately God's work; the transformation of human hearts is God's work; redemption and renewal and resurrection and the beatific intimacy of eternity is God's work. And this work enfolds me, inundates me, and operates deep within me *here and now*, in this very moment.

There is no need, therefore, to be stirred to restless agitation, to make complicated plans or unrealistic resolutions, to live so stretched to the future that I fail to abide in the present. There is no need, either, to feel far from God because of my frailty, my limitations, even my struggles with sin. However closed I may be, however narrowed because of selfishness, fear, and the clothing of self-protection that keeps me from basking in the light of his gaze and letting myself surrender into his welcoming embrace...he is always close to me, always looking with love, always communicating himself tenderly and lovingly. And for him, past, present, and future are indivisibly united in his single, time-transcending, world-cradling gaze. Yes, from the bosom of his own eternity—an everlasting Now in which all things, already, are fully consummated in the love of Father, Son, and Holy Spirit—he is present to me in my own limited, created "now."

There is no need for anything, therefore, but for me to pronounce my "yes" to his love *now*, welcoming his gift and giving myself to him in response. This "yes" spoken in the sacrament of the present moment, this "yes" held and cradled by the fullness of God's presence to me in his own eternal "Yes," is joined with the everlasting "yes" that shall be mine in eternity. And through baptism I am *already* caught up into the innermost embrace of the Trinity, already breathing with the Father and the Son their one Spirit. Let me, therefore, simply lean into this Love that gazes upon me, this Love that embraces me, this Love that kisses me and breathes into me the eternal cherishing and delight of God. Through my "yes" awakened and sustained by his own "Yes," he will pervade my whole life, inundate my whole being, and, little by little—in the sacred fullness of each succeeding moment as it intersects with the fullness of eternity—he will transfigure me and unite me perfectly to himself, until the "now" of the present moment becomes, definitively, the Now of his Eternity. And there I shall be, forever, in the Love of the Three who have created me, redeemed me, and united me to themselves in the most total intimacy of reciprocal belonging, and in which, also, I am united to every other created person and to the whole cosmos, made new in the light of eternal beauty, of infinite love.

Let us simply praise him for his beauty and goodness, and rejoice already in his happiness, in the perfect bliss which is his, undimmed, from eternity to eternity, and which is ours too, by his gift, and shall be ours, forever without end:

Glory to the Father, and to the Son, and to the Holy Spirit,
as it was in the beginning, is now, and will be forever. Amen.

PRAYERS OF SURRENDER

I.
Holy Trinity, God of Love, I accept the love You have for me,
this Love pouring forth from Your inmost Heart,
this Love ever burning within You
—the flames of perfect acceptance
and mutual surrender,
the joyful fire of intimate communion,
embrace of consummate love!
I accept in trust and simplicity
this Love that enfolds and penetrates me,
as it flows out to flood the entire world,
to inundate, fill, and save each and every heart.

Jesus! I accept the gift flowing
from Your Crucified and Risen Heart.
I accept Your embrace of loving compassion,
and I in turn embrace You
in compassion and in grateful love.
Accepting, Lord, this all-encompassing Love,
I lovingly surrender all I am to You,
to the Father and the Holy Spirit too.
Inundate all of me, my inmost heart,
its every silent movement, its every stirring, its every beat
—to beat in Yours, and Your Heart, Jesus, in mine.
Fill my mind, my every thought, with Your presence,
transfigured, transformed in pure love,
and may my will, too, be perfectly conformed to Yours,
one, in You, with the will of the eternal Father;
may my every affection, desire, and experience
accord entirely with You,
so that I may not only will, but thirst, with all that I am,
seeing, thinking, feeling, yearning, in every moment,
as You and the Father see, think, feel, and yearn
in that blessed intimacy that You share eternally, as one.
Live freely and fully, Lord, in my very body,
in my every slightest movement,
my breath and my heartbeat deep within,
in word and silence, in solitude and community,
in work and deed, in stillness and repose,
in every gladness and every sorrow,
in suffering and in joy
—in the joy and peace of love
that is deeper still,
burning in the heart of all things
and enfolding each and all of us,
yes, deep within my breast!—

in the unceasing prayer, the hymn of love,
rising from my inmost heart, filling all I am,
and receiving, unreservedly, the outpouring of Your Love,
flowing forever, freely, from the Trinity's embrace!

Let it be in me, wholly, entirely, now and forever,
in everything, as You desire, my God, my Love...
Flood and inflame, possess and transform,
shelter and embrace, in the tenderness of sweet love,
in gentle mercy, loving compassion,
in Your own compassionate Heart, Jesus,
and the compassionate Heart of our heavenly Father,
and the ardent passion and gentle breath of the Holy Spirit!
Enfold me—and every heart!—embrace the entire world,
and draw us, my God,
into the inmost heart of Your eternal embrace,
into the depths of Your life of love and blessed communion,
Father, Son, and Holy Spirit,
forever and forevermore. Amen!

II.
Father, I thank you for having heard me; I know that you always hear me. So I am certain that I have already received from you what I have asked, through Christ your Son, in whose Name all beauty, goodness, and truth have been bestowed upon us. So I praise you, I love you, I trust in you, I put all my hope in you, I adore you in your infinite radiance. Totus tuus!

Let a ceaseless hymn of thanksgiving resound from my inmost heart, from my very flesh, and from the very fabric of my life at each moment, and forever! Glory to you, Father, Son, and Holy Spirit! Love poured out into our hearts, touching, healing, and making new, transfiguring us to participate in your very own life as Trinity, as everlasting Love and Communion: glory, praise, and adoration to you!

Grant me to seek, love, and live only your beauty, goodness, and truth, in all things, so as to be all yours with total transparency, with complete devotion, with joyful trust, ardent desire, and complete loving surrender. Totus tuus! I trust you. I desire you. I love you. Forgive me all of my sins; illumine the darkness of my mind; guide my inmost heart in the freedom of your truth; give me always the joy of your salvation; and through me, let sinners return to you.

Yes, let innumerable hearts turn to you, trust you, desire you, love you! Ravish your beloved children with the vision of your own Beauty, console them with the light of your cherishing gaze, and draw them with the fragrance of your holiness. Save us, O God, and we shall be saved, and shall praise you forever: eternal Triune God, infinite immensity, humble intimacy, boundless outpouring, sweet anointing filling every space of heart and life, Father, Son, and Holy Spirit, praise to you forever and ever, for eternity without end. Amen.

III.

Eternal God, Father, Son, and Holy Spirit, infinite Love and everlasting Intimacy, pure Goodness and delightful Bliss, radiant Beauty and undying Truth, your poor and weak child, a redeemed sinner and cherished beloved, opens himself anew to your gaze of love. This gaze bathes me with cherishing tenderness in my utter littleness, and summons me to the fullness of life, to complete sanctification and transfiguration in you.

I allow you to love me, this day, this moment, and I respond to this love —by your grace—with all that I am. Aware of your infinite thirst to love and to be loved, and thirsting too, myself, through the thirst you have placed within me, I give you my love, my life, my prayer, my poverty, my weakness and sin, my suffering, my joy, my hope and desire, my faith and trust, my love and total surrender—everything, in all circumstances and at every moment, forever—to be only all yours, now and eternally, and in you to be opened wide in love, tenderness, and affirmation, in the pure light of your own gaze, for the whole of creation and for each one of your precious and beloved children. Totus tuus!

I thank you, Father, for the immeasurable gift of your love, and for all of existence flowing from your paternal hands. I thank you for the grace of adoption and espousal that you have given to me, to all of your children, in Christ. Let all of your desires be fulfilled in me and in all of your children, on earth as it is in heaven, until earth is taken definitively into heaven's embrace. I thank you above all for creating me and redeeming me—Father, Son, and Holy Spirit—to partake in your own divine nature, to participate in the innermost mystery of your life as Trinity: in the complete transparency of the cherishing gaze of reciprocal delight, in the total mutual surrender of perfect gift, and in the consummate intimacy of mutual belonging, sweetest embrace, and true indwelling, breathing with the Son and the Father their one Holy Spirit.

Let it be! Let it be always and forever, in me and in all persons, even in the shadows and sufferings of this life, your love present touching, redeeming, healing, sanctifying, transfiguring, divinizing, and bringing to fullness of life. Hold us always, and carry us throughout life, until we are home with you in your eternal joy, yes, until the whole cosmos is carried to everlasting consummation in the heart of your Triune embrace, and all things are permeated and fulfilled in the vibrancy of your infinite Love and everlasting Intimacy. Glory to you, Father, Son, and Holy Spirit, now, and throughout all eternity! Amen.

IV.

Eternal Trinity—perfect Love and Intimacy, Father, Son, and Holy Spirit—grateful for the gift you bestow upon me and upon all of your children, particularly the gift of your very self, and aware of your infinite thirst to love and to be loved, and thus to grant us full access into the heart of your own life, I offer myself totally to you, now and forever, to be all yours and for you, and, in you, to be for each one of your precious children. Possess me, transfigure me, divinize me in your love, that your thirst may be satisfied, that I myself may find fullness of happiness in you, and that abundant fruit may be borne for the salvation and sanctification of all. Glory be to you forever and ever, born of the trust-filled and loving praise of human hearts, lifting up the entire creation to you, Father, Son, and Holy Spirit. Amen.

V.

Holy Trinity, I give myself totally to you anew, now and forever, to respond with love to your Divine Love, with thirst to your infinite thirst. I offer myself to satiate this thirst with my life and my love, with my participation in your own life; I offer myself unreservedly, without conditions or limit, but according to your will for me, for the good of my brothers and sisters, and for all of the desires in your heart as you gaze with love upon this broken, bleeding, but beautiful world.

I surrender myself to you in atoning love born of, and conformed to, the perfect Love of Christ—Incarnate, Crucified, Risen, and Eucharistic—for the reunification of Christians, and for the ever more transparent holiness of your Church and all of her members. And through this and alongside this, that the whole world may come to believe, and, believing, to rejoice. There are so many things that you deeply desire or that bring pain to your heart; for all of these I offer myself, to be wholly joined to your divine thirst, and, through my own thirst, my own love, suffering, and prayer, conformed to that of Christ, to let you bear more abundant fruit in the hearts of your children throughout the world. I offer myself to you that the light may shine in the darkness, love may overcome hate, truth may illumine and correct error, purity may be born from sin through repentance and transformation, peace may overcome conflict and division, healing may come to broken hearts, lives, and relationships, and all things may be made new in Christ through the Holy Spirit, that we ourselves, and the whole universe, may return to you, Father, to share eternally in the inmost life of the Trinity, a life of everlasting joy in perfect love and intimacy. Amen.

END NOTES

1. Thomas Dubay, S.M. *Fire Within: St. Teresa of Avila, St. John of the Cross, and the Gospel – On Prayer* (San Francisco: Ignatius Press, 1989), 196-197.

2. The quote from Joseph Langford in the footnote is from "D'une Thérèse à l'autre...," pp. 38-45, quoted in Jacques Gauthier *I Thirst: Saint Thérèse of Lisieux and Mother Teresa of Calcutta* trans. Alexandra Plettenberg-Serban (Staten Island, New York: Alba House, 2005), xxii and 25.

3. Joseph Langford, *Mother Teresa's Secret Fire: The Encounter That Changed Her Life, and How It Can Transform Your Own* (Huntington, Indiana: Our Sunday Visitor Publishing Division, 2006), 96, 99.

4. Ibid., 117-120.

5. Offertory of the Mass of the Feast of the Sacred Heart. Quoted in Michael E. Gaitley, MIC, *33 Days to Morning Glory* (Stockbridge, Massachusetts: Marian Press, 2011), 81.

6. Ibid.

7. *Letters of Saint Thérèse of Lisieux,* vol. II, translated by John Clarke, O.C.D. (Washington, D.C.: ICS Publications, 1988), 995.

8. Among many other examples, we can include St. Margaret Mary Alacoque: "He made me rest for a long time on His divine breast, where He showed me the marvels of His love and the unspeakable secrets of His sacred heart that had always been hidden before. He opened them to me there for the first time, in a real and tangible way. ... He said to me, 'My divine heart is so impassioned with love for humanity, and for you especially, it cannot contain the flames of its burning charity inside. It must spread them through you, and show itself to humanity so that they may be enriched by the previous treasures that I shared with you.' Afterwards, He asked for my heart. I begged Him to take it and He did, placing it in His own adorable heart. He let me see it there like a little atom consumed in a burning furnace. Then He returned it to me in a burning heart-shaped flame and placed it where it had been."(*Autobiography of St. Margaret Mary,* trans. The Sisters of the Visitation (Rockford, IL: TAN Books, 1968), 69. Quoted in Gauthier, 64)

9. Mother Teresa's Letter to the Missonaries of Charity family, 25th March 1993, © 2011 Missionaries of Charity Sisters, c/o Mother Teresa Center. As quoted in *33 Days to Morning Glory* by Fr. Michael E. Gaitley, MIC, with the first paragraph placed later in the text, 70-72.

10. Sr. Miriam James Hiedland, S.O.L.T., *Loved As I Am: An Invitation to Conversion, Healing, and Freedom through Jesus* (Notre Dame, Indiana: Ave Maria Press, 2014), 95.

11. Quoted in Langford, 79.

12. Paul Glynn, S.M. *A Song for Nagasaki: The Story of Takashi Nagai* (San Francisco: Ignatius Press, 2009), 188-189.

13. Ibid., 257-258.

14. Ibid., 232-233.

15. Joseph Ratzinger, *Introduction to Christianity,* trans. J.R. Foster (Ignatius Press: San Francisco, 2004), 267-268.

16. All quotes in this reflection: Pope John Paul II, *Memory and Identity: Conversations at the Dawn of a Millennium* (New York: Rizzoli, 2005), 27-30.

17. As quoted in the Office of Readings of the Liturgy of the Hours, Friday of the 7th Week of Easter.

18. Quoted in Mother Teresa *Jesus is My All in All: Praying with the "Saint of Calcutta"* ed. And intr. Fr. Brian Kolodiejchuk, M.C. (New York: Doubleday, 2008), 36.

19. Father Iain Matthew, *The Impact of God: Soundings from St John of the Cross* (London: Hodder & Stoughton, 1995), 25-26.

20. All quotes in this section from Matthew, 28-30.

21. **THE EYES OF LOVE**
(italics is the voice of Christ, the Son, and bold is the voice of the Father)
I.
My Father, those eyes of love
gaze upon me so intensely,
eyes of goodness and of grace,
eyes that, looking,
bestow the beauty that they see.
I am—because you see me,
and I am exactly as you see.
The goodness you desire,
you yourself beget in me;
the radiance of my countenance
is only a reflection of your own—
of that face, which, shining brightly,
always gazes out: upon your Son.

Son, my only-begotten One,
the radiance of your countenance
wounds my deepest Heart:
for in the face, I gaze deep within,
in the eyes, I read the Heart.
And in your Heart, my Son,
I see indeed only one,
your Heart and mine.

One Heart, for mine flows from you,
an effusion of Love,
like water flowing down
from the heights, cascading,
dancing, upon the depths of water below—
yet how can words express how this water
flows up again to you, united with the Source,
in the very act by which it comes forth?
Acceptance, reciprocal surrender,
these are one, Father, between you and I.
Ah, yes, you give me beauty,
so that I may be Beautiful—

—Ah, yes, I am captured by your Beauty,
to give myself to you!
My Heart is drawn by Love's magnetism
to communicate all to you, my Son.

And mine, by receiving,
cannot but pour itself out again to you.

**A glance, a single moment's look,
communicates all, my Love.
Seeing once, I see through and through,
and this moment lasts forever—
an eternity of love.**

Seen once, I am seen forever,
known, I am known entirely,
and I know you, Father,
even as I am known.

**Known, my Son, in this Love,
this Look, this Gaze,
exchanged between you and I,
in our Communication of self,
where, given, received,
we are, and will be,
in the single moment of eternity, one:
in the Spirit of Love who belongs to us both,
in whom, together, we belong.**

II.
My Father, these eyes of love,
mine and yours, gaze out—
upon a world—and, looking,
they create.
In gazing, in a single glance,
which is never-ending contemplation
and radiant, unceasing delight,
we clothe in beauty the creatures
whom we have lovingly made.
Clothe, yet not from without alone,
for eyes of love always look within.

**My Son, you see that the most precious
of my creatures,
the children made to share
in our own image and likeness,
in the radiance of that Beauty, given—
have not seen in what lies true love:
ah, look, my Son, they desire not to receive!
They think they must grasp,
must make beauty, goodness,
as if it were their own,
as if—ah!—as if it were not pure gift.**

I look, Father, but in them

I still see beauty, hidden,
but enduring and true.
Who can take it away?
Beauty, but buried deep within
the shame of the fallen heart.
Come, Father, let us go to them,
you and I, and our Spirit too.
Let us seek them out,
let us dwell within,
after making them again our own,
and open up,
in acceptance, in reciprocal surrender,
those hearts enclosed in fear.

Yes, my Son,
I am drawn by the magnetism of love!
Ah! how my Heart aches for them
— as yours does as well.
Go, you first,
draw near to them,
and I will be in you.
Draw near and walk among them,
love them as you have been loved by me.
Give the Spirit whom I have given to you;
pour him out
as he has poured forth into your Heart,
eternally,
cascading, like an immensity of water,
falling,
into the poverty of the human heart.
And he will prepare a place for you,
for me,
to dwell there among them,
to pitch our tent in their very place of exile,
pilgrims in a strange land,
so that,
already, in their very place of wandering,
they may be citizens of the blessed homeland,
children,
in the mansions where we dwell.

—The abode, Father, which is your very bosom,
that blessed embrace of love!
I go, that they may return here to this place.

III.
The dust of our roads,
kicked up by the feet of God—
what is this marvel?
The water drawn from our wells
to quench the thirst of the eternal Fountain!

He is here among us,
eating at our table,
laboring at the same burdens as we.
He feels the same hunger,
fasting,
the same thirst,
parched by the desert heat.
What is this?
Tempted to turn stones into bread,
to show a display of power,
to fall down in adoration before the power of evil
so as to share in its domain?
No, but he is different.
He is bound by the same limitation and weakness,
yet is free from our chains—
a free Man in a world of slavery,
born to set us free.

More than this,
there is something deeper,
don't you see?
A power goes forth from him,
not like what the world calls power.
Those who draw near,
they feel it,
those who are simple, weak,
they know.
It is love they feel,
and mercy,
the compassion burning in the Heart of God,
aflame in the Heart of this One
who is present among us,
a child of his mother,
a brother to us all.
The Father of eternal glory
is reflected in his face;
the Bridegroom of all,
the same who led us through the desert
so many centuries ago.
He is here.

How can eternal and infinite Love
be contained by the limits of time,
by the boundaries of our space?
He rises early, very early in the morning
to go into the hills to pray.
Exhausted, he falls asleep
on a cushion in our boat!
Then, awaking, a single word of his
stills the elements which no creature obey.
Who then must this be?

There, in his eyes,
is a mysterious glimmer,
a piercing gaze, which looks,
not to judge or condemn,
but to love and to accept.
Do you not feel?
He does not look to discern
whether there is anything lovable in you
—for he already knows what he will find there—
but he looks to awaken the beauty
slumbering deep within.

I know, I, who have leaned against his breast.
I have felt there mysteries unspeakable,
I have seen things unseen,
touched what cannot be touched.
Who can read this Word,
written into the lines of our history?
Who can hear his voice,
echoing in the wind as it rustles in the trees?
Before our world was,
HE IS.
Our whole creation is like a parchment
on which is written one word:
Son.
For when our God looks upon us,
what does he see?
He sees the image of his well-Beloved,
the One begotten of him from eternity to eternity.
We are all like a scroll held in his hand,
like the blood that flows through his veins,
surging from and returning to that precious Heart.
We are all...ah, what wonder...
a bride he has made, and come,
to espouse lovingly to himself.

This precious Body,
yes, it is the body of every man and woman.
The two shall become one flesh,
God and humanity,
in the Body of the Son.
What is this?
This Body sweats drops of Blood!
What?
It is by fierce scourges rent.
Look at him—no, look away!
Ah, what can one do?
Run, hide? Stand and pray?
This is my body, broken, rent.
But this is the Body belonging to the Son of God.

Power of love, here mocked
and condemned to indignity.
Here, silent like a lamb led to slaughter,
the Word who never ceases to sound.
Listen...
can you hear his silence speak?
Carrying that terrible burden
up the hill of our death.
Do you feel the beams
pressed against your shoulders,
yet, at the same time,
lifted from you?
What he carries, he takes from us.
What we carry, it now belongs to him.
What exchange is this—
the Innocent is condemned,
tortured, crucified,
that the guilty may go free?
Love enters into the abyss of our lovelessness,
and, as a lamp on a lampstand,
is raised aloft in our darkness.
Healing rays of love,
heartbeat surging right up against our own...
This narrow, suffocating heart
within my breast,
expands on contact with his.
Yes...through union with him
I am again made innocent, pure.

Ah...nails pierce the sacred flesh!
This meek lamb gives hardly a cry,
but see the tears streaming down his cheeks?
All of humanity is gathered here.
We all watch this spectacle,
played out before our eyes.
It is something we always knew,
yet something we never knew,
nor could have even imagined.
The ugliness and pain of our sin,
we see...but disarmed
in the outstretched arms of Love.
Yes, raised up for every eye to see—
in this way he descends into the depths,
the depths of our hearts,
where he makes a home,
wedding himself to our creaturely poverty,
yet overcoming the poverty of sin
and transforming it into the poverty of love.

IV.
My Heart yearns, dearest Father,

that they may be with me where I am.
I have come among them—
here I am now,
yet I have not left your side.
I taste the bitter drink of sin,
but from your bosom, the Wellspring of Love,
I never cease to drink.
Your face, Father, is veiled to them,
not because you hide it,
because they have lost the ability to see—
and I must go beyond the veil
that through love it may be rent,
granting them to see again,
as they are seen by us, lovingly,
learning thus, in us, to love.
Yes, so we have desired,
and so I desire now.
This is a sanctuary of mystery
so awesome, so amazing.
Love alone can taste it,
how One can experience in his Heart
both suffering and joy,
the pain of separation
yet the union which nothing can tear asunder.
I surrender to you here,
affixed to this Cross,
breathing forth my last...
this breath, dear God!
It is our Spirit, filling the lungs of humanity.
It is the flame of love
thawing the heart frozen by sin and fear.
It is the light of Love
illumining the darkest place.
Yes, they can know
—immersed in the immensity of love—
this mystery of pain and joy...
more, they can know
the joy deeper than every pain or strife,
which I have known before them.
For in me, I have opened up the path,
the way of love,
which penetrates every substance
and transforms it into itself,
which floods all with the fountain of eternal joy.
For you gaze, Father,
with those piercing eyes of love,
and, even when our eyes grow dim,
that glance of love sees as in brightest day
—and carries us, as a child in its mother's arms,
tranquil and secure,
resting against her bosom,

into the fullness of your embrace!

V.
Ah, my Son!
Today I have begotten you.
Now: the Today of eternity
and that of time
meet...

As the Light of your gaze,
Father,
pierces the depths of the tomb,
the depths of the place of death
—and gives life,
the Dawn from on high shining upon creation,
breaking the bars of hell,
shattering the chains that bind,
illumining the tombs of those who sleep.
I rise, Father,
I come to you!
And in my Heart, my flesh,
I carry every person!

You stand with them, my Son.
In you, Love abides in the very fabric
of redeemed creation.
Your Heart beats silently, gently
—and mine in You—
in the depths of every heart,
in the slightest stirring of the breeze,
the whistling of the birds,
the voice of man, woman, child.
The sunrise, casting its rays over the earth,
the tender warmth, the golden hue:
this is the gaze of my Son,
victorious over death,
coming as a Bridegroom from his tent
to take his Bride unto himself—

—to bring her to you, my Father,
enfolding her in my arms,
so that she may be where I am,
to behold my glory that you have given me
in your love for me
before the foundation of the world.
That she may share,
fully and completely,
in the radiance of this single glance of love
that passes for all eternity
between you and I,
in this knowledge and intimacy

which is ours in the Spirit of Love.
Right here, in the midst of this
silent dialogue,
she abides...
I in you, and you in me,
and she, in us both,
one...in the bliss of eternal Love.

22. Quoted in Mother Teresa *Jesus is My All in All*, 24.
23. Father Iain Matthew, *The Impact of God: Soundings from St John of the Cross* (London: Hodder & Stoughton, 1995), 52.
24. Ibid., 55-57.
25. A Carthusian, *The Way of Silent Love,* trans. An Anglican Solitary (Herefordshire, England: Gracewing Publishing, 2008), 90-93.
26. Langford, 250, 252-255.
27. A SINGLE ACT OF PURE LOVE

I.
You touched me so deeply through these words, my God,
when I was young, and so ravished by you;
and they still stand true before me today,
though now purified and clarified, made transparent,
correcting the imbalance and the unnecessary dichotomy,
and harmonizing all in love's true center, its heartbeat,
in the embrace of the Heart of Jesus Christ,
in your own Trinitarian heartbeat as Father, Son, and Spirit.

For it is true that your work alone redeems the world,
your work alone saves sinful hearts from sin
and wounded hearts from the shackles of their fear,
and accomplishes all other good, whatever it may be,
as a gratuitous gift pouring out from your generosity,
even if such gifts appear to be, and are,
mediated through human prayer and activity.

One act of pure love is worth more than all other works put together:
this is simple truth, for every person in every single life.
What can we truly give to you, but ourselves, but love,
but the openness of heart to receive your gift,
your outpouring of your very self, in the Spirit, into us,
harnessing our reciprocal gift to you in response?

Yes, what do you desire but wedding human hearts to yourself,
but intimacy, communion in the life of the divine Persons,
each one of your children breathing forth the Holy Spirit
in union with the eternal breathing of the Father and the Son?

What sacred happiness, what breathtaking beauty, what glory,
that you have made us to breathe with you the very Breath you breathe,
already in this life, though imperfectly, and for all eternity
in the undimmed fullness and unmediated embrace of everlasting Joy!

And this mystery of sharing in your life and love,
it touches us, not just in the apex of our humanity,
the still-point of the spirit beyond our bodies and our life,
but rather descends into the rich fabric of our everyday experience,
sanctifying it all from within, making it holy:

that these bodies of flesh are temples of the spirit,
that our work, activity, play, and rest
becomes a ceaseless act of pure love, born of love's purity,
and our very human communion with one another
is a transparent reflection and participation
in your own eternal life of intimacy as Father, Son, and Spirit.

Yes, each person can find their life written in these words,
their longing to encounter, at the heart of every moment,
the heartbeat of gratuitous intimacy and joy,
the playful communion of love, the kiss of Lover and beloved.

It is for this that we, your children, long:
the pure for-its-own-sake-ness of love and communion,
which alone gives meaning to all else, in fullness,
and also transcends all else in the pure togetherness of hearts in love.

And this will be our everlasting gladness when this life is passed,
and the whole world is re-created, made new,
in perfect transparency to the uncreated life of the Trinity,
and each and every created thing, and person,
affirmed and cherished uniquely precisely in this space.

II.
And you also speak to me, uniquely, through these words,
and yet so far beyond them, too, in the heart,
telling me anew of your loving plan for me, your gift,
that my heart's desire and spirit's song for so long
has been guided by you, and by you matured.

For you indeed do wish for me to abide, uniquely,
in a place of solitude, silence, prayer, and play,
at the heart of my littleness and poverty,
for my sake and for the sake of all the world,
in the midst of the humble destitution of my life,
in which you are my only security and safety,
in whom my frailty and smallness is cradled in your love,
and my human communion, too, sheltered and safeguarded
in its unique sacredness, its holiness in your sight,
as your gift, your manifestation, your delight.

A life of pure love, gratuitous and free,
useless in the eyes of the world, but precious in your sight:
the beauty of prayer and togetherness.

So simple it is, so vulnerable, so small,
but the most important thing of all,
made present in each and every life, uniquely,
is made present for me too, here.

You give this gift to me, to abide in me, and to bear fruit,
in living my humble life of prayer, in illness and incapacity,
in the stillness of the heart at rest, and its longing dilation,
in ceaseless wonder and play born of faith,
in the joy of filial belovedness and nuptial belonging,
in the gratuitous wonder that is your gift to us,

in the pure love of which the words speak, so beautifully,
and yet also more human, more humble, more flesh-and-blood;
and in equal measure, though secondarily,
flowing from this primal place of intimacy, God, with you,
you manifest this gift, and make it live,
in the beauty of human communion,
in looking with your eyes of love upon the person
entrusted to me by you, to be with me here,
and in her loving, with you, all the world,
that the world may find and know your goodness and love,
and find fulfillment in your embrace eternally.

Yes, this most humble and simple life, my God,
is a witness, also, for all persons, of that central mystery,
that pure gratuity of love and intimacy that you desire
to have with us, Bridegroom of the bride, Father of the child,
the intimacy for which you have created us, union with you,
the true and everlasting rest of the restless heart,
and oh...so beautiful and lovable in yourself,
eternal Beauty, eternal Goodness, you who are Love!

And this central mystery is also manifest, alive,
in looking out, from this most intimate embrace,
upon your world with the light of your own gaze,
alive and active, so rich, so full, so beautiful,
affirming and cherishing each person with your own love,
and playing in every moment and every thing,
in the gaze of lighthearted contemplation, your delight,
and lifting all up into the consummating space of your embrace.

And, finally, it is manifest in your desire
for us to have such intimacy, such blessed communion,
in you, with one another, children of the same Father,
man and woman, son and daughter, siblings and friends,
sheltered and held in the communion that is yours,
made present in us, among us, and carrying us, at last,
to consummation in you who are eternal Intimacy:
Father, Son, and Holy Spirit, without end.
28. Langford, 280.
29. **A SINGLE DROP**
I.
I look upon your face, my Son,
upon the abyss of your mystery,
which is so deep that I could lose myself in it
were it not but a perfect reflection
of the abyss that I am.
Behold! today I have begotten you,
in this ceaseless day of eternity,
which has no dawn and no dusk,
no beginning or end,
but is endless fullness of life and of love.
But indeed, it bears within it such richness,
such abundance of grace,
that all the hues cast by the rising sun
across the morning sky,
lighting up the earth with brilliance,

and all the dancing colors streaking across heaven,
filling the air at the closing of the day,
all the changes of seasons and times,
all forms of weather—thunderclap,
lightning-beams, the gentle dripping of the rain,
the wind, the calm, the heat and the gentle cool—
are all like so many reflections
of that single light,
undivided, pure,
which passes eternally from me to you,
and from you to me.

Like gathering moisture which distills
into a single drop,
upon the edge of a leaf in the early morning dew—
so love distills,
my Father,
as the gift of creation.
The whole ocean of divinity,
majestic, immense,
the roaring of the waves,
so great, yet so calm
that they cannot be heard by mortal ears,
becomes but a single drop of water,
falling.

The single mystery becomes refracted light,
the One, many and multifaceted.
Yet abundance, too, becomes so small,
the infinite and uncontainable,
veiled in forms of flesh, plant, animal, and earth.
Yet man and woman, above all, my Son,
in our image we create,
breathing into them our Spirit—life.
How can a tiny mirror reflect the whole expanse of sky?
However you position it, won't it reflect but a part?

They reflect, dear Father,
not by way of containing
—as a glass contains water,
or even as the shores contain the sea—
but as gazing eyes contain the sky
with its immensity of stars,
or as a glance of love
enfolds in the heart's embrace
the mystery of the beloved.

II.
My Son, they reflect this image, this likeness,
because I breathe upon them
the Breath that passes eternally between you and I,
and when I look,
I imprint upon them
—as light waves caught within the eye—
the image of my Beloved One.
It is in you, Son, that I alone create.

But they are, Father,
more than a passing ray of light
succeeded by darkness,
or a glance which the mind soon forgets.
I dwell among them: the enduring Word of God.

**Dwell, Son:
be the Word made flesh.
Yes! The light is more**
than a mere reflection upon the glass.
Knit together in the womb,
spirit, flesh, sinews, and bone,
a Son is conceived in time
by a lowly mother—a Son
who is begotten from all eternity
by the eternal Father.
Born, in a single moment,
in a poor and lowly manger,
you who are born eternally
in my sheltering bosom, so full of love.

This is my body,
taken from her who reflects the light of love,
radiantly refracted in so many ways
throughout the history of the world,
concentrated again in her,
like a single intense beam of light,
sealing a marriage between God and man.
A scroll with writing on both front and back,
a library with more books than the world could contain,
is now contained in that soft flesh
of a little child.
I AM.

III.
A silent glance, a look of love
between mother and child,
shares in that eternal glance
between you and I,
my Son.

Here is more than words can express,
however much time or ink one has—
yet less.

**Deeper within,
in the depths of love,
less is more.**

Less, my Father,
less I will be,
deeper, further into their lives,
until all words and activity
—the whole life of a man—
reaches but a single point:

LOVE.

**The Spirit is breathed silently
from that failing, broken body
upon a Cross.
Ah...
This says all...**

And yet...

And yet, my Son.

The undivided light
breaks forth anew,
to gather from the four corners
into the fullness of the light's embrace—

**—the eternal Breath of Love
between you and I,
silently.**

Father,
all becomes a single gift,
accepted from your hands,
and given, in this flesh of mine,
to those whom you have given me.

**All of life, the whole of man,
yes—the whole of God—
distilled, my Son, to a single point,
where less is more,
where All is contained within the least,
a bit of bread, a drop of wine:**

This is my Body,
this, my Blood...

Printed in Great Britain
by Amazon